VALUING ROLES
HOW TO ESTABLISH RELATIVE WORTH

Michael Armstrong and Ann Cummins

KOGAN
PAGE

London and Philadelphia

First published in Great Britain and the United States in 2008 by Kogan Page Limited

120 Pentonville Road
London N1 9JN
United Kingdom
www.kogan-page.co.uk

525 South 4th Street, #241
Philadelphia PA 19147
USA

ISBN 978 0 7494 5077 9

British Library Cataloguing-in-Publication Data

A CIP record for this book is available from the British Library.

Library of Congress Cataloging-in-Publication Data

Armstrong, Michael, 1928–
    Valuing roles : how to establish relative worth / Michael Armstrong and Ann Cummins.
        p. cm.
    Includes bibliographical references.
    ISBN 978-0-7494-5077-9
    1. Job evaluation. 2. Human capital. 3. Employees—Rating of. I. Cummins, Ann. II. Title.
    HF5549.5.J62A76 2008
    658.3'06—dc22

2007042311

Typeset by JS Typesetting Ltd, Porthcawl, Mid Glamorgan
Printed and bound in India by Replika Press Pvt Ltd

Contents

Acknowledgements

We acknowledge the invaluable contributions of the following to this book:

Peter Christie, Hay Group
David Conroy, Mercer
Chris Corrin, Anglo American
Carole Hathaway, Watson Wyatt
Jamil Hussain and Martha How, Hewitt
· Sue Millsome, e-reward
Geoff Nethersell, Hay Group
Julie Sleeman, Chichester College
Gayle Spear and Jim Crawley, Towers Perrin
Tascha Tinneveld, Greenpeace International
Giles Tulk and Ben Pullenayegum, PricewaterhouseCoopers

Introduction

This book is about role valuation, which we define as a formal or informal method of placing roles in a grade or pay structure, or deciding on the rate of pay for an individual role (spot rates). Although the book is concerned with all aspects of role valuation as defined below, much of it deals with formal job evaluation schemes.

APPROACHES TO ROLE VALUATION

There are basically three approaches to establishing the value of roles in an organization:

1. *Job evaluation* – using traditional formal schemes such as point-factor rating or job classification, and newer developments such as analytical matching to determine internal relativities and define organization structures and career paths. These are usually coupled with analyses of market rates to inform decisions on pay structures and rates of pay. Some consultants and organizations use the term 'levelling' as an alternative.

2. *Market pricing* – relying entirely on external comparisons to determine internal rates without using any form of job evaluation to assess internal relativities. This has been termed 'extreme market pricing' by Ellis *et al* (2004) to distinguish it from the market rate analyses that are carried out in conjunction with job evaluation.

3. *Informal role valuation* – deciding on grades or levels, rates of pay and internal relativities in ways that are not based on explicit schemes of evaluation or the systematic analysis of market rates.

PURPOSE OF ROLE VALUATION

Role valuation defines relativities and may be used to establish comparable worth. Even in organizations that do not have a formal basis for deciding on the worth or value of roles, decisions about what to pay people are made all the time. This 'worth' may be explicit or hidden. It may be based on an analysis of the responsibilities of role holders and the demands made upon them, or comparisons with external market rates, or a combination of these. Evaluating 'worth' leads directly or indirectly to where a role is placed in a level within a hierarchy and can therefore determine how much someone is paid. The performance of individuals also affects their pay but this is not a matter for role valuation, which is concerned with valuing the roles people carry out, not how well they perform their roles.

However, as we emphasize throughout this book, role valuation is increasingly being used for broader purposes than simply providing the basis for pay decisions. It can provide valuable information and guidance on career ladders and organization structures and a useful link to corporate IT systems.

ROLE VALUATION OPTIONS

There are many options in role valuation. For example, in the United Kingdom the effect of powerful equal pay legislation has been to emphasize the benefits of traditional analytical job evaluation schemes over other types. In contrast, the tendency in the United States has been to prefer market pricing. The need to achieve 'comparable worth' may be recognized there, but market considerations are commonly deemed to be more important.

There is a diverse range of organizational factors that influence choice, so there is unlikely ever to be a standardized approach to role valuation. This book therefore covers the whole spectrum of how organizations value roles – what gets taken into account and the advantages and disadvantages of different methods. It recognizes that organizations have different drivers that will influence the decision on which type of approach to use and therefore the language they will use to describe role valuation. The aim is to set out the criteria that can be used when making a choice and then to provide guidance on how to develop and implement the methodology that best meets the needs and circumstances of the business.

We also recognize in this book that role valuation is increasingly an international process that involves different considerations than those present when operating a scheme in one country.

PLAN OF THE BOOK

Part 1 provides a general background to role valuation, including a discussion of the factors that affect the process and a description of the process itself.

Part 2 is concerned with the development and implementation of the various formal methods of job evaluation dealing with:

▌ choosing an approach (Chapter 3);

▌ the general considerations to be taken into account in developing a formal job evaluation scheme (Chapter 4);

▌ rolling out, implementing and maintaining a scheme following its design and testing (Chapter 5);

▌ the steps required to design formal point-factor and matching job evaluation schemes (Chapters 6 and 7);

▌ the use of market pricing (Chapter 8);

▌ the schemes offered by consultants (Chapter 9).

Part 3 covers how job evaluation is applied as a means of achieving equal pay for work of equal value, informing the design of grade and pay structures, and in international firms.

Part 4 includes an analysis of the results of the 2007 survey of job evaluation conducted by e-reward and a number of case studies. It concludes with a review of trends and issues in role valuation.

The appendices consist of a bibliography and examples from a number of organizations of a point-factor job evaluation scheme, a job questionnaire, a project programme, an appeals procedure and a job evaluation policy statement.

REFERENCE

Ellis, C M, Laymon, R G and LeBlanc, P V (2004) Improving pay productivity with strategic work valuation, *WorldatWork Journal*, Second Quarter, pp 56–68

Part 1

The Process of Role Valuation

1

Valuing roles: approaches and issues

This chapter contains an introduction to the approaches and issues involved in valuing roles. The aim is to provide a background to the more detailed descriptions of role valuation methodology in the rest of this book. The chapter starts with introductory discussions of the purpose of role valuation and a broad description of the methods available – formal job evaluation, market pricing and informal or semi-formal approaches. In the next two sections of the chapter two fundamental questions concerning role valuation are examined. First, are we valuing jobs, roles or people, or all three? Second, what do we mean by 'value'? The answers to these questions can significantly affect how role valuation is carried out.

The most common approach to role valuation, at least in the United Kingdom and Europe, is formal job evaluation, which is distinguished from market pricing and other methods. Formal/traditional schemes are what most people think of when they refer to job evaluation. The features of the main formal schemes are described in the next chapter, but as an introduction it is useful to review the basic considerations that affect the operation of any of these schemes. The next section of this chapter therefore examines how formal job evaluation works as a comparative, judgmental, structured and analytical process and the extent to which it is scientific, objective and a satisfactory measurement tool. The case for job evaluation as a systematic process can seem to be self-evident but over the years its limitations have been much discussed and these are reviewed in this section.

The final part of the chapter builds on the general considerations dealt with so far by examining the key issues that need to be addressed in planning and operating any type of role valuation, namely:

▌ assessing reliability and validity;

▌ the felt-fair principle;

▌ the meaning and significance of the term 'comparable worth';

▌ reconciling the need to be internally equitable with the need to be externally competitive.

THE PURPOSE OF ROLE VALUATION

It has been asserted by Gupta and Jenkins (1991) that the basic premise of role valuation is that certain roles 'contribute more to organizational effectiveness and success than others, are worth more than others and should be paid more than others'. The imperative to provide equal pay for work of equal value is an important additional premise.

Specifically, role valuation aims to:

▌ generate the information required to develop and maintain an internally equitable grade and pay structure by establishing the relative value of roles or jobs within the organization (internal relativities) based on fair, sound and consistent judgements;

▌ provide the data required to ensure that pay levels in the organization are externally competitive by making valid market comparisons with jobs or roles of equivalent complexity and size;

▌ ensure transparency so that the basis upon which grades are defined, jobs graded and rates of pay determined is clear to all concerned.

Role valuation can have a number of other different purposes, depending upon the needs of the organization, its environment and its culture. These include:

▌ supporting the description of career paths and providing a frame-work for talent management; in some cases there may be no formal link between role valuation and the pay system;

▌ taking into account the fact that 'extreme' market pricing often fails to provide the broader understanding of organization design and structure required to explain and manage career progression and therefore using formal job evaluation to bring back some internal structure;

▌ facilitating human capital measurement by providing a basis for allocating people to levels in an organization in order to generate the data required to analyse the value added by its human capital;

▌ supporting the introduction of new management information systems such as SAP or PeopleSoft, which require a field for job levels within the system in order to generate standard reports;

▌ in the United Kingdom, conducting a risk assessment of the like-lihood of an equal pay claim to indicate any actions required to prevent a claim or to offer a defence.

METHODOLOGY

There are many different approaches to role valuation, from the simple to the sophisticated. It can be conducted through a formal job evaluation scheme – a systematic arrangement that specifies the criteria for making judgements and how those criteria should be used. This is the meaning attached to the term 'job evaluation' in this book to distinguish it from market pricing and less formal methods of valuing roles. At the other extreme it can operate on an entirely informal basis. Formal schemes can be used with varying degrees of informality just as an element of formality can be added to an informal approach. Different methods can be combined. The focus may be on internal relativities – the initial concern of traditional job evaluation, or external relativities with market rates – market pricing, or a combination of the two. Role valuation is sometimes described as 'levelling' to indicate that it can involve defining the levels in an organizational hierarchy and allocating roles to those levels.

Although formal job evaluation may work systematically, it should not be treated as a rigid, monolithic and bureaucratic system. It should instead be regarded as an approach that may be applied flexibly.

Process – how job evaluation is used – can be more important than the system itself when it comes to producing reliable and valid results. This book often focuses on formal schemes but this does not mean that we underestimate the importance of using them informally when appropriate.

JOBS, ROLES AND PEOPLE

Jobs, Roles & People is the title of a book by Pritchard and Murlis (1992) of the Hay Group, in which the initial point is made that:

> As organizations and the roles of people within them change, so too, job evaluation has to adapt to meet their changing needs… The emphasis has moved away from organizations based on many layers of tightly defined hierarchy to ones which are more organic and flexible, where people-centred and performance-driven approaches to organization design are dominant.

The authors follow up this point later with the statement that: 'Within these organizations there is a need to move away from restrictively defined "jobs" to more broadly defined "roles", with an emphasis on flexibility and making maximum use of people and their abilities.'

We agree that a distinction should be made between jobs and roles and that the focus should be on the people in these roles. These matters are discussed below.

Jobs and roles

The terms 'job' and 'role' are often used interchangeably. But they are different and this needs to be recognized in the valuation processes used.

A *job* is an organizational unit, which consists of a group of defined tasks or activities to be carried out or duties to be performed. *Job descriptions* spell out what job holders are required to do. They are prescriptive and inflexible, giving people the opportunity to say: 'It's not in my job description', meaning that they only need to do the tasks listed there. Because they are more concerned with tasks than outcomes and with the duties to be performed rather than the competencies required to perform them (technical competencies covering knowledge and skills, and behavioural competencies), they provide an inadequate basis for valuing the work that people do.

A *role* refers to the part people play in their work – the emphasis is on the outcomes of what they do, the technical competencies required to do it (what they need to know and be able to do) and, often, the behaviours expected of them (behavioural competencies). *Role profiles* define these outcomes and competencies. They can be applied flexibly because they do not prescribe in detail the tasks to be carried out in achieving outcomes. When used in formal job evaluation schemes, role profiles may include an analysis of the role in terms of the factors included in the scheme (a 'factor' is a common characteristic of roles that refers to the responsibilities exercised by role holders and the demands made upon them when carrying out their work).

It can be argued that the term 'role' should only be used for know-ledge workers and others where there is a close relationship between the work done and the competencies required, while the term 'job' should be reserved for those carrying out clearly prescribed and specified work. But this would mean creating two classes of people in an organization, which could be both divisive and demeaning. We prefer to use the term 'role', although we have to accept that people commonly refer to job evaluation or 'levelling', not role evaluation.

People

It is often said that formal job evaluation is concerned only with jobs, not people. In one sense this is true in so far as it is the level of the work people do that is measured in formal evaluation schemes, not the performance of individuals in those jobs. But this statement implies that people have nothing to do with the level of work they do, which is ludicrous. As Plachy (1987a) comments, 'roles are created according to the strengths and limitations of the people who design and fill them'.

The case for focusing job evaluation on people as well as jobs was put by Lawler (1991):

> The job evaluation approach is based on the principle that people are worth what they do. In many cases this may not be the most desirable cultural value for an organization. It tends to depersonalize people by equating them with a set of duties.

The importance of adopting a people-based approach was also stressed by Pritchard (1995):

> A major feature of today's more fluid organizations is that the work people actually do is determined not just by the conventional idea of a 'job', but also

by their own capability – 'people make jobs'. A basic tenet of traditional job evaluation is the separation of jobs and people; this may no longer be possible in a flexible organization.

It is people, not jobs, that add value, and it is people who have value in the marketplace. As Lawler (1991) put it: 'Jobs do not quit organizations and jobs are not hired by other organizations… The key compensation issue from a human resources perspective concerns what an individual is worth, not what a job is worth.'

The implications of this focus on roles and people are, first, that role valuation should reflect the existence of role flexibility and not be constrained by over-concentration on rigidly defined jobs; and second, that the market worth of individuals is a factor that must be taken into account in setting their rates of pay.

THE MEANING OF VALUE

The *Concise Oxford English Dictionary* defines value as 'worth' and worth as 'of value equivalent to'. Value, like beauty, can be said to be in the eye of the beholder. It has a number of different meanings, namely the concepts of intrinsic value, relative value, the labour theory of value, market value and strategic value.

Intrinsic value

The belief that jobs have intrinsic value that belongs naturally to them because of what they are has strongly influenced traditional job evaluation methods. This particularly applies to schemes in which the value of jobs is measured by scoring them, thus indicating that the worth or 'size' of a job is so many points. But job evaluation points have no meaning in themselves and therefore cannot be used in absolute terms to define the value of a job. The leading pragmatist John Dewey (1916) did not accept intrinsic value as an inherent or enduring property of things. Intrinsic value, he claimed, is always relative to a situation.

Relative value

The value of anything is always relative to the value of something else. It is this notion that governs the comparative nature of role valuation, which aims to establish the relative value of roles to one another so that internal equity can be achieved. The rates of pay for roles within the organization are also compared with those outside the organization (market rate comparisons) so that pay levels can be competitive. A grade structure (a sequence or hierarchy of grades, bands or levels into which roles of comparable worth are placed), can signify that the roles grouped into one grade are of greater value than the grade below and of lower value than the grade above. But it can also define levels of responsibility in an organization and the competencies required to perform at each level, thus producing a career structure. A pay structure, which will be influenced by market comparisons, attaches financial values to roles and, where appropriate, pay ranges to grades.

Labour theory of value

The labour theory of value originated by Karl Marx (1867) treats labour as a commodity and states that the value of a product depends on the amount of labour required to produce it. Nielsen (2002) argues that 'job content' based evaluation methodology, ie valuing jobs by reference to the duties carried out by job holders, is a Marxist approach and is no more relevant today than most of the other views expressed by Marx on political economy. This is because valuing jobs according to their content ignores market considerations.

Market value

The price of anything is related to the perceived value of the article to the buyer or seller, but it is ultimately governed by the laws of economics. It was stated by Hicks (1935) that: 'Wages are the price of labour and thus, in the absence of all control, they are determined, like all prices, by supply and demand.' However, the way in which these laws apply is affected by the degree to which transactions are carried out in what economists call 'perfect' or 'imperfect' markets. A perfect market is one in which both buyers and sellers have equal power and full knowledge of prevailing prices and there are no restrictions on transactions. An imperfect market is one that is affected by the relative power of suppliers, where knowledge of prices may be limited and there are restrictions on trade, limitations on entry, etc.

The rate of pay for a job or a person is a price like any other, and rates in the external market (market rates) are affected by demand and supply considerations operating in what is likely to be an imperfect market. These affect rates of pay within organizations (the internal market) because they influence the ability of those organizations to attract and retain the sort of people they need. This is the argument used by those such as Nielsen (2002) who support market pricing:

> Typical job evaluation systems set the prices of jobs by looking at factors that bear no relation to and are abstractions from the jobs themselves. Thus they abrogate the laws of supply and demand that set the prices of goods and services in the marketplace.

Strategic value

The concept of strategic value was formulated by Robert Heneman of Ohio State University and Peter LeBlanc of Sibson Consulting (2002; 2003) and developed by Ellis *et al* of Sibson Consulting (2004). The premise is that a key factor in determining the value of a position is its impact on 'current and future business success', ie its strategic value. However, when explaining their work valuation theory they recognized that the value of work also depends on 'talent market value' (the value that other organizations place on the work) and 'competency value' (the knowledge, skills, abilities and other attributes related to effective employee performance).

Implications

The meanings attached to value can be complementary (intrinsic value, labour theory, strategic value) or contradictory (labour theory and market value, intrinsic and relative value). To a greater or lesser extent, they can all influence beliefs about what role valuation is attempting to value and how to set about it. For example, belief in the prime significance of market value may lead to a focus on market pricing (assessing rates of pay by reference to the external market rates for comparable roles); belief in intrinsic value or labour theory could lead to the use of traditional job content evaluation techniques; belief in relative value might encourage the use of analytical matching (comparing jobs factor by factor) or market pricing; and belief in strategic value encourages the strategic work valuation approach advocated by Ellis *et al* (2004). These beliefs are often subliminal but need to be articulated to achieve a satisfactory and understandable basis for valuing roles.

FORMAL JOB EVALUATION

Traditionally, job evaluation has provided the basis for decisions on what people should be paid for the work that they do (not how well they do it). But typical formal schemes such as point-factor rating, analytical matching and job classification do not directly establish rates of pay. They are concerned with assessing internal relativities, informing the design and maintenance of grade structures and determining the levels of jobs in organizations (this process of 'job levelling' informs the development of career pathways). It is usual, although not universal, to attach pay ranges or brackets to these grades that indicate the rates of pay for roles and are determined separately on the basis of some form of market rate analyses. However, what Ellis *et al* (2004) call 'extreme market pricing' can be used formally to price roles solely on the basis of market rates with no regard to internal relativities.

How formal job evaluation works

Formal job evaluation involves comparative, judgmental, structured and analytical processes, as discussed below.

Job evaluation as a comparative process

Job evaluation deals with relationships, not absolutes. It does this in one of the following ways:

▌ job to job – jobs are compared with other jobs in order to decide whether their value is greater, lesser, or the same, as in ranking, whole job matching and market pricing;

▌ job to scale – jobs are compared with a scale, which could be a graduated scale of points attached to a set of factors, as in point-factor rating, or a defined hierarchy of job grades, as in job classification;

▌ factor to factor – jobs are analysed into factors and compared factor by factor with grade or role profiles analysed under the same factor headings, as in analytical matching.

Job evaluation as a judgmental process

Job evaluation requires the exercise of judgement in interpreting data on jobs and roles, comparing one job to another and comparing jobs against scales or factor by factor. It can be described as a subjective process carried out within an objective framework.

Job evaluation as a structured process

A formal job evaluation scheme is structured in the sense that a framework is provided that aims to help evaluators make consistent and reasoned judgements. This framework consists of language and criteria used by all evaluators, although, because the criteria are always subject to interpretation, they do not guarantee that judgements will be either consistent or rational.

Job evaluation as an analytical process

Job evaluation is or should be based on a factual description of the characteristics of the jobs under consideration. This means that although judgemental, at least the judgements are informed. However, schemes may be described as analytical in the sense that jobs are analysed and compared in terms of defined factors, or non-analytical in the sense that 'whole jobs' that have not been analysed by factor are compared with one another. Properly designed and executed analytical schemes can help to ensure that judgements are structured and consistent.

Questions about formal job evaluation

Is job evaluation scientific?

Job evaluation has been dismissed by Clarke (1987) as a 'pseudo science'. Plachy (1987b) comments that: 'Job evaluation is not a scientific system. It is a human system. Human beings make mistakes. They lose their objectivity and consistency, no matter how hard they try, no matter how great their integrity.' Job evaluation is not a science at all in the sense defined by the *Concise Oxford English Dictionary* as a connected body of demonstrated truths or with observed facts classified under general rules. The only part of this definition that applies to formal job evaluation is the reference to 'observed facts'. A systematic approach to job evaluation is based on information about jobs, not on assumptions.

Is job evaluation objective?

It is often claimed that although formal job evaluation is not scientific, it at least aspires to being objective by attempting to base judgements on the analysis of established facts uncoloured by the feelings or opinions of the evaluator. But these feelings cannot be eliminated and it is therefore difficult to avoid subjectivity. As the Equal Opportunities Commission (EOC) states (2003): 'It is recognized that to a certain extent any assessment of a job's total demands relative to another will always be subjective.'

Every step in a formal job evaluation process involves value judgements based on the interpretation of data presented in the form of words. As Plachy (1987a) notes: 'People give words the meaning they wish, sometimes intellectually, most of the time emotionally.' Job evaluation is based on the 'facts' presented in job descriptions or role profiles. But these can be partial representations of reality, in both senses of the word.

The most common job evaluation method (point-factor rating, as described in Chapter 2) depends utterly on the 'factor plan', which includes definitions of the different levels at which each of the 'factors' in the scheme can be present in a job. But the words used to convey meaning in factor level definitions are always subject to interpretation. Madigan and Hills (1988) have explained that: 'Evaluation processes merely provide a means for structuring judgements about internal pay systems. Whether a particular pay system is valid is a matter of judgement.' Armstrong and Baron (1995) commented that: 'The best that can be said of (formal) job evaluation is that it helps to make value-judgements explicit and requires evaluators to assess them within a framework.' Although this might reduce subjectivity by aiming to produce a consistent and systematic basis for evaluation, it does not make the process objective.

A fundamental aim of any process of job evaluation is to ensure, as far as possible, that consistent judgements are made based on objectively assessed information. But to refer to an evaluation as 'judgemental' does not necessarily mean that it is inaccurate or invalid. Correct judgements are achieved when they are made within a defined framework and are based on clear evidence and sound reasoning. This is what job evaluation can do if the scheme is properly designed and properly applied.

Is it all about measurement?

It is claimed by Heneman and LeBlanc (2002) that traditional job evaluation and market pricing attempt to measure, not determine, value. Job evaluation certainly cannot determine the value of jobs – it already exists – although the situation is confused because there are a number of ways of defining value, as discussed earlier in this chapter. They are also correct in saying that job evaluation attempts to measure value. The key word in that statement is 'attempts'.

The assumption made by the most popular forms of job evaluation such as point-factor schemes and the Hay Guide Chart method is that it is possible to measure or 'size' job value or worth. In job evaluation circles, reference is often made to the 'size' of jobs. But the ordinal (rank-ordered) numbers used in such schemes have no meaning in themselves and do not, because they cannot, represent any unit of measurement such as the number of items produced. It was noted by Emerson (1991) that: 'Ordinal structure without any ties to an empirical measuring system conveys the image of precision without providing any real, substantive measuring tool.' Points give an impression of accuracy, but this is an illusion. The numerical scores are based on value judgements and do not produce mathematical certainty.

It is perhaps preferable to regard job evaluation as a process for *comparing* job values. Some form of measurement in the form of points scores may be used to assist in comparisons but these do not define value on their own.

The limitations of formal job evaluation

It was argued by Phelps Brown (1962) that 'job evaluation is only a painstaking application of the way in which people do think and act about relative pay'. This statement implies that even analytical job evaluation may do no more than provide a rationalization for the assumptions people have already made about relativities between jobs. Crystal (1970) wrote that: 'Essentially, job evaluation boils down to organized rationalization.'

Critics writing in the 1980s and 1990s emphasized that job evaluation can be cumbersome, bureaucratic, inflexible, time-consuming and inappropriate in today's organizations. Lawler (1986) asserted that job evaluation can create unnecessary and undesirable pecking orders and power relationships in organizations. He also claimed that people realize that creatively written job descriptions can lead to pay increases (he calls this 'point grabbing' in point-factor schemes). Quaid (1993) suggested that job evaluation functions as a rationalized, institutional myth and considers that it:

> provides organizations with a set of language, rituals and rhetoric that has transported an otherwise impossible and indeterminate process to the realm of the possible and determinable. In this way, what job evaluation seems to do is to code and re-code existing biases and value systems to re-present them as objective data.

Grayson (1987) believed that job evaluation systems have usually been designed on the basis of traditional assumptions about work: 'The result is job evaluation schemes which are seen to be too slow, inflexible, unhelpful in implementing change and more geared to preserving the status quo.'

Incomes Data Services (1991) summarized the arguments against job evaluation as follows:

> The most damning charge against job evaluation for employers and employees alike, is that it simply measures the wrong things. The idea that the focus should be measuring the job, not the job holder, runs counter to the way in which work is increasingly organized. More and more functions and businesses are subject to rapid change and depend on groups of employees to deploy their skills in a flexible way. The established systems fail to measure what is important in the contribution of these 'knowledge workers'.

Comments like these contributed to or were prompted by the general malaise about job evaluation prevalent at the time. However, things have moved on. There is less reliance on the continuous use of elaborate and time-consuming formal job evaluation schemes. They may still exist but only in a supporting role. Processes such as analytical matching that are much less elaborate have come to the fore. The emphasis is more on flexible roles than rigidly defined jobs. If used in the right way, computer-aided job evaluation as described in Chapter 2 can reduce the cumbersome nature of traditional schemes and simplify administration. It is more generally acknowledged that the need to be externally competitive and therefore to consider the implications of market rates is a necessary part of the process of valuing roles. This especially applies in the United States, although in the United Kingdom attention has been drawn by the Equal Opportunities Commission to the fact that over-reliance on market rate analysis can perpetuate discrimination. But the issue of reconciling internal equity with external competitiveness is still with us, as discussed later in this chapter.

ROLE VALUATION ISSUES

The process of valuing roles is never straightforward. The limitations of formal job evaluation listed above need to be recognized and overcome, and there are problems with market pricing and informal methods, which will be discussed in Chapter 2. What is being valued needs to be understood. There are no easy solutions and role valuation projects can go badly wrong, although this is more often because of the process of developing and applying the scheme than the design of the scheme itself. The main issues that have to be addressed are discussed below, and methods of dealing with them are considered in subsequent chapters of this book.

Assessing the reliability of role valuation

Role valuation is reliable when it produces consistent results; for example, a role is assigned into the same grade or level by different evaluators. A reliability study requires that jobs are evaluated by two or more evaluators using the same job content information. Research carried out in the United States by the National Academy of Sciences, as reported by Risher (1989), established that inconsistencies can easily arise which, in some pay structures, could mean more than a 20 per cent difference in pay. Inconsistencies take place because of unreliable job data, factor plans that include ambiguous wording, or unreliable job evaluators.

Assessing the validity of role valuation

Role valuation is valid when it leads to sound and defensible decisions on the value of roles. The intention is to provide the basis for an equitable and competitive approach to paying people. Where there is a formal grade structure, this means indicating the correct grade for a role, but this begs the question of what constitutes a 'correct' grade. As pointed out by Arvey (1986) it is important to understand that when people talk about validity in formal job evaluation they are not necessarily referring to the specific scores resulting from the use of a job evaluation instrument. Instead they are referring to the kinds of inferences and decisions made on the basis of those scores: 'There is nothing inherently valid or invalid about a set of scores – they are simply a set of scores.' It is contended by Risher (1989) that:

> The only measure of system validity is management's assessment: 'Does it meet our business needs?' From this perspective each system should be uniquely configured to 'fit' the employer's compensation strategy, organization structure and planned career paths.

However, there are three approaches to validation that try to be more scientific:

1. *Criterion-related validity* – this attempts to determine the degree of correlation between the evaluation and the market rate for the role. But correspondence between internal and external relativities can be misleading, even irrelevant, because the conditions prevailing in the internal and external markets that establish relativities can be quite different. In any case, accurate market rate information is not always readily available.

2. *Content validity* – in an analytical (factor-based) scheme this attempts to show that the factors represent all the important role characteristics. But whether they do or not is a matter of opinion – it cannot be proved. Even if the right set of factors exists it does not necessarily mean that a valid result will be obtained.

3. *Construct validity* – a construct is a theory created to explain and organize existing knowledge. Construct validation looks at the system itself. If it is meant to measure job value, is that what it measures? Do factor ratings give an accurate indication of perceived role value? A test for construct validity can in theory be conducted by evaluating a set of jobs in an established hierarchy (ie, one in which relative values have been agreed) using two or more evaluation methods, but this can be an unacceptably elaborate process and still lead to inconclusive results.

These three approaches to validation are all flawed and most organizations resort to a fourth method, that of face validity. In effect, this involves making the statement that if it looks or feels right then it must *be* right. The illogicality of this is obvious but it provides the basis for the most commonly used method of validation, namely the 'felt-fair test', as discussed below.

The felt-fair test

The felt-fair test is derived from the felt-fair principle formulated by Eliot Jaques (1961). He suggested that: 'There exists an unrecognized system of norms of fair payment for any given level of work, unconscious knowledge of these norms being shared among the population engaged in employment work.' This view about pay perceptions was supported by his research, but the concept has been hijacked by job evaluators who commonly use it to test the results of a job evaluation exercise – if the grade or rank of a job after evaluation is felt to be fair then it *is* fair. Used in this way the felt-fair test is simply a means of establishing face validity.

The problem is that people have preconceptions about the relative value of jobs. They support the results of role valuation that confirm these conceptions and reject those that don't. A felt-fair approach used by management may simply reproduce the present hierarchy with which they are perfectly happy, having been living with it for some time. It may be governed by traditional beliefs on the hierarchy of jobs and thus inequities in the existing grade and pay structure may be perpetuated.

Advocates of market pricing assert that it obviates the need for spurious attempts to validate formal job evaluation. They claim that market rates are ascertainable facts not subject to the judgements present in traditional approaches. However, this claim is specious; judgements have to be made about market rate data, just as they have to be made in any type of role valuation. Market pricing cannot guarantee valid results.

Equity and competitiveness

In a sense, role valuation is always about comparing the worth of one role with another, and the concept of 'comparable worth' (a phrase used more frequently in the United States than the United Kingdom) focuses attention on delivering internal equity – equal pay for work of equal value – through role valuation. This raises the issue of the choice between internal equity and external competitiveness.

The tension between these two highly desirable aims of role valuation has created major divisions in the role valuation world between those who favour traditional job evaluation with some reference to external market rates, those who advocate 'extreme market pricing', ie relying entirely on external market rate data to inform internal rates of pay, and those who set out to reconcile the irreconcilable by trying to do both at once.

Powerful arguments and powerful beliefs are brought to bear by those who support market pricing. One of the writers of this book, when presenting the case for job evaluation to the trustees of a large charity, was told, somewhat rudely, by the chairman (a businessman) that 'he (the writer) should get into the real world – the only thing that counts is being competitive'.

In the United States many commentators emphasize the importance of the external market. Nielsen (2002) takes exception to the fact that traditional job evaluation is not concerned with external relativities, which, he claims, are what really matter. Research conducted by Heneman (2001) in the United States in 2000 showed that 'market pricing is fast replacing traditional job evaluation as a preferred method of job evaluation'. But in a later article, Heneman, together with LeBlanc (2002), stated that: 'We believe that it is premature to abandon traditional job evaluation for market pricing.' That is why they advocate replacing job evaluation with 'work valuation', which takes account of both internal and external factors. Our research indicates that there is increasing support in the United States for the use of some form of internal valuation or process of levelling to provide a structure for market pricing.

In the United Kingdom the focus tends to be more on internal equity as established by job evaluation, although this varies between sectors – highly competitive finance or high-tech companies tend to be more concerned with competitive pay. Of course, in other sectors market rates are taken into account when attaching pay ranges to grade structures or pricing individual roles, but 'extreme market pricing' does not have the support it attracts in the United States. There are a number of reasons for this, the most important being the greater focus on equal pay in the United Kingdom. Another factor is the strength of the trade unions in the United Kingdom, especially in the public sector. They believe strongly in internal equity and tend only to look outside the organizations with which they are concerned when negotiating increases to base rates. Perhaps in the United Kingdom there is also a stronger philosophical belief in fairness as represented by equitable pay within organizations, a belief captured by Eliot Jaques (1961) that persists today.

REFERENCES

Armstrong, M and Baron, A (1995) *The Job Evaluation Handbook*, CIPD, London

Arvey, R D (1986) Sex bias in job evaluation procedures, *Personnel Psychology*, **39**, pp 315–35

Clarke, K (1987) as reported in *The Times*, 17 March, p 6

Crystal, G (1970) *Financial Motivation for Executives*, American Management Association, New York

Dewey, J (1916) Objects of valuation, *Journal of Philosophy*, **15**, pp 9–35

Ellis, C M, Laymon, R G and LeBlanc, P V (2004) Improving pay productivity with strategic work valuation, *WorldatWork Journal*, Second Quarter, pp 56–68

Emerson, S M (1991) Job evaluation: a barrier to excellence, *Compensation & Benefits Review*, January–February, pp 4–17

Equal Opportunities Commission (2003) *Good Practice Guide – Job Evaluation Free of Sex Bias*, EOC, Manchester

Grayson, D (1987) *Job Evaluation in Transition*, ACAS, London

Gupta, N and Jenkins, G D (1991) Practical problems in using job evaluation to determine compensation, *Human Resource Management Review*, **1** (2), pp 133–44

Heneman, R L (2001) Work evaluation: current state of the art and future prospects, *WorldatWork Journal*, **10** (3) pp 65–70

Heneman, R L and LeBlanc P V (2002) Developing a more relevant and competitive approach for valuing knowledge work, *Compensation & Benefits Review*, July/August, pp 43–47

Heneman, R L and LeBlanc P V (2003) Work valuation addresses shortcomings of both job evaluation and market pricing, *Compensation & Benefits Review*, January/February, pp 7–11

Hicks, J R (1935) *The Theory of Wages*, Oxford University Press, Oxford

Incomes Data Services (1991) *IDS Focus*, No 60, IDS, London

Jaques, E (1961) *Equitable Payment*, Heinemann, Oxford

Lawler, E E (1986) 'What's wrong with point-factor job evaluation?', *Compensation & Benefits Review*, March–April, pp 20–28

Lawler, E E (1991) Paying the person: a better approach to management?, *Human Resource Management Review*, **1** (2), pp 145–54

Madigan, R M and Hills F S (1988) Job evaluation and pay equity, *Public Personnel Management*, **17** (3), pp 24–38

Marx, K (1867, translated in 1976) *Capital*, Harmondsworth, Penguin

Nielsen, N H (2002) Job content evaluation techniques based on Marxian economics, *WorldatWork Journal*, **11** (2), pp 52–62

Phelps Brown, E H (1962) *The Economics of Labour*, Yale University Press, Newhaven, CT

Plachy, R J (1987a) The point-factor job evaluation system: a step by step guide, part 1, *Compensation & Benefits Review*, July–August, pp 12–27

Plachy, R J (1987b) The point-factor job evaluation system: a step by step guide, part 2, *Compensation & Benefits Review*, September–October, pp 9–24

Prichard, D (1995) What's new in job evaluation, *The Human Resource Management Yearbook*, AP Services, London

Pritchard, D and Murlis H (1992) *Jobs, Roles & People*, Nicholas Brealey, London

Quaid, M (1993) *Job Evaluation: The myth of equitable settlement*, University of Toronto Press, Toronto

Risher, H W (1989) Job evaluation: validity and reliability, *Compensation & Benefits Review*, January/February, pp 22–36

2

Role valuation: methodology

The role valuation methods described in this chapter fall broadly into two categories: formal and informal.

Formal methods comprise job evaluation schemes that can operate singly or be combined. Job evaluation schemes are concerned with internal relativities and the associated process of establishing and defining levels in an organization ('levelling'). An alternative approach is 'extreme market pricing', in which formal pay structures and individual rates of pay are entirely based on systematically collected and analysed information on market rates and no use is made of job evaluation to establish internal relativities. This is what we mean when we refer to 'market pricing'. We distinguish between this and the process of collecting and analysing market rate data used to establish external relativities, having already determined internal relativities through formal job evaluation. Formal schemes may be used by a single organization or they may be developed for a whole sector, eg higher education (HERA), further education (Gauge) or local authorities.

Informal approaches price roles either on the basis of assumptions about internal and external relativities or simply by reference to going market rates when recruiting people, unsupported by any systematic analysis. There are, however, degrees of informality. A semi-formal approach may require some firm evidence to support a market pricing decision and the use of role profiles to provide greater accuracy to the matching process.

Formal job evaluation schemes can be either analytical or non-analytical; these are covered in the first two parts of this chapter. Market pricing is dealt with in the third part of the chapter, and informal, combined approaches and 'levelling' are discussed in the next three parts. The penultimate part of the chapter examines how computer-aided job evaluation works to support the process, and the final part lists the parties involved in role valuation.

FORMAL ANALYTICAL JOB EVALUATION SCHEMES

Analytical job evaluation is based on a process of breaking down whole jobs into a number of defined elements or factors such as responsibility, decisions and the knowledge and skill required. These are assumed to be present in all the jobs to be evaluated. In point-factor and fully analytical matching schemes jobs are then compared factor by factor either with a graduated scale of points attached to a set of factors or with grade or role profiles analysed under the same factor headings.

The advantages of an analytical approach are, first, that evaluators have to consider each of the characteristics of the job separately before forming a conclusion about its relative value and, second, they are provided with defined yardsticks or guidelines that help to increase the objectivity and consistency of judgements. It can also provide a defence in the United Kingdom against an equal pay claim (the 'job evaluation study defence'). The main analytical schemes as described below are point-factor rating, analytical matching and factor comparison. A number of management consultants have their own analytical schemes, sometimes referred to as 'proprietary brands'. These are described in Chapter 9.

Point-factor evaluation

Point-factor schemes are the most common forms of analytical job evaluation. They were used by 70 per cent of the respondents to the e-reward 2007 job evaluation survey who had job evaluation schemes. The basic methodology is to break down jobs into factors or key elements representing the demands made by the job on job holders. It is assumed that each of the factors will contribute to the value of the job and is an aspect of all the jobs to be evaluated but to different degrees.

Each factor is divided into a hierarchy of levels. Definitions of these levels are produced to provide guidance on deciding the degree to which the factor applies in the job to be evaluated. Evaluators consult the role profile or job description, which should ideally analyse the role in terms of the scheme's factors. They then refer to the level definitions for each factor and decide which one best fits the job.

A maximum points score is allocated to each factor. The scores available may vary between different factors in accordance with beliefs about their relative significance. This is termed 'explicit weighting'. If the number of levels varies between factors, this means that they are 'implicitly weighted', because the range of scores available will be greater in the factors with more levels.

The total score for a factor is divided between the levels to produce the numerical factor scale. Progression may be arithmetic, eg 50, 100, 150, 200, etc or geometric, eg 50, 100, 175, 275 and so on. In the latter case, more scope is given to recognize the more senior jobs with higher scores.

The complete scheme consists of the factor and level definitions and the scoring system (the total score available for each factor and distributed to the factor levels). This comprises the 'factor plan'.

Jobs are 'scored' (ie, allocated points) under each factor heading on the basis of the level of the factor in the job. This is done by comparing the features of the job with regard to that factor with the factor level definitions to find out which definition provides the best fit. The separate factor scores are then added together to give a total score that indicates the relative value of each job and can be used to place the jobs in rank order.

A point-factor scheme can be operated manually – a 'paper' scheme – or computers can be used to aid the evaluation process, as described later in this chapter. An example of a point-factor scheme developed for a large trade union is given in Appendix B.

Analytical matching

Like point-factor job evaluation, analytical matching is based on the analysis of a number of defined factors. There are two forms of analytical matching. One is role profile to grade/level profile matching, the other is role profile to benchmark role profile.

In *role to grade analytical matching*, profiles of roles to be evaluated are matched to grade, band or level profiles. Reference is made to a grade structure incorporating the jobs covered by the evaluation scheme.

This consists of a sequence or hierarchy of grades, bands or levels that have been defined analytically in terms of a set of factors that may correspond to the job evaluation factors in a point-factor scheme or a selection of them. They may also or alternatively refer to levels of competency and responsibility, especially in job and career family structures, as described in Chapter 11. Information on roles is obtained by questionnaires or interviews and role profiles are produced for the jobs to be evaluated under the same headings as the grade or level profiles. The role profiles are then 'matched' with the range of grade or level profiles to establish the best fit and thus grade the job.

In *role to role analytical matching,* role profiles for jobs to be evaluated are matched analytically with benchmark role profiles. A benchmark role or job is one that has already been graded as a result of an initial job evaluation exercise. It is used as a point of reference with which other roles or jobs can be compared and valued. Thus, if role A has been evaluated and placed in grade 3 and there is a good fit between the factor profile of role B and that of role A, then role B will also be placed in grade 3. Roles are analysed against a common set of factors or elements. Generic role profiles, ie those covering a number of like roles, will be used for any class or cluster of roles with essentially the same range of responsibilities, such as team leaders or personal assistants. Role to role matching may be used in combination with role to grade matching.

In both these methods a decision on fit may be governed by a protocol, as in the National Health Service (NHS) Agenda for Change Programme, or it may be based on a general review of all the factorized information on roles, leading to an overall comparison with level or benchmark role profiles.

Analytical matching may be used to grade jobs or place them in levels following the initial evaluation of a sufficiently large and representative sample of benchmark roles. This can happen in big organizations when it is believed that it is not necessary to go through the whole process of point-factor evaluation for every job, especially where 'generic' roles are concerned. When this follows a large job evaluation exercise such as in the NHS, the factors used in analytical matching may be the same as those in the point-factor job evaluation scheme that underpins the analytical matching process and can be invoked to deal with difficult cases or appeals. In some matching schemes the number of factors may be simplified, for example some higher education institutions clustered related factors in the HERA scheme together, reducing the number of factors from 14 to seven.

However, analytical matching may not necessarily be underpinned by a point-factor evaluation scheme, which can save a lot of time in the design stage as well as when rolling out the scheme. In this case the approach is based on a matrix in which profiles or definitions of the grades or levels are defined analytically in terms of a number of factors but no points are attached to levels and the jobs are not scored as in a point-factor scheme. Instead, role profiles are matched analytically by role to grade matching and/or role to role matching as described above. In effect, as modelled in Figure 2.1, this method means slicing a conventional factor plan horizontally and assembling the factor definitions level by level, which produces level profiles containing the definitions for the factors at each level. In practice, as in the extract from a matrix developed for a charity given in Table 2.1, the starting point may be directly to form a matrix through the analytical level definitions without preparing a factor plan. In this case the matrix can be turned into a factor plan by slicing it vertically, which was done in the charity referred to above to provide a check on the validity of the matrix.

Factor comparison

The original factor comparison method compared jobs factor by factor using a scale of money values to provide a direct indication of the rate for the job. It was developed in the United States but is not used in the United Kingdom. The Hay Guide Chart profile method is described by the Hay Group as a factor comparison scheme, but, apart from this,

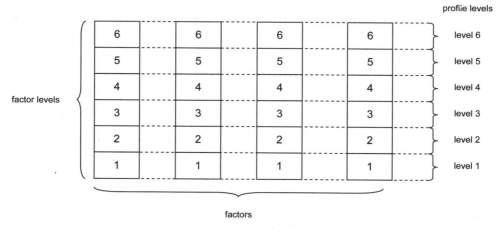

Figure 2.1 Model of analytical matching matrix

Table 2.1 Extract from an analytical matching matrix

	BAND 5
Scope	Work is varied and focuses on the achievement of service delivery or technical/specialist departmental goals.
	Deals with problems or issues that need detailed information gathering, investigation and analysis, including assessment of benefits and risks of different courses of action: expected to make direct contribution to improved performance, whether through own area of work or through participation in cross-disciplinary projects.
	Manager agrees priorities and gives guidance on business issues, but role holder is expected to resolve most technical/operational issues unaided.
Impact of decisions	Internal impact: decisions, recommendations or actions impact on the effectiveness of operations and/or quality of service provided by the department and may set a precedent for future decisions. Impact may extend to other areas of organization or the department's ability to meet departmental objectives in the short to medium term.
	External impact is typically localized to a geographic area or department, influencing perceptions of departmental effectiveness or quality of service over the short to medium term.
Resources	May have delegated budgetary responsibility; may allocate resources, input to the planning or budgetary process or advise on budget spend, allocation or use of resources.
	May have personal or team income target.
Interpersonal skills	Develops and maintains professional relationships on behalf of organization; may be involved in developing new business relationships.
	Requires ability to have a constructive dialogue and persuade or advise colleagues, external representatives or clients in a wide variety of circumstances, tailoring approach to audience/stakeholder/client needs and views.
People skills	May have formal responsibility for others or be involved in providing advice to line managers on a broad range of people-related issues; for line managers this includes direct responsibility for conducting performance reviews and developing action plans to improve the performance of others, whether staff or volunteers; may direct the work of others and take responsibility for ensuring that work quality and professional standards are maintained.
Applied knowledge and skill	Applies deep or broad level of specialist or technical expertise.
	Will be called on as a source of expertise, both within and outside own area. This is particularly so for specialist roles that have no people responsibilities.

the only form of factor comparison now in use is graduated factor comparison, which compares jobs factor by factor with a graduated scale. The scale may have only three value levels – for example lower, equal, higher – and no factor scores are used. This is a method often used by the independent experts engaged by employment tribunals to advise on an equal pay claim. Their job is simply to compare one job with one or two others, not to review internal relativities over the whole spectrum of jobs in order to produce a rank order. Independent experts may score their judgements of comparative levels, in which case graduated factor comparison resembles the point-factor method except that the number of levels and range of scores are limited, and the factors may not be weighted.

Graduated factor comparison can be used within organizations if there is a problem of comparable worth and no other analytical scheme is available. It can also be used in a benchmarking exercise to assess relativities across different categories of employees in the absence of a common analytical job evaluation scheme, as long as the factors used are common to all the job categories under consideration.

Tailor-made, ready-made and hybrid schemes

Any of the schemes referred to above can be 'tailor-made' or 'home grown' in the sense that they are developed specifically by or for an organization, a group of organizations or a sector, eg further education establishments. The 2007 e-reward survey showed that only 20 per cent of the schemes were tailor-made (this was 37 per cent in the e-reward 2003 survey).

A number of management consultants offer their own 'ready-made' schemes, as described in Chapter 9. They are often called 'propriet-ary brands'. Consultants' schemes tend to be analytical (point-factor, factor comparison or matching) and may be linked to a market rate database. They often provide for computer-aided schemes. As many as 60 per cent of the respondents to the e-reward survey used these schemes.

Hybrid schemes are consultants' schemes that have been modif-ied to fit the particular needs of an organization – 20 per cent of the e-reward respondents had such schemes. Typically, the modification consists of amendments to the factor plan or, in the case of Hay, to the Hay Guide Chart.

It is also possible to develop a computer-aided approach in con-junction with a tailor-made job evaluation scheme using software provided by a consultant such as Link or Pilat, although this is not strictly a hybrid scheme in the sense described above.

FORMAL NON-ANALYTICAL SCHEMES

Non-analytical job evaluation schemes enable whole jobs to be compared in order to place them in a grade or a rank order – they are not analysed by reference to their elements or factors. They can stand alone or be used to help in the development of an analytical scheme. For example, the paired comparison technique described later can produce a rank order of jobs that can be used to test the outcomes of an evaluation using an analytical scheme. It is therefore helpful to know how non-analytical schemes function even if they are not used as the main scheme.

Non-analytical schemes operate on a *job to job* basis in which a job is compared with another job to decide whether it should be valued more, or less, or the same (ranking and 'internal benchmarking' processes). Alternatively, they may function on a *job to grade* basis in which judgements are made by comparing a whole job with a defined hierarchy of job grades (job classification) – this involves matching a job description to a grade description. The e-reward 2007 survey showed that only 14 per cent of respondents' schemes were non-analytical (21 per cent in 2003).

Non-analytical schemes are relatively simple but rely on overall and potentially more subjective judgements than analytical schemes. Such judgements will not be guided by a factor plan and do not take account of the complexity of jobs. There is a danger therefore of leaping to conclusions about job values based on *a priori* assumptions that could be prejudiced. For this reason, non-analytical schemes do not provide a defence in a UK equal pay case.

There are four main types of non-analytical schemes: job classification, job ranking, paired comparison (a statistical version of ranking), and internal benchmarking.

Job classification

This approach is based on a definition of the number and characteristics of the levels or grades in a grade and pay structure into which jobs will be placed. The grade definitions may refer to such job characteristics as skill, decision making and responsibility, but these are not analysed separately. Evaluation takes place through a process of non-analytical matching or 'job slotting'. This involves comparing a 'whole' job description, ie one not analysed into factors, with the grade definitions to establish the grade with which the job most closely corresponds. The difference between job classification and role to grade analytical matching as described above is that in the latter case, the grade profiles are defined analytically, ie in terms of job evaluation factors, and analytically defined role profiles are matched with them factor by factor. However, the distinction between analytical and non-analytical matching can be blurred when the comparison is made between formal job descriptions or role profiles that have been prepared in a standard format which includes common headings for such aspects of jobs as levels of responsibility or knowledge and skill requirements. These 'factors' may not be compared specifically but will be taken into account when forming a judgement. This may not satisfy the UK legal requirement that a scheme must be analytical to provide a defence in an equal pay claim.

Job ranking

Whole job ranking is the most primitive form of job evaluation. The process involves comparing whole jobs with one another and arranging them in order of their perceived value to the organization. In a sense, all evaluation schemes are ranking exercises, because they place jobs in a hierarchy. The difference between simple ranking and analytical methods such as point-factor rating is that job ranking does not attempt to quantify judgements. Instead, whole jobs are compared – they are not broken down into factors or elements, although, explicitly or implicitly, the comparison may be based on some generalized concept such as the level of responsibility. Job ranking or paired comparison ranking as described below is sometimes used as a check on the rank order obtained by point-factor rating.

Paired comparison ranking

Paired comparison ranking is a statistical technique used to provide a more sophisticated method of whole job ranking. It is based on the assumption that it is always easier to compare one job with another than to consider a number of jobs and attempt to build up a rank order by multiple comparisons.

The technique requires the comparison of each job as a whole separately with every other job. If a job is considered to be of a higher value than the one with which it is being compared it receives two points; if it is thought to be equally important, it receives one point; if it is regarded as less important, no points are awarded. The scores are added for each job and a rank order is obtained.

Paired comparisons can be done factor by factor and in this case can be classified as analytical. A simplified example of a paired comparison ranking is shown in Table 2.2.

Table 2.2 A paired comparison

Job reference	a	b	c	d	e	f	Total score	Ranking
A	–	0	1	0	1	0	2	5=
B	2	–	2	2	2	0	8	2
C	1	0	–	1	1	0	3	4
D	2	0	1	–	2	0	5	3
E	1	0	1	0	–	0	2	5=
F	2	2	2	2	2	–	10	1

The advantage of paired comparison ranking over normal ranking is that it is easier to compare one job with another than to make multiple comparisons. However, it cannot overcome the fundamental objections to any form of whole job ranking – that no defined standards for judging relative worth are provided and it is not an acceptable method of assessing equal value or comparable worth. There is also a limit to the number of jobs that can be compared using this method – to evaluate 50 jobs requires 1,225 comparisons. Paired comparisons are occasionally used analytically to compare jobs on a factor by factor basis.

Internal benchmarking

Internal benchmarking is what people often do intuitively when they are deciding on the value of jobs, although it is not usually dignified in job evaluation circles as a formal method of job evaluation. It simply means comparing the job under review with any internal job that is believed to be properly graded and paid (an internal benchmark) and placing the job under consideration into the same grade as that job. The comparison is made on a whole job basis without analysing the jobs factor by factor. It can be classified as a formal method if there are specific procedures for preparing and setting out role profiles and for comparing profiles for the role to be evaluated with standard benchmark role profiles.

MARKET PRICING

As explained at the beginning of this chapter, we make a distinction between 'extreme market pricing' and the normal process of obtaining data on market rates to inform decisions on pay structures and individual rates of pay. Extreme market pricing directly prices jobs within the organization by means of a systematic analysis of market rates (external relativities). Internal relativities reflect relativities in the marketplace and conventional job evaluation is not used. An organization that adopts this method is said to be 'market driven'. Techniques are described in Chapter 8. This approach has been widely adopted in the United States. It is associated with a belief that 'the market rules OK', disillusionment with what was regarded as bureaucratic job evaluation, and the enthusiasm for broad-banded pay structures (ie structures with a limited number of grades or bands, as described in Chapter 11). It is a method that often has appeal at board level because of the focus on the need to compete in the marketplace for talent.

Market rate analysis may be associated with formal job evaluation. The latter establishes internal relativities and the grade structure, and market pricing is used to develop the pay structure – the pay ranges attached to grades. Information on market rates may lead to the introduction of market supplements for individual jobs or the creation of separate pay structures (market groups) to cater for particular market rate pressures.

The acceptability of market pricing is dependent on the availability of robust market data and, when looking at external rates, the quality of the job to job matching process, ie comparing like with like. It can therefore vary from analysis of data by job titles to detailed matched analysis collected through bespoke surveys focused on real market equivalence. Extreme market pricing can provide guidance on internal relativities even if these are market-driven. But it can lead to pay discrimination against women where the market has traditionally been discriminatory. It does not satisfy UK equal pay legislation. To avoid a successful equal pay claim in the United Kingdom, any difference in pay between men and women carrying out work of equal value based on market rate considerations has to be 'objectively justified', ie the employment tribunal will need to be convinced that this was not simply a matter of opinion and that adequate evidence from a number of sources was available. In such cases, the tribunal will also require proof that there is a business case for the market premium to the effect that the recruitment and retention of people essential to the organization was difficult because pay levels were uncompetitive.

INFORMAL ROLE VALUATION APPROACHES

Roles are valued informally when there is no attempt to use any of the formal methods described above. This is often the case in small or start-up businesses. Larger organizations may also prefer to value roles informally because they feel that they can achieve an acceptable result (at least to the management) without wasting time on formal job evaluation or market pricing. The most common informal approaches are examined below.

Informal internal benchmarking

Informal internal benchmarking takes place when on appointment, promotion or transfer to a different job a person's pay is determined by reference to the pay of another person who is thought to be in a job of comparable worth. No formal and detailed comparisons are made between the responsibilities of the person involved and those of the person in the job that is being used as a benchmark. It is assumed by some process of intuition that the jobs are similar and that this provides adequate guidance on the appropriate rate of pay. Allowance may be made for the level of experience or skill of the person whose pay is being determined as against that of the individual with whom he or she is being compared, but again this is done intuitively.

Informal job slotting

Informal job slotting takes place when a defined grade structure already exists and jobs are simply allocated to grades without any precise comparison with a grade definition of the features of the job. This may be associated with informal benchmarking – comparing the job to be allocated with jobs that have already been graded.

Informal market pricing

Informal market pricing takes place when some account is taken of perceived market rates for comparable jobs. These are often collected from dubious sources such as advertisements.

Comment

Informal benchmarking or slotting may possibly produce reasonably equitable results, and informal approaches based on market pricing may ensure that pay levels are reasonably competitive. They save time and trouble and can be attractive to smaller and start-up businesses. But they rely mainly on intuitive judgement and can lead to unequal pay. They may also result in over- or under-payment because of the inadequate nature of the market rate data.

COMBINED APPROACHES

There are three basic ways of combining the above approaches:

1. *Point-factor rating/analytical matching* – point-factor rating or an analytical proprietary brand is used to evaluate benchmark posts as the basis for designing a grade structure in which grade profiles are defined analytically, and the remaining posts are graded by analytical matching.

2. *Point-factor rating/job classification* – point-factor rating or an analytical proprietary brand is used to evaluate benchmark posts as the basis for designing a grade structure in which grades are defined non-analytically and the remaining posts are graded by slotting them into grades on a whole job basis.

3. *Formal job evaluation/market rate comparison* – formal job evaluation is supplemented by information on market rates when developing pay structures, deciding on market supplements (additions to the base rate to reflect market rates), and fixing individual rates of pay.

The first two types of combination are used when it is believed that time will be saved by not extending benchmark point-factor rating to a large number of other posts. Some form of market rate analysis is commonly used when developing a pay structure following the initial job evaluation.

LEVELLING

'Levelling' is a term often used by consultants to describe a process of identifying and defining the levels of work that exist in an organization. It may serve as the basis for a pay structure, but, increasingly, levelling provides guidance on career mapping, organizational analysis, developing and describing international organization structures, and providing a link to an information technology system such as PeopleSoft or SAP.

When it is used simply as a means of defining pay structures, 'levelling' could be regarded as no more than a euphemism adopted by consultants who want to dissociate themselves from the negative connotations of traditional job evaluation schemes. But it is more meaningful when the focus is on the career mapping, organizational and IT applications mentioned above. Defining an organization structure in levels may express the philosophy of a business about how it should be organized and the career steps that are available to its people.

In practice, levelling uses established job evaluation techniques such as analytical matching or job classification and may be underpinned by point-factor rating. It starts with a decision on the number of levels required, which could be based on a ranking exercise using either point-factor scheme scores or whole job ranking. Alternatively, an *a priori* decision may be made on the number of levels required by a study of the organization structure, which may be supported by a role profiling exercise. This decision may be amended later after the level structure has been tested. Levels may be defined in terms of job evaluation factors or a selection of them. Sometimes, as in the Unilever example given below, only a single descriptor is used. In cases where the focus is on career mapping as well as or instead of pay determination, the level definitions or profiles may be defined in ways that clearly establish the career ladder, often in a career or job family. The definition may express what people are expected to know and be able to do at each level (technical competencies) and/or they may refer to behavioural competencies. The aim is to produce a clear hierarchy of levels that will ease the process of allocating roles to levels and define career progression steps in and between families.

An example of levelling is provided by Unilever, which rejected the notion of broad-banding and introduced its 'work level' structure. This is a variation of broad-grading using different nomenclature and a special approach to defining levels. There are six work levels, each subdivided into a number of pay grades. The levels were determined according to the idea of the time-span of discretion developed by Eliot Jaques (1961) and also measure the strategic importance of particular jobs. The three principles underlying levels are:

1. The major tasks of any job fall into a single work level. This is the case despite the fact that a job may include a mixture of tasks, with an executive making strategic decisions also undertaking less demanding administrative tasks.

2. At each successive higher work level, decisions of a broader nature are taken in an increasingly complex environment. Discretion and the authority required to do the job also increase, and more time is required to assess the impact of these decisions. Assigning jobs to work levels involves identifying the decisions that are unique to a job. This helps to highlight differences in management decision making and accountability, which in turn allows the management structure to be more clearly delineated.

3. Each work level above the first requires one and only one layer of management. A layer of management is necessary only where a manager makes decisions that could not be taken by subordinates, who may be more than one level below their boss. The company's work levels approach ensures that job holders take decisions that cannot be taken at a lower level.

The example of level definitions in Table 2.3 is taken from the Peabody Trust framework. The complete framework also has headings for expertise and eight competencies.

COMPUTER-AIDED JOB EVALUATION

Computer-aided job evaluation uses computer software to convert information about jobs into a job evaluation score or grade. It is generally underpinned by a conventional point-factor scheme. The 'proprietary brands' offered by consultants are often computer-aided.

Table 2.3 Level definitions for accountability – Peabody Trust

---

ACCOUNTABILITY

The type and level of work carried out by the role holder; the results for which the role holder is accountable; the degree to which work is prescribed; the amount of freedom to act

---

A
- Provide basic administrative and support services
- Work largely prescribed, freedom to act fairly limited
- Role requirements clearly defined

B
- Provide fairly complex administrative and support services
- Work largely standardized
- Some freedom to decide on methods and priorities

C
- Provide complex administrative and support services or technical support
- Some diversity in role requirements
- Act within specific and detailed policy and procedural guidelines

D
- Manage certain operations within function or provide professional services in a key area
- The work is diverse
- Act within broad policy guidelines

E
- Manage a function or department within an operational or technical area or is the main provider of professional advice and services in a key aspect of the Trust's activities
- The work is highly diverse
- Freedom to act within broad policy frameworks

F
- Head of a major function or department, making a major impact on the performance of the Trust
- The work is complex and involves making a broad range of highly diverse decisions
- A considerable amount of independent action is required within the framework of Trust strategies and plans and subject only to general guidance

G
- Take part in creating a shared vision and mission for the Trust
- Take part in formulating the Trust's strategic goals
- Formulate strategies for the function for which the Management Team member is responsible
- Gain support for organizational and functional strategies
- Ensure that functional strategies are implemented and that strategic goals are achieved

Computers may be used simply to maintain a database recording evaluations and their rationale. In the design stage they can provide guidance on weighting factors through multiple regression analysis, although this technique is not used as extensively as it used to be.

Methodology

The software used in a fully computer-aided scheme essentially replicates in digital form the thought processes followed by evaluators when conducting a 'manual' evaluation. It is based on defined evaluation decision rules built into the system shell. The software typically provides a facility for consistency checks by, for example, highlighting scoring differences between the job being evaluated and other benchmark jobs.

There are two types of computer-aided evaluation. The first is schemes in which the job analysis data are either entered direct into the computer or transferred to it from a paper questionnaire. The computer software applies predetermined rules to convert the data into scores for each factor and produce a total score. This is the most common approach.

The second is interactive computer-aided schemes in which the job holder and his or her manager sit in front of a PC and are presented with a series of logically interrelated questions, the answers to which lead to a score for each of the built in factors in turn, and a total score.

The case for computer-aided job evaluation

In a point-factor scheme that is not computer-aided, jobs are often evaluated by a panel that may include a broadly representative group of staff as well as line managers and one or more members of the HR department. The panel will have been trained in interpreting the factor plan and applying this in the evaluation of the job descriptions or questionnaires provided. The panel studies the job information and, by relating this to the factor level definitions and panel decisions on previous jobs, debates and agrees the level (and hence the score) that should be allocated for each factor. To save time, individual members of a panel may have carried out evaluations prior to panel meetings. This is a well-understood process that has been tried and tested over more than 50 years and, properly applied, is generally accepted as a good approach by all concerned.

The problem with the panel approach is chiefly the way it is applied, leading to the criticisms of job evaluation outlined in Chapter 1. The most common failings or disadvantages are:

▮ *Inconsistent judgements* – although the initial panel may be well trained, panel membership changes and, over time, the interpretation of the factor plan may also change. The presence or absence of a particularly strong-minded member may influence panel decisions.

▮ *Inadequate record of decisions* – each allocated factor level will, of necessity, be recorded, but panels do not always conform to good practice by maintaining a record of how each decision was reached (a rationale). If an 'appeal' is lodged, it can be difficult to assess whether or not the original panel took account of whatever evidence is presented in support of the appeal. The Gauge system of job evaluation helps to overcome this difficulty by recording the decision-making process.

▮ *Staff input required* – a panel of six or seven people (a typical size) may take an hour or more to evaluate each job if a traditional job by job approach is used. Ten person-hours or so could thus be spent evaluating each job. This is a substantial cost for any organization.

▮ *Time taken to complete the process* – assembling a quorum of trained panel members may take several weeks and, if their evaluations are subject to review by some higher-level review team (to minimize the risk of subsequent appeals), it can take two or three months to complete the whole process.

Incorporating computer-aided job evaluation into the process from the outset can help to overcome these problems. Depending on the type of scheme, it can achieve greater consistency – the same input information gives the same output result. It can also increase the speed of evaluations, reduce the resources required and provide facilities for sorting, analysing and reporting on the input information and system outputs, and record keeping (database).

However, it is worth remembering that the system can only support the job evaluation process by using the rules and algorithms that have been built in to it. Human judgement is still required to design the scheme in the first place and to ensure that accurate job information is entered. In practice there is no such thing as 'computerized' job evaluation – only computer-aided evaluation.

The capabilities that can be found across a range of software packages are summarized in Table 2.4.

The software platforms have moved on considerably in recent years. Whereas initial computer-aided job evaluation schemes used to require the installation of a software package on a stand-alone PC or server, most consultancy firms offering a computer-aided scheme now provide for internet, intranet or PC access. The advantage of

Table 2.4 Software job evaluation applications

Support to scheme design	
Development of weightings/scoring	Paired comparison to support development of weightings. Use of software package to develop weighting, eg SSPS for multiple regression analyses (often manipulated by consultant as part of development process – not part of client software package).
Data management	
Record keeping	Record of individual evaluation responses. Maintaining library of benchmark roles.
Data entry	Direct import of job questionnaires completed manually. Direct online responses to questionnaire by job holder or analyst; may be accompanied by guidance and the ability to refer to similar jobs (sometimes called an 'expert' system). Direct online responses that are tailored to responses already entered (an 'interactive' system)
Job descriptions/profiles	Ability to write job descriptions using a standard template, or evaluation responses generate a profile that is based on an adapted form of wording from the evaluation scheme.
Progress checking	System records status of all scores, eg provisional, final and multiple scores for the same job where it is evaluated separately by more than one evaluator prior to evaluation team review.
Analysis and reporting	
Scoring	Calculation of evaluation scores using predetermined scoring/weighting – either built into standard package or agreed with client and built into software (usually on basis that client does not have access to the scoring model to make any changes).
	Sophisticated scoring capability, including ability to build relationships between responses to separate questions.

Table 2.4 Software job evaluation applications *(continued)*

Tailored reporting	Rank order listings either by total job score or factor by factor, either in order of calculated points score or by factor level entered (A, B, C, etc). Analysis of evaluation results by function, gender or other pre-determined elements. Inter-site/division comparisons. Ability to generate customized reports.
Quality review	Quality checking of data entry for missing information. Identification of inconsistent scores, eg outside of pre-defined parameters, or unusual relativities between jobs (eg manager scores less than subordinate on decision making).
Additional applications linked to job evaluation	
Pay modelling	Modelling grades, salaries and costs of new pay structure (typically includes scattergrams, lines of best fit).
Equal pay review	Analysis by gender, disability, race or age for pay elements of total package, allowances and other benefits.
Competencies	Provides a link between job requirements and individual performance expectations and required behaviours.
Survey link	Direct link to consultants' pay database, based on evaluation points or bandings.

web-enabled systems is that the software is updated automatically, so there is no need to have to install the latest upgrade on site.

A web-enabled or intranet system means that organizations can devolve the administration of their scheme around the organization or, where relevant, around the world. Where this is the case, the package will invariably provide for a range of security settings. This will typically allow for some locations or users to have read-only access; others will be able to enter and amend data for the jobs under their jurisdiction only; while at the highest level the system 'administrator' will have complete access to all records in the system.

The case against computer-aided job evaluation

For some organizations the full approach is a too expensive and elaborate process for them to be bothered with. Others do not want to abandon the involvement of employees and their representatives in the traditional panel approach. There is also the problem of transparency in some applications. This is sometimes called 'the black box effect' – those concerned have difficulty in understanding the logic that converts the input information to a factor level score. Interactive systems such as those offered by Pilat Consultants (Gauge) and Watson Wyatt aim to overcome this difficulty.

It is perhaps for these reasons that less than half the respondents to the 2007 e-reward survey had computer-aided schemes, and over half of those used computers simply to maintain job evaluation records.

THE PARTIES INVOLVED

The parties involved in role valuation are:

- *senior managers* who determine or agree on the policy;
- *front-line managers* who play an important part in implementing and maintaining role valuation and should take part in the design of a formal scheme;
- *employees* who are affected by role valuation and, through representatives, may be involved in the design and operation of a scheme;
- *trade union or staff association representatives* who are usually consulted on the scheme and participate in its design;
- *HR or reward specialists* who advise on the role valuation policies and practice, take part in selecting the approach and any external advisers, and are involved in the planning, management and implementation of the project, often as project leaders;
- *project team/panel chair* who chairs project team meetings and job evaluation or role matching panels;
- *project team members* who take part in designing and implementing the scheme;
- *job or role analysts* who obtain information about jobs and roles and produce job descriptions or role profiles (this may be done manually or with the aid of computers, see above);
- *evaluators* who are the individuals who evaluate jobs or roles, review and moderate results and hear appeals – they may be

members of a job evaluation, matching, moderating or appeals panel, or facilitators, managers and employees in an interactive scheme;

∎ *external advisers* who provide expertise and experience in developing and operating role valuation.

CHOICE OF APPROACH

When deciding on how roles should be valued, either when doing it for the first time in a considered way, or when reviving an existing scheme, there is always choice – on the type of approach and on how it should be applied. The considerations affecting this choice are discussed in the next chapter.

REFERENCE

Jaques, E (1961) *Equitable Payment*, Heinemann, Oxford

Part 2

Developing Job Evaluation

3

Choice of approach

The fundamental choice is between using formal or informal methods of valuing roles. This may not be a conscious decision. A company may use informal methods simply because that's what it has always done and because it never occurs to its management that there is an alternative. But it may decide deliberately that an informal or semi-formal approach fits its circumstances best.

Alternatively, a formal approach may be preferred and there is plenty of choice. The aim of this chapter is to provide guidance on making the choice between a formal and informal approach, and if the former is preferred, which method should be used.

The chapter covers:

- the factors that affect the choice;

- a decision tree on selecting the approach;

- reviewing present arrangements;

- deciding whether to retain, modify or replace a formal or informal approach;

- defining objectives;

- drawing up a specification;

- evaluating alternative formal approaches;

▌ choosing between a tailor-made, ready-made or hybrid scheme;

▌ using external help;

▌ planning and resourcing the development programme.

FACTORS AFFECTING CHOICE

The method of role valuation used will depend first on the objectives of the exercise, second on contextual factors (the environment of the organization), and finally on the degree to which any of the methods available meet the objectives and fit the context.

Objectives of role valuation

The use of role evaluation can have a number of purposes, as discussed in Chapter 1. These include determining the level or grade of jobs, developing and maintaining pay structures, achieving equal pay for work of equal value (and creating a defence against an equal pay claim), providing a framework for career planning, and contributing to organizational analysis and design. The objectives will affect the choice of scheme and need to be defined.

Contextual factors

Context is all important. It consists of the type of organization, its size, complexity and culture, the work carried out in it and its structure. It may also be influenced by the employee relations climate. The approach in international firms may differ from those operating in any one country. External pressures from legislation and trade unions may also affect the choice. Whatever the methodology, it must fit the organization's context.

The type, size and complexity of the organization

Some types of organizations are more likely to use formal job evaluation than others. Public and private bureaucracies prefer an ordered existence. The survey conducted by e-reward in 2007 established that job evaluation is much more widespread in the public services and voluntary sectors (79 per cent) than in the private sector (51 per cent).

Smaller organizations are less likely to use formal job evaluation than large and complex ones. A small business may believe – rightly or wrongly – that it does not need the support of an elaborate job evaluation scheme to run its pay system.

Organization culture

The core values of organizations will affect their attitude to job evaluation. Those that believe strongly in equity, fairness and transparency may be more inclined to use a formal scheme, and while sensitive to market rates will not allow their pay system to be driven by them. Organizations whose values are dominated by the need to achieve competitive advantage and enhance shareholder value may be less inclined to give prominence to the ideal of internal equity.

Work and organization structure

Job evaluation is more likely to be used formally where the work is relatively structured, prescribed or routine, as in public and private bureaucracies and manufacturing. It is less likely to occur in organizations largely staffed by knowledge workers (eg research and development) or creative workers (eg advertising agencies).

Employee relations

Job evaluation is often used in organizations with strong unions representing professional, administrative or manual workers. This is one reason why job evaluation is more common in the public sector, which is more strongly unionized than other sectors. However, in the United Kingdom unions representing manual workers and prison officers, fire fighters and police officers have traditionally been suspicious of job evaluation, even hostile to it. Some of them have felt that it is a management ploy that will be used to undermine their ability to influence pay decisions. This view is less prevalent today in amalgamated 'white collar' and workers' unions and in the public sector unions representing administrative staff, but it still exists in some quarters, such as the Prison Officers' Association.

International firms

International firms have a variety of practices depending on their structure and management processes. Some may prefer to use a formal system to ensure a degree of uniformity in dealing with grade and pay issues, for example the pay of local staff, expatriates and third-country nationals in their international units or subsidiaries. They may also be interested in role valuation as a means of developing international career pathways.

The approach adopted may be a traditional formal scheme coupled with market pricing through local pay surveys. Some international organizations use the services of management consultants to establish rates of pay in different countries using a common structure of grade levels. Details of consultants' schemes are provided in Chapter 9 and further information on how roles are valued in international firms is given in Chapter 12.

The external environment

The approach to role valuation will be affected by the labour market – if it is highly competitive, market pricing is more likely to be favoured. It will also be affected by equal pay legislation and, sometimes, the views of the national trade unions.

The impact of the factors

How the factors affect the choice of approach is summarized in Table 3.1

Table 3.1 Factors affecting choice of approach

Approach	Factors affecting choice
More likely to be in favour of formal job evaluation	• Larger, more complex, more bureaucratic organizations • Strong values in favour of equity, fairness and transparency • Positive trade union influence • Need to meet equal pay requirements, eg reviews • In an international firm; policy on the degree to which a uniform approach is required influenced by the need to make cross-border comparisons
More likely to be in favour of extreme market pricing	• A highly competitive labour market • The existence of high-quality market data
More likely to adopt an informal approach	• Smaller and start-up organizations • Hostility to job evaluation – unnecessary, cumbersome, bureaucratic • Belief that the market is all-important, without resorting to extreme market pricing

DECIDING ON THE APPROACH TO ROLE VALUATION

A decision tree/flow chart for selecting which approach to adopt is given in Figure 3.1 and the main stages are discussed below.

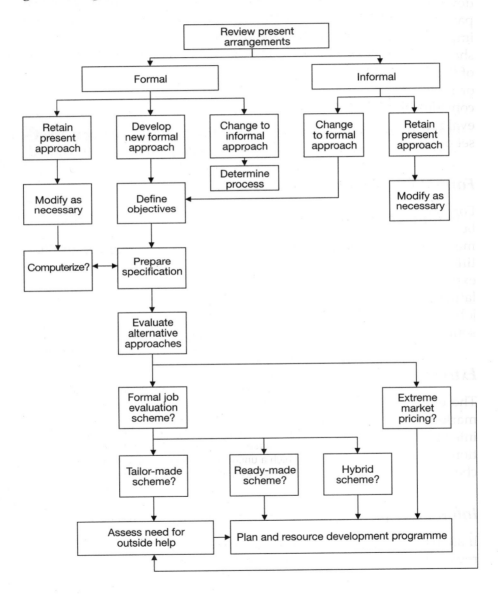

Figure 3.1 Stages in deciding on the approach to role valuation

REVIEW PRESENT ARRANGEMENTS

The starting point is an analysis of the present arrangements in order to establish the extent to which they are fit for purpose, ie how far they provide a clear, logical, fair and generally acceptable basis for developing and maintaining an equitable and competitive grade and pay structure that fits the organization's aims and context without imposing unacceptable costs or administrative burdens. The analysis should identify any specific problems and be followed by a diagnosis of the causes of the problems to indicate a course of action: to replace or revise the present approaches or to retain them. The points to be considered with regard to the three main approaches – formal job evaluation, extreme market pricing and informal role valuation – are set out below.

Formal job evaluation schemes

Formal job evaluation schemes can decay. The factors may no longer be appropriate, job descriptions can be inflated and scores may be manipulated, which can lead to inequities and 'grade drift' (unjustifiable upgrading). Schemes can be bureaucratic, time-consuming and expensive to operate. The checklist on page 54 contains questions relating to these and other typical problems that can arise in established job evaluation schemes, especially if they have been functioning for some time.

Extreme market pricing

The effectiveness of extreme market pricing, ie relying entirely on market rate data to determine competitive rates of pay and, in effect, internal relativities, depends largely on the validity of the data. Questions need also to be asked about how it impacts on internal equity. A checklist is set out on page 55.

Informal approach

If an informal approach exists, the checklist on page 55 can be used to review its effectiveness.

Checklist for reviewing the effectiveness of a formal job evaluation scheme

1. Does the scheme show any general signs of decaying?
2. In an analytical scheme, are the factors still appropriate in the light of changes in roles and the way in which work is organized, or new approaches to defining the core values and competencies of the organization?
3. In a points scheme, is there any evidence of 'point grabbing', ie using inflated role profiles or job descriptions to acquire the extra points needed to achieve an upgrading?
4. Does the scheme lead to or fail to control grade drift?
5. Are the results obtained by the scheme consistent, ie similar roles are valued the same in different functions or over time?
6. Has operating the scheme become a 'cottage industry', ie a time-consuming and paper production process that creates unnecessary work and not added value?
7. Do employees understand how the scheme operates and how it influences grade and pay decisions?
8. Are employees and their representatives cynical about the scheme or openly hostile to it because they feel it functions unfairly or inconsistently?
9. Does the scheme provide a satisfactory basis for maintaining an equitable grade and pay structure?
10. Will the scheme provide an adequate defence in an equal pay case?

DECIDE WHETHER TO RETAIN, MODIFY OR REPLACE

The answer to these checklists will provide guidance on whether the formal scheme or the informal approach should be retained with, possibly, some modifications, or whether it needs to be replaced.

Retain, possibly with modification

Analysis of the present arrangements may indicate that they are perfectly satisfactory, but there will be few situations in which no improvements can be made, at least to the process of operation if not the approach itself.

Checklist for reviewing the effectiveness of extreme market pricing

1. Does the process ensure that pay levels are competitive?
2. Are the sources of information about market rates valid and reliable?
3. Has a good sample of benchmark roles been used for external comparisons?
4. Have good external matches been obtained for those benchmark roles?
5. Is the approach used to price roles for which external data are not available satisfactory?
6. Have the data been interpreted properly to allow for variations in information from different sources?
7. Does the use of market pricing result in any significant internal inequities?
8. Does the use of extreme market pricing leave us vulnerable to a successful equal pay claim?
9. Do managers and employees understand how market pricing works?
10. Do they accept the results as fair and equitable?

Checklist for reviewing the effectiveness of an informal approach to role valuation

1. Do we believe that relying on managerial judgement on internal and external relativities to determine rates of pay produces results that satisfy both management and employees?
2. Are we confident that we have got internal relativities right?
3. Do our methods of tracking and responding to information on market rates produce a competitive pay structure as indicated by our ability to attract and retain good quality people?
4. Have we got the right information to develop and maintain an equitable grade and pay structure?
5. Are we vulnerable to an equal pay claim?

Improving a formal job evaluation scheme

Improvements to a formal job evaluation scheme can be made by giving more guidance and training to managers and evaluators, monitoring the inputs to job evaluation (role profiles) and outcome of evaluations more carefully, exercising closer control over upgrading following job evaluations, streamlining job evaluation procedures, spending time on communicating how the scheme works, using analytical matching as the main process for evaluating roles (relegating the basic scheme to a support function), or making minor amendments to the factor plan (replacing a considerable part of it would constitute a new scheme).

It may also be decided that introducing a computer-aided system would diminish administrative burdens and provide for more consistency in judgements of value.

Improving extreme market pricing

Possible improvements to extreme market pricing include:

▌ ensuring that a representative sample of jobs is used as benchmarks for external comparisons;

▌ reviewing existing and potential sources of market data to ensure that they are valid and reliable (see also Chapter 8);

▌ reviewing methods of interpreting and presenting data so that they give clear guidance on any actions necessary;

▌ reviewing methods of pricing non-benchmark jobs for which no market data are available.

Possible improvements to an informal approach

Improving an informal approach probably means adding a degree of formality to decision making. Arrangements can be made for internal comparisons to be made by comparing specially prepared role profiles for the role under consideration with role profiles for benchmark roles – this could be described as internal benchmarking. External comparisons with market rates can be based on a more systematic review of data – going beyond reference to advertisements to scanning published survey material. These actions would mean in effect that a semi-formal approach has been adopted.

Replace present approach

It may be decided that tinkering with the present arrangements will do little good and the approach should be replaced. The choice will be between replacing an existing formal job evaluation scheme with a new scheme, moving from formal job evaluation to market pricing or vice versa, or changing from formal arrangements to informal ones or vice versa. The factors affecting this choice will be the organization's context, including its values, size and complexity, the national or international nature of its operations and the degree to which it is competing for high-quality people, as summarized above in Table 3.1.

If it is also believed that a revised grade structure is required, for example reducing the number of grades, this is a further argument for introducing a new scheme. This decision should not be taken lightly. New schemes can take a lot of time, trouble and money to develop and install and can cause disruption and dissatisfaction.

Points for consideration – formal job evaluation

A checklist of the points to be considered when deciding whether to retain or introduce formal job evaluation is given below.

Checklist of points to be considered when deciding whether to introduce a formal job evaluation scheme

Do we need formal job evaluation for any of the following reasons?

1. The present approach results in inequitable rates of pay.
2. A grade structure is required that is based on a systematic, logical and fair process of determining relativities.
3. A sounder and more defensible method of grading jobs is required.
4. Without it we are vulnerable to an expensive equal pay claim.
5. It is required to inform equal pay reviews.
6. Employees or their representatives are pressing for a fairer and more transparent method of making grade and pay decisions.

Points for consideration – extreme market pricing

The questions affecting the choice of extreme market pricing are simply:

1. Is our main concern the need to be competitive in the job market-place?

2. Do we believe that formal job evaluation schemes are a waste of time and money?

3. Are we certain that we can get good market rate data?

4. Do we believe that market pricing will produce an internally equitable pay structure?

5. Do we care whether pay is internally equitable or not?

Question 5 may not be posed as crudely as this, but a negative answer, even if not stated explicitly, may underpin the decision to go for market pricing. It may be felt that such an answer is deplorable in terms of achieving equal pay for work of equal value within the organization, but it represents the approach adopted by many businesses that adopt market pricing.

Points for consideration – informal approach

The questions to be answered when considering whether to retain an informal approach to role valuation or move to a new one are:

1. Are we satisfied that we can price jobs without a formal scheme?

2. Do we believe that an informal approach will enable us to offer competitive rates of pay?

3. Would an informal approach create internal inequities and would it matter if it did?

DEFINE OBJECTIVES

If it is decided that a new formal approach (a job evaluation scheme or extreme market pricing) is required, it is necessary to be clear about what is to be achieved from the new scheme before producing a specification of requirements.

A guide to the possible objectives that might be set was provided by the respondents to the 2007 e-reward survey of job evaluation. The most common objectives were:

▌ Provide basis for design and maintenance of rational and defensible pay structure.

▌ Ensure equitable pay structure.

▌ Help in management of job relativities.

▌ Ensure the principle of equal pay for work of equal value.

▌ Assimilate newly created or changing jobs into existing structures.

▌ Compare internal pay levels with market rates.

▌ Harmonize pay structures as a result of merger or acquisition.

Other objectives not mentioned by the respondents were to provide a basis for career planning, or to enable the better analysis of the organization's population by levelling, ie defining levels of responsibility and how roles fit into them.

SPECIFICATION

The specification provides the basis for evaluating the different approaches and for briefing consultants. It flows from the objectives and has to fit the circumstances and culture of the organization. The specification should set out what the scheme is intended to achieve, the type of scheme required (eg analytical), whether it should be a computer-aided system, and any concerns of management, staff or trade unions that may affect it. An example of a specification drawn up for a large local authority is given in Table 3.2.

Table 3.2   Example of a job evaluation scheme specification

The job evaluation scheme should:

- overcome the problems of the present arrangements, namely: inappropriate factor plan, inability to control grade drift;
- provide the information needed to develop a new pay structure with fewer grades;
- be analytical;
- be based on a factor plan aligned as far as possible with the competency framework;
- be computerized to minimize the time and resources used to administer it;
- be acceptable to the trade unions.

Computer-aided job evaluation

An early choice should be made on whether to use a computer-aided process and if so, which software and supplier should be selected (a checklist on the points to be considered when selecting a supplier is given in Chapter 9). Knowing the input and other requirements of the software system in advance should minimize the work and time required to convert the basic paper design to the computer process. The arguments to be considered for and against computer-aided evaluation are summarized in Table 3.3.

Table 3.3 Arguments for and against computer-aided job evaluation

Arguments for	Arguments against
• Improve consistency	• Can be costly and time-consuming to develop and test
• Can be based on existing factor plan	• Consistency depends on the quality of the inputs (ie the role analyses) to the process
• Ease administration	• The time taken in moderating initial results can be as high if not higher than in a non-computerized scheme
• Save time and resources	• Conventional computerized schemes (ie those that are not interactive) may not be transparent – the process of reaching a conclusion may be hidden in the system (the 'black box' effect)

EVALUATE ALTERNATIVE FORMAL APPROACHES

The first choice is between a formal job evaluation scheme and extreme market pricing. The factors affecting this choice are set out in Table 3.1 above. Essentially, market pricing is selected when the prime requirement is to be competitive rather than equitable. External help may be required.

If it is decided to use a formal scheme, choices have to be made between an analytical and non-analytical approach and the different types of scheme. This means weighing up the advantages and disadvantages listed in Tables 3.4 and 3.5 and making a selection against a set of criteria.

The arguments in favour of analytical schemes carry most weight, at least in the United Kingdom where the e-reward 2007 survey established that 87 per cent of the job evaluation schemes used by respondents were analytical. A more detailed comparison of the various analytical and non-analytical methods is given in Table 3.5.

Table 3.4 Comparison of analytical and non-analytical approaches to job evaluation

Approach	Features	Types	Advantages	Disadvantages
Analytical	Decisions are made about the relative value or size of jobs by reference to an analysis of the level at which various defined factors or elements are present in a job. The set of factors used in a scheme is called the *factor plan*, which defines each of the factors used (these should be present in all the jobs to be evaluated), the levels within each factor and, in point-factor schemes, the scores available at each level.	• Point-factor • Analytical matching • Combined • Factor comparison	• Systematic • Provide evaluators with defined yardsticks, which help to increase the objectivity and consistency of judgements • Provide a defence against an equal pay claim	• Can be expensive and time-consuming to design or implement • Can be over-complex • Do not ensure either complete objectivity or consistency
Non-analytical	Whole jobs are compared to place them in a grade or a rank order – they are not analysed by reference to their elements or factors.	• Job classification • Job ranking • Non-analytical matching	• Can be developed quite easily • Provide a simple and quick method of grading jobs or establishing relativities (rank orders)	• Rely on overall and potentially subjective judgements that may be insufficiently guided by a factor plan and do not take account of the complexity of jobs • No defined standards for judging relative worth are provided • Do not provide a defence in an equal pay case

Table 3.5 Comparison of formal approaches to job evaluation

Scheme	Characteristics	Advantages	Disadvantages
Point-factor rating	An analytical approach in which separate factors are scored and added together to produce a total score for the job that can be used for comparison and grading purposes.	As long as they are based on proper job analysis, point-factor schemes provide evaluators with defined yardsticks that help to increase the objectivity and consistency of judgements and reduce the over-simplified judgement made in non-analytical job evaluation. They provide a defence against equal value claims as long as they are not in themselves discriminatory.	Can be complex and give a spurious impression of scientific accuracy – judgement is still needed in scoring jobs. Not easy to amend the scheme as circumstances, priorities or values change.
Analytical matching	Grade profiles are produced that define the characteristics of jobs in each grade in a grade structure in terms of a selection of defined factors. Role profiles are produced for the jobs to be evaluated, set out on the basis of analysis under the same factor headings as the grade profiles. Role profiles are 'matched' with the range of grade profiles to establish the best fit and thus grade the job.	If the matching process is truly analytical and carried out with great care, this approach saves time by enabling the evaluation of a large number of jobs, especially generic ones, to be conducted quickly and in a way that should satisfy equal value requirements.	The matching process could be more superficial and therefore suspect than evaluation through a point-factor scheme. In the latter approach there are factor-level definitions to guide judgements and the resulting scores provide a basis for ranking and grade design, which is not the case with analytical matching. Although matching on this basis may be claimed to be analytical, it might be difficult to prove this in an equal value case.
Job classification	Non-analytical – grades are defined in a structure in terms of the level of responsibilities	Simple to operate; standards of judgement when making comparisons are provided in the	Can be difficult to fit complex jobs into a grade without using over-elaborate grade definitions; the

Table 3.5 *(continued)*

Scheme	Characteristics	Advantages	Disadvantages
	involved in a hierarchy. Jobs are allocated to grades by matching the job description with the grade description (job slotting).	shape of the grade definitions.	definitions tend to be so generalized that they are not much help in evaluating borderline cases or making comparisons between individual jobs; does not provide a defence in an equal value case.
Combined approach	Point-factor rating is used to evaluate benchmark posts and design the grade structure, and the remaining posts are graded either by analytical matching or job classification.	Combines the advantages of both methods.	Can be more complex to explain and administer. If job classification is used rather than analytical matching, the disadvantages set out above apply, so there may be more of a need to revert to the full point factor scheme in the event of disagreement.
Ranking	Non-analytical – whole job comparisons are made to place them in rank order.	Easy to apply and understand.	No defined standards of judgement; differences between jobs not measured; does not provide a defence in an equal value case.
Internal benchmarking	Jobs or roles are compared with benchmark jobs that have been allocated into grades on the basis of ranking or job classification and placed in whatever grade provides the closest match of jobs. The job descriptions may be analytical in the sense that they cover a number of standard and defined elements.	Simple to operate; facilitates direct comparisons, especially when the jobs have been analysed in terms of a set of common criteria.	Relies on a considerable amount of judgement and may simply perpetuate existing relativities; dependent on accurate job/role analysis; may not provide a defence in an equal value case.

Criteria for choice

The main criteria for selecting a scheme are that it should be:

▌ *Thorough in analysis and capable of impartial application* – the scheme should have been carefully constructed to ensure that its methodology is sound and appropriate in terms of all the jobs it has to cater for. It should also have been tested and trialled to check that it can be applied impartially to those jobs.

▌ *Appropriate* – it should cater for the particular demands made on all the jobs to be covered by the scheme.

▌ *Comprehensive* – the scheme should be applicable to all the jobs in the organization, covering all categories of staff, and, if factors are used, they should be common to all those jobs. There should therefore be a single scheme that can be used to assess relativities across different occupations or job families and to enable benchmarking to take place as required.

▌ *Transparent* – the processes used in the scheme should be clear to all concerned, from the initial role analysis through to the grading decision. If computers are used, information should not be perceived as being processed in a 'black box'.

▌ *Non-discriminatory* – the scheme should meet equal pay for work of equal value requirements.

▌ *Ease of administration* – the scheme should not be too complex or time-consuming to design or implement.

The decision may be to use one approach, for example point-factor rating or analytical matching. But an increasing number of organizations are combining the two: using point-factor rating to evaluate a representative sample of benchmark jobs (ie jobs that can be used as points of comparison for other jobs) and, to save time and trouble, evaluating the remaining jobs by means of analytical matching.

CHOICE BETWEEN A TAILOR-MADE, READY-MADE OR HYBRID SCHEME

Whichever formal job evaluation scheme is selected, the next choice is whether to develop a specially designed tailor-made scheme, a 'ready-made' consultant's scheme (proprietary brands) as described in Chapter 9, or a 'hybrid' scheme (a modified consultant' scheme). The advantages and disadvantages of each approach are summarized in Table 3.6.

Table 3.6 Pros and cons of different approaches to introduction

Approach	Advantages	Disadvantages
Ready made A consultant's 'proprietary' brand	• Tried and tested, with an established reputation • The consultants can draw on extensive experience of implementing similar schemes • Does not require intensive design effort • May link to pay database • Computer support may be available as part of the package • Consultancy may have international network and database	• Factors may not suit the requirements, characteristics and culture of the organization • May not lead to high level of internal ownership • May be difficult to explain rationale for scoring and weighting • Can lead to ongoing reliance on external provider • May include elements or supporting processes that do not meet organizational requirements, eg lengthy job descriptions
Tailor-made A scheme specially designed for the organization	• Reflects the values and language of the organization – focuses on what is important • Fits the particular needs at the time • Participative design process likely to lead to greater buy-in • No ongoing reliance on external provider • Can be aligned to competency framework	• Needs investment of considerable time and resources to develop scheme • Unless expertise is available in-house, needs external support to develop
Hybrid A proprietary scheme modified to a degree (eg amended factor plan) to fit the organization's particular needs	• Enables the proprietary scheme to be customized to a degree • Draws on external experience, so saves on design time • Gives a starting point to the design process, but gives opportunities to engage employees	• Needs careful design input and implementation to avoid same risks as for proprietary scheme • Need to avoid 'cherry picking' factors or scheme design elements that do not logically hang together

USING OUTSIDE HELP

An early decision is whether to use an external resource. It may well be worthwhile getting support where in-house expertise is non-existent or limited. Many people are exposed to a new job evaluation scheme only once or twice in their careers, whereas a good external adviser will have experience of applying job evaluation schemes in many different settings and can provide an in-depth knowledge of both technical design issues and the potential pitfalls around putting in a new scheme.

Support can come from a range of sources, including consultants, ACAS (in the United Kingdom) and employers' associations. In making a decision about which external adviser to use, consideration needs to be given to what role they will play. This can take the form of supplying a packaged solution, as in a consultant's proprietary scheme. Alternatively, the adviser can act as project leader in the development of an in-house scheme, or can provide support by facilitating the process that will help the organization develop its own scheme. The level of support can vary from providing hands-on input to acting as a sounding board during the development programme.

The following checklist will help the decision about which consultant or adviser to use.

Checklist for choosing a consultant or adviser

▮ How closely does the adviser's view of their role match the organization's own expectations?
▮ Depending on the degree of customization required, what is the adviser's experience in proprietary, customized or tailor-made schemes?
▮ How well does their experience relate to the organization/sector?
▮ To what extent does the prospective adviser focus on the technical aspects of scheme design, compared with the non-technical aspects?
▮ What is their level of familiarity with equal pay for work of equal value issues?
▮ What tests do they recommend as a matter of course to ensure that the scheme will not be biased?
▮ To what extent will the organization want to be dependent on the external adviser in the future?
▮ If the scheme is to be computer-aided, to what extent does the computer support the process? Can the provider guarantee good on- and off-site support and training? Can they provide reference sites?

▌ How does the consultant charge for and record their fees? What happens if the scope of the project changes? Are they clear about how they charge for additional expenses, for example is there a standard loading for overheads? Do they charge separately for administrative/secretarial time? What is the licence or purchase fee for any software-related support and to what extent does this vary between stand-alone and networked versions?

▌ Last but by no means least, what is the 'fit'? Does the style of the consultant or adviser suit the organization? Bear in mind that the success of a project is not only related to the technical design of the scheme but also to the organizational credibility of the scheme, which can be enhanced through communication, consultation and involvement. An external adviser can have a significant impact on the development and implementation process in this regard.

A checklist of points to be considered when selecting a ready-made consultant's scheme – a 'proprietary brand' – is set out in Chapter 9.

PLAN AND RESOURCE THE DEVELOPMENT PROGRAMME

There are choices on how the development of job evaluation should be planned and resourced, which will be influenced by whether or not consultants are used and the availability of internal expertise. Choices will have to be made on involvement (the use of joint working parties or project teams) and the communications strategy. These are considered in Chapters 4 to 7.

4

Developing a formal job evaluation scheme

This chapter starts with an overview of the process of developing a formal job evaluation scheme from design through roll-out to implementation. It then reviews basic design principles and goes on to examine the general considerations affecting the structure and management of a design project. The roll-out of job evaluation to all staff and implementing the scheme, including the application of assimilation and protection policies and the development of appeals procedures, is dealt with in Chapter 5. The specific considerations involved in the design of point-factor and matching schemes are covered in Chapters 6 and 7 respectively, and market pricing is dealt with in Chapter 8.

THE DEVELOPMENT PROCESS

The development process consists of three stages: design, roll-out and implementation.

Design

The design stage involves developing and testing the basic scheme. There are four design options:

1. A factor plan for a point-factor scheme that can be used to evaluate benchmark posts and design a grade structure.

2. A framework for an analytical matching scheme consisting of a grade structure in which grade and role profiles have been defined analytically, ie in terms of job evaluation factors.

3. A grade structure with non-analytical grade definitions for a job classification scheme.

4. A combination of a point-factor scheme with an analytical matching scheme or a job classification scheme.

The process includes designing and testing a 'paper' scheme, possibly developing a computer-aided version of the paper scheme and testing that version, applying the scheme to a sample of test or benchmark posts, designing the grade structure, conducting a survey of market rates to inform the design of a pay structure that may consist of pay ranges added to the grade structure (broad-banded structures as described in Chapter 11 may be treated differently).

At this early stage consideration can usefully be given to developing operational procedures and implementation policies and procedures (assimilation, protection and appeals, as described in Chapter 5), especially if they have to be agreed with trade unions.

Evaluation roll-out

The roll-out phase involves evaluating any jobs not treated as benchmarks in the design stage. This may mean using the full scheme. Alternatively, the programme can be completed through a simpler evaluation process, such as analytical or non-analytical matching, or by applying faster evaluation techniques such as a computer-aided questionnaire instead of a paper-based version.

Implementation

The implementation stage involves:

▌ agreeing policies on assimilation to the new structure and protection of existing pay (preliminary consideration of these could usefully have been given in the design stage);

▌ assimilating jobs to the grade and pay structure and establishing if any need to be 'red-circled' because they are paid more than the upper limit of their new grade, or 'green-circled' because they are paid less;

▊ calculating the cost of implementation, which can amount to as much as 3 to 4 per cent of payroll because some people may be paid more but no one is likely to be paid less immediately – if the costs are unacceptable it may be necessary to reconsider the grade structure and re-assimilate jobs;

▊ establishing arrangements for the use of the scheme after implementation, including how to evaluate new or changed jobs and the appeals process;

▊ informing individuals how they are affected by the new structure;

▊ considering any appeals against gradings.

A flow chart of the development process is shown in Figure 4.1.

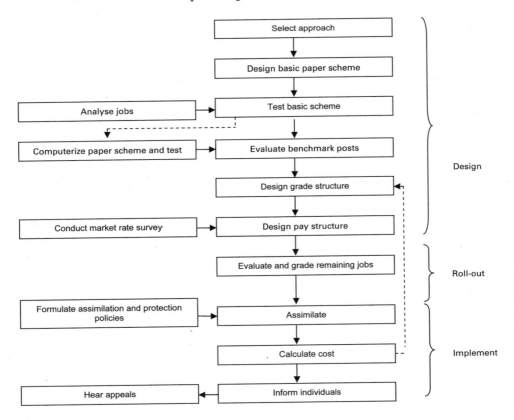

Figure 4.1 Development sequence

The development process should be based on agreed principles of design and implementation. It involves creating a project structure, project planning and management, establishing how many jobs there are in the organization, analysing jobs or roles, communication and managing implementation.

DESIGN PRINCIPLES

The following principles should be taken into account in the design stage:

▌ the scheme should be based on a thorough analysis of the jobs to be covered and the types of demands made on those jobs to determine what factors are appropriate in the context of the organization's working environment and culture;

▌ the scheme should facilitate impartial judgements of relative job values;

▌ factors or the grade/band elements in a matching/classification scheme should cover the whole range of jobs to be evaluated at all levels without favouring any particular type of job or occupation and without discriminating on the grounds of gender, race, disability or for any other reason – the scheme should fairly measure features of female-dominated jobs as well as male-dominated jobs;

▌ through the use of common evaluation criteria and methods of analysis and evaluation, the scheme should enable benchmarking to take place of the relativities between jobs in different functions or job families;

▌ the scheme should be simple to operate;

▌ the scheme should be transparent; everyone concerned should know how it works – the basis upon which the evaluations are produced;

▌ special care should be taken in developing a grade structure to ensure that grade boundaries are placed appropriately and that the allocation of jobs to grades is not discriminatory;

▌ plenty of time should be allowed for the design programme.

DESIGN PRACTICE

The advice in the form of dos and don'ts on design practice offered by the practitioners who responded to the e-reward 2007 survey on job evaluation is given below:

∎ Do seek senior management commitment.

∎ Do discuss with managers at all levels.

∎ Do communicate, communicate, communicate.

∎ Do consult and communicate widely and prepare the organization for major changes in pay relativities.

∎ Do tell everyone what you are doing, and why.

∎ Do consult with the business, explain the process and what sort of things are measured, do explain what job evaluation is all about – ie dispel some of the myths.

∎ Do consult with employee representatives at an early stage – ideally set up a working party.

∎ Do ensure you engage with managers so that they feel ownership of the approach.

∎ Do seek specialist advice.

∎ Do adopt a scheme that will serve the business model of your business.

∎ Do allow more time than you think you need.

∎ Do plan, plan and plan again; staff are naturally very suspicious, so pilot test to identify any snags; be transparent about how it works in as far as you can.

∎ Do ensure that it meets your organization's needs, that the consultants understand your organization and that it's simple – don't think that complicated is better.

∎ Do have realistic timescales.

∎ Do ensure that each step of the design is understood by all and that there is no room for misinterpretation of what the design is trying to achieve.

∎ Do ensure it offers a robust justification of outcomes.

∎ Do stick firmly to what you want to get out of it and don't compromise this.

∎ Don't take shortcuts, exclude trade unions, or keep staff in the dark about the process.

∎ Don't over-complicate.

∎ Don't compromise on what you intend to get out of it; don't think it is the means to solve all your problems; don't exclude employee involvement.

∎ Don't just hand over design to consultants; get buy-in from management.

These practical tips and the principles that affect them need to be taken into account in the detailed design and implementation of schemes as described in later chapters. The rest of this chapter is concerned with the various activities involved in the development programme, namely the fundamental starting point of job and role analysis, structuring the project, involving people, project planning and management and, importantly, communicating.

JOB AND ROLE ANALYSIS

All formal job evaluation schemes are based on an analysis of jobs or roles. The first step is to know how many jobs or roles exist in the organization. Clarifying this early on can help enormously in project planning as it may influence the approach taken to job/role analysis and roll-out of the evaluation scheme. Although this would seem to be a basic piece of organizational information, it is surprising how few organizations can immediately say how many distinct jobs or roles there are. This is for a number of reasons: job titles tend to evolve over time to fit individuals, organization charts may not be up to date, job titles in the payroll system may not match job titles in the human resources (HR) information system, and some organizations pay fixed-term or hourly paid staff through departmental budgets rather than centrally – so there may be incomplete or duplicate records.

Before embarking on a job evaluation project it is therefore necessary to review job lists. Unless it is known that HR data are accurate, it is helpful to ask senior line management to review the list of job titles for their area of responsibility rather than to rely entirely on information held within the HR department. Reviewing this list will help to identify where, for evaluation purposes, jobs can be clustered together and evaluated as a single role.

Job or role information can be obtained in a number of ways, and it is important to decide early in the planning phase how this will be done. Traditionally, job evaluation was based on the information contained in job descriptions or role profiles, whether pre-existing or developed specifically for job evaluation. However, increasingly questionnaires are used as the basis for evaluation. Techniques for job or role analysis are described later in this section.

Job descriptions

Traditional job descriptions contain an overview of the job and its place in the organization structure followed by detailed descriptions of duties and responsibilities. When used to inform analytical job evaluation they should include an analysis of the job demands in terms of each of the factors or elements in the scheme.

If the organization already has job descriptions in place they may possibly provide a basis for evaluation. But existing descriptions are often inadequate, out of date and unusable because they have not been written to a consistent format. Moreover, they will typically not support a factor analysis or analytical matching process. It is therefore almost always necessary to start afresh by deciding on a new standard format and conducting a job analysis programme.

Role profiles

Increasingly, organizations are taking the opportunity presented by a job evaluation exercise to redefine the way that work is described; switching away from a detailed job description to a role profile that focuses on the required skills, behaviours and outcomes or deliverables of the role, rather than on the detailed tasks that must be performed. As discussed in Chapter 1, the concept of a 'role' rather than 'job' focuses on what is needed to deliver organizational objectives by setting out the behavioural expectations as well as the expected outcomes, rather than the minutiae of how the work needs to be done. The aim is to give more career development opportunity to employees in the role by focusing on the delivery of outcomes rather than how they get there. It also provides for organizational flexibility by not detailing working methods and tools.

Role profiles have the advantage of being more enduring documents than job descriptions as they do not need amending each time the duties of the role change. Neither do they require the level of detail found in some job descriptions, as they are not so task focused. Changes in technology or organization do not have so much of an impact on broadly defined role responsibilities. For these reasons it is possible to generate generic role profiles that capture information on a number of roles that might previously have been described using separate job descriptions. For example, one vehicle leasing company reduced over 180 job descriptions down to just over 50 role profiles. On the other hand, some organizations are wary of prejudging the outcome of job evaluation and use the results of the job evaluation exercise to create generic role profiles as a follow-on from the job evaluation project. This is particularly so where there are concerns that the scheme will lack credibility if staff might believe that they have been force-fitted into generic profiles – many people like to believe in the 'uniqueness' of their own job.

One of the authors reviewed a job list in a university that had an art department job title of 'model – clothed'; the next on the list was 'model – unclothed'. This led to a discussion about how different the jobs were in practice or whether the difference was one that might be reflected in a special payment.

Options for gathering job/role information

There is a choice of methods, including using a job description or role profile, written questionnaires, structured interviews and computer-aided interviews. In developing the scheme, it may be worth trialling more than one method, as this will inform the process used for rolling-out the scheme across the organization and for future evaluations, post-implementation.

Job description or role profile

Job descriptions or role profiles can be used as the basis for evaluating jobs if they are designed to capture the job evaluation criteria that are included in the evaluation scheme. If the use of pre-existing job descriptions or profiles is preferred it is advisable to test evaluate a number of roles against the criteria before committing to this approach.

Where this was done in one not-for-profit organization it immediately became apparent that the quality of information contained in the existing job descriptions was not going to be adequate, so it decided to use a questionnaire instead.

Where job descriptions or profiles are rewritten to meet the evaluation criteria these can be drafted by job holders, but as they provide a summary of the organization's role requirements they should be approved through line management – perhaps with one or two tiers of review. In order to have a more controlled and quality assured process some organizations use line managers to write all job descriptions/role profiles. Where this is the case the new job descriptions or profiles should be agreed with the job holder.

Written questionnaire

Increasingly organizations are attracted by a questionnaire-based approach rather than using job descriptions or role profiles because embarking on a complete rewrite of the organization's job descriptions may seem to be a formidable and time-consuming task. Instead a questionnaire may be used, with a commitment to review the design of job descriptions or role profiles on completion of the job evaluation project, using the information drawn from the questionnaires.

The type of questionnaire more commonly used in the development phase asks for narrative responses to questions that relate to each factor, evaluation criteria or element in the matching matrix. They may be given to employees for completion on the basis that they know best how the job is done, or to the line manager, or, ideally, to both as a shared task to complete. An example of a questionnaire is given in Appendix C.

The risk of giving the questionnaire directly to job holders is that individuals tend to focus on their own role and can find it difficult to think about their role relative to others in the organization. This can produce misleading patterns of responses, depending on the perceived importance of the role – it allows for individuals to 'talk up' or downplay their roles. From an equal value perspective this gives rise to concern as there is, at least, anecdotal evidence that men are more likely to talk up their roles than women. As a result the process needed to subsequently validate self-completed questionnaires can be a long one.

For this reason it is better to validate the completed questionnaire through the line manager, or to get the manager and job holder to complete the questionnaire together. Where there are multiple job holders it can be helpful to get a group of them together to generate the questionnaire responses, ideally using a facilitator to support the process, whilst allowing individuals to comment on any individual variation from the common responses.

Another approach to gathering evaluation information through questionnaires is by using a multiple-choice type questionnaire, rather than obtaining a written description of the job. The questions may be based directly on the factor levels in a factor plan. This approach is used by some proprietary schemes. The questionnaire may even ask the completer of the questionnaire (typically either the job holder or manager) to make a tick against the appropriate factor level for the job. There are risks in this approach because the individual is effectively evaluating the job, without any knowledge of the context. If the options are written in terms of the factor level descriptions, the language can appear quite abstract to job holders and they may feel that they have not been given sufficient opportunity to describe their job. Also, a multiple-choice questionnaire is unlikely to give enough background context about a job to be able to validate whether the draft scheme is picking up all characteristics of a job effectively – although this may not be a problem if there are good job descriptions or role profiles.

Therefore, although this approach may be used to speed up evaluations for a scheme that has been fully developed and tested, it is unlikely to be a satisfactory tool for use during the scheme development process.

Structured interview

Alternatively, questionnaires can be used as the basis for a structured interview with job holders – either directly sharing the questionnaire with the job holders, or using an interview guide based on the questionnaire, administered by job analysts. The results of the interview are then written up in full after the interview. Sharing a questionnaire with job holders can increase the transparency of the process, giving it to job holders either before the interview or during it. Where there are multiple incumbents an interview can take place with a representative sample of them. When this is the case it can be helpful to have two interviewers. It is advisable to allow around an hour and a half to two hours for employee interviews. However, there will always be exceptions. In one organization interviews were typically taking around three hours, although this was exceptional. The time taken tends to be influenced by the culture and style of the organization, and this should be factored into the timetable. However, when allocating resources it is advisable to plan for no more than two interviews a day in order to allow time to write up the outcomes.

Computer-aided analysis

Interactive computer-aided systems as described in Chapter 2 use a set of online questions. This enables a more sophisticated questioning approach whereby job holders are only asked questions that relate directly to their job, rather than all the questions embedded in the scheme. If the same initial question on a factor is answered differently, the next question that appears will be different. This approach does not rely on job descriptions. An output of the interview is likely to be some form of job profile, based on the interviewee's answer.

However, even when the final scheme will be computer-aided, it is likely that the initial development of the 'paper' scheme will use a more traditional questionnaire approach to test the factors, before building these into the computer tool.

The parties involved in job analysis

The parties involved in job analysis may be:

▌ *The job holder* who knows how the job is done in practice.

▌ *The job holder's manager* who should have an overview of what is required of the job holder.

▌ *The manager's manager* who may be used in a signing-off capacity or to resolve any differences between the job holder and his or her manager.

▌ *A trained analyst* who may interview job holders, facilitate discussions between the job holder and the line manager, and help to resolve differences; analysts may be drawn from the project team, the HR function, or a broader group of trained employees.

▌ *Trade union representatives* who may be involved as observers to the job analysis process, or sit in on interviews if requested by the job holder(s).

Whoever is involved in the initial development of the scheme will need to be given guidance or formally trained. This will include a combination of the following activities depending on the type of scheme chosen and who plays what role: guidance on how to conduct interviews or complete/verify questionnaires, the need to distinguish between individual performance and the job requirements, and awareness training on how to avoid discrimination.

STRUCTURING THE PROJECT

The development project should be structured to ensure that there is proper guidance and control and that expertise is deployed effectively. Consideration has to be given to the extent, if at all, to which employees should be involved in the project (see the next section of this chapter).

Large projects typically have quite a formal structure with a steering group overseeing the programme, a sponsor who is concerned with directing the programme, and a project team involved in the more detailed development of the scheme. There may be a project leader, who could be full-time, and possibly project administrators, who could be part-time. Job evaluation or matching panels may be set up to roll-out and maintain the scheme.

Less elaborate structures may be more appropriate in smaller projects. There could be no steering group, although the board or senior management team may exercise overall control. The project may be conducted by a small team (two or three line managers and an HR specialist) or even by HR alone, although that is undesirable – a recurring theme in the advice given by respondents to the e-reward 2007 job evaluation survey was to avoid treating job evaluation as a black art understood and managed by HR on its own. The various roles in a large job evaluation project are described below. The composition of the various groups or teams will be affected by the policy of the organization on involvement.

The steering group

The steering group makes policy decisions about the development of the scheme and exercises overall control of the project. It will approve proposals on the scheme's overall design and the development programme and will review progress at key stages of the project. Depending on the approach taken to employee involvement in the evaluation process, the steering group in a large organization may include a combination of the project sponsor (see below) and representatives of senior and middle management and employees. In a small organization, or in a tightly controlled project, the steering group may be the senior management team or directors. Schemes developed for a sector such as local government have a balance of employer representatives and national trade union officials.

The project team

The role of the project team is to:

▌ provide ideas and input at all stages of the scheme design, for example drawing up the factor plan or matching elements;

▌ function as a sounding board for the detailed design work that takes place outside the project team meetings;

▌ take part in tests of the proposed scheme;

▌ review the outcome of tests and progress generally;

▌ act as an advocate for the project;

▌ help with communicating information about the project to employees.

Terms of reference should be prepared for the team that set out their authority and responsibilities.

Individual members may also act as job analysts, obtaining details of jobs as a basis for evaluation. The project team can evolve into a job evaluation panel that is concerned with the roll-out and implementation of job evaluation once the scheme has been designed.

Careful consideration should be given to the composition of the project team. It could consist of managers, other employees, the project manager and administrator and, where appropriate, an outside adviser. The team should be led or chaired by someone who is recognized internally as being objective and capable.

If there are recognized trade unions or a staff association, their representatives could also be included in the project team. This helps to gain their commitment to the outcome of the project. Many trade unions are willing to be involved 'without prejudice' in scheme development in a non-negotiating forum, often as full project team or steering group members, but they usually retain the formal right to negotiate on the scheme outcomes. Full union engagement is encouraged by the ACAS guidelines, which state that 'in the event of an equal value claim, a jointly agreed analytical scheme is more likely to be regarded as fair by an employment tribunal'.

Selecting members who represent a diagonal slice across the organization by level and by function works well in offering different perspectives during scheme development. In addition, gender balance should be taken into account. As the EOC *Good Practice Guide* states:

> It is recognized good practice in job evaluation to include in these groups a representative sample of people from the spread of jobs covered by the scheme. A fair representation of women in all job evaluation groups and discussions is strongly recommended as a means of reducing the probability of sex bias.

As well as ensuring broad representation, it is necessary to think about what kind of expertise will support the project. For example, a project team might include members with:

▮ knowledge of the organization's previous grading or job evaluation history;

▮ internal communications experience;

▮ specific organizational responsibility for equality or diversity;

▮ spreadsheet or financial modelling skills (particularly in small projects where the project team may also be involved in pay design);

▮ HR knowledge.

The size of the project team will vary from one organization to the next. There is a balance between ensuring broad representation and keeping the team to a workable size. Experience suggests that teams of more than 10 people can be less effective in providing the scope for all team members to make an equal contribution. However, more than 10 may be needed to ensure full representation, for example in a unionized environment where several unions are represented and want to be involved. On the other hand, a team of less than six or seven is unlikely to be representative of the organization.

The evaluation team

Whether the scheme is a point-factor or a matching scheme, a group of evaluators is commonly but not universally used to conduct the initial evaluations. Even where the evaluation system eventually becomes an entirely computer-aided process a team approach is still likely to be used for the initial test evaluations. Historically, the language of job evaluation has referred to such a group as a 'panel', but it may well be the project team that conducts these initial evaluations, or the project team together with a broader group of trained staff.

In large projects a moderating or review group may also be established to review initial evaluations to ensure consistency, especially where there is more than one evaluation panel or the evaluation is computer-aided. Where a matching process is used it is likely that it will initially be tested by the project team centrally, with subsequent matching conducted at divisional/department level, facilitated by HR.

The project sponsor

The project sponsor is usually a senior manager who provides top management perspective and knowledge. The sponsor acts as a communication link to the board or senior management team, ensures that resources are made available, gives a steer on tactics and matters of principle, and may chair the steering group.

The project leader

The project leader is responsible for the overall management of the project. He or she prepares timetables, ensures that resources are available, monitors and reports to the steering group on progress, focuses the activities of the project team, deals with the problems that inevitably arise, liaises with any external advisers who may be involved, and directs the activities of staff attached to the project, for example the project administrator, role analysts or evaluators.

The project administrator

The project administrator provides administrative support. This is particularly helpful in large projects that need careful coordination, for example in administering and tracking the job analysis process. Two of our case study companies commented on the need for accurate job information, and how time-consuming it can be to maintain it. This includes monitoring progress in evaluating individual jobs and reconciling job titles or reference codes so that the same job can be tracked across different documents, including the computer system (if used) or progress tracking spreadsheet, HR/payroll system, organization charts and job descriptions or role profiles. As ABC Limited found, up-to-date record keeping is especially important if the organization is in a state of flux and job titles or departmental structures are changing during the course of the project.

INVOLVING PEOPLE IN THE PROJECT

Serious consideration needs to be given to the extent to which line managers and union or employee representatives should be involved in designing, rolling-out and implementing the scheme. There are very strong arguments for involving line managers who will have a large part to play in bringing to bear their knowledge of the jobs being evaluated and will be directly concerned in the administration of the scheme. There is also much to be said for involving trade union and staff representatives and this will almost certainly be inevitable when there is a recognized trade union.

Even if there are no unions, the adage 'people support what they help to create' should be remembered. It certainly applies to the development of a job evaluation scheme. People are deeply concerned with the outcomes of job evaluation, and their confidence in the process and understanding of how it works will be increased if they, or at least their representatives, have been involved in its development. Involvement and consultation enhance the credibility of the scheme and ensure that different perspectives are taken into account. In a unionized organization the involvement of full-time union officials needs to be considered. There is much to be said for at least consulting them. They can bring a broader perspective to bear and it is as well to have them on your side. In many cases, especially in large public sector projects, union officials will want to be actively involved. Arrangements for involvement should be built into the structure of the project. Consultation can be carried out through the usual trade union channels, focus groups and employee surveys.

Involvement may be desirable but it usually takes more time and it may be difficult to do in some situations, for example with international firms. Some organizations, especially non-unionized ones and international firms, have therefore foregone involvement and rely on good communication, explaining the purpose of the scheme, how it works and how people will be affected by it.

PROJECT PLANNING

Project planning means appreciating the principles involved, identifying and defining the activities required, resourcing the project, estimating times for completing each stage of the project, and drawing up and maintaining a project timetable.

Project planning principles

The principles to follow in drawing up a project plan are:

▌ Allow plenty of time – it is likely to take longer than you think.

▌ Identify the key stages in the projects – the events that have to take place and the activities required to make those events happen.

▌ Clarify any interdependencies between stages.

▌ Define the criteria to be used to assess whether satisfactory progress has been made.

▌ Identify the key decisions to be made.

▌ Identify the responsibilities for managing the project, conducting each stage, monitoring and reporting on progress, reviewing progress and making decisions.

▌ Remember when planning the project that a frequent major cause for delay is getting decisions agreed by steering groups or higher authorities.

▌ Allocate a timescale for each stage.

▌ Set out when 'milestone' meetings will need to take place at which progress will be reviewed and decisions made.

▌ Build communication into the project plan from the outset. Job evaluation implementation starts at project inception, as early communication sets the scene for how credible the scheme will ultimately be. It is often helpful to have a separate communication plan that runs alongside the technical development plan.

▮ Develop project control systems. Take account of organizational style and culture in developing the plan. Try to make a realistic assessment of how many drafts of the scheme will be needed before it is signed off. Is the organization highly analytical? How feasible is it to drive decisions through the steering group or senior management team, and to what extent are they likely to want to see a number of iterations/drafts at each stage? Build in contingency time, as appropriate.

Activities

The activities in relation to the technical aspects of scheme design should be listed as a series of steps. For example, in a large computer-aided point-factor scheme the steps might be:

1. Agree deliverables, process and timetable.

2. Design paper scheme, eg develop a factor plan.

3. Test the paper scheme.

4. Convert the paper scheme to a computer-aided scheme.

5. Test the computer-aided scheme.

6. Select benchmark jobs.

7. Analyse benchmark jobs.

8. Evaluate benchmark job posts.

9. Design the grade structure.

10. Grade benchmark posts.

11. Conduct market rate survey.

12. Design the pay structure.

13. Agree implementation policies.

14. Estimate the cost of assimilation.

15. Develop analytical matching process.

16. Evaluate and grade non-benchmark jobs.

17. Calculate the cost of implementation.

18. Decide individual grades and pay.

19. Provide information generally on the new structure and pay arrangements, including assimilation and protection policies.

20. Inform individuals of their grade and pay and, if applicable, arrangements for progressing them to their new pay scale or how their pay will be protected.

21. Hear appeals.

For a small organization undertaking an analytical matching scheme, the steps might be:

1. Agree deliverables, process and timetable.

2. Design scheme.

3. Test scheme and information gathering process across a representative range of jobs.

4. Amend scheme and finalize information gathering process.

5. Analyse jobs or roles.

6. Evaluate jobs or roles.

7. Finalize the band/grade structure.

8. Design and cost pay structure.

9. Agree assimilation arrangements and ongoing process for future evaluations.

10. Inform individuals of their grade and pay and, if applicable, arrangements for progressing them to their new pay scale or how their pay will be protected.

11. Hear appeals.

Resourcing

An early decision needs to be made on what resources will be required to complete a job evaluation project. It is wise not to underestimate this. The largest financial outgoings are likely to be the cost of buying in external support and software, if needed. However, at least as important as the financial cost is the internal time commitment (opportunity costs). Clearly, the resources required depend on the scale and complexity of the project and the target for its completion. Resource requirements are interrelated with the timetable. This aspect of project planning may be iterative – looking at what resources can be made available, considering the desirable timescale and adjusting resources or the timetable to obtain a reasonable balance between the two.

The internal resources required will be HR or reward management staff, job analysts, job evaluators, project administrators, communication specialists and project team members. Project team members should be told how much time they may have to spend on the project to ensure that they can commit to the project's demands. The level of commitment needs to be made clear to all other interested parties, as the scheme design and testing may involve a large number of employees who are not part of the project team. It is also worth thinking about whether to have an additional reference group to challenge the development work undertaken by the project team. One non-unionized charity set this up from representatives of their regional consultative committees. At key stages in the project the group met the HR director and one or two other team members, and the external adviser, as appropriate. Their purpose was to be an independent challenge to the design team and to look at the development work from an employee perspective, providing input on scheme design and the development process, and making suggestions about staff communication.

Estimating the time required

When drawing up a project plan it is first necessary to determine the time required. The variables that will affect the time taken need to be taken into account. These are:

▌ the type of scheme – the design and implementation of a tailor-made point-factor scheme will involve the most work, but time can be saved through using a computer-aided approach or by rolling out the scheme through matching;

▌ the number of benchmark posts to be analysed and evaluated;

▌ the total number of non-benchmark jobs to be analysed and evaluated – the use of matching rather than full job evaluation can reduce the time taken on evaluation;

▌ the internal and external resources available;

▌ any other major organizational initiatives taking place that may result in a clash of priorities.

The estimate of time for developing a point-factor scheme, possibly using matching during implementation, would cover the following activities in the development programme.

Design and test scheme

This would include designing the factor plan, identifying and analysing test jobs, testing the scheme on those jobs, and iterations as necessary. This has been known to take two years in a very large and complicated process with union involvement. More typically, it can take between three and six months in a normal project, less in a small organization. An important determinant of timing is the process used to gather job information. Also, the evaluation process itself will impact on time. A matching process is likely to take less time, both in development and design, because, depending on the approach used, there is less need to pin each job down precisely against each element and level in the evaluation matrix.

Design and test a computer-aided system

If it is decided to use a computer-aided system, this will need to be based on the paper scheme designed at an earlier stage. The time varies according to the system used, but it is unlikely to take less than three months in an average sized project and in major schemes has taken six months or more. However, some of this time can be offset by the time saved in job analysis and, with some systems, in the evaluation itself.

Identify and analyse benchmark posts

This step involves identifying the total number of jobs in the organization, determining the number of test or benchmark posts to be analysed and evaluated, and then calculating the time taken for analysis of the benchmark jobs. This would include activities such as getting questionnaires completed, conducting interviews and preparing the job analyses for the evaluation team. Other than where the process involves inputting a limited range of responses to pre-set questions (eg some computer-aided questionnaires), job or role analysis can be time-consuming. Basic information has to be obtained, preferably from both job holders and their managers. The use of questionnaires may speed this up, but not if the questionnaires are supplemented by interviews. The role profile and job description have to be drafted, or completed questionnaire or interview results written up, and then usually – and preferably – approved by both the manager and the individual. Differences of opinion on the content of the role often occur and have to be resolved by the analyst – if used – in conjunction with the line manager and the job holder(s), as appropriate. Where no analyst has been used, HR may be involved in a quality review of completed questionnaires or job descriptions/role profiles, and facilitating differences between the line manager and job holder. The time taken for each role may total half a day and even more, particularly if there are central quality controls.

Although questionnaires are generally considered to be quicker to complete than writing a new job description or role profile, it will depend on the verification processes used. What will be different is how the activity is dispersed throughout the organization. Take the following examples:

▌ Analyst interviews job holder and writes new role profile/job description or interview notes using standard template (4 hours); manager and job-holder review (1 hour each) – total 6 hours.

▌ Job holder writes role profile (4 hours), verified by line manager (1 hour – total 5 hours.

▌ Manager writes role profile (3 hours), reviewed by job holder (1 hour), verified by next level line manager or HR for consistency (1 hour) – total 5 hours.

▌ Job holder completes structured questionnaire (3 hours), manager reviews and verifies it (1 hour) – total 4 hours.

None of the above allows for the additional time needed if the reviewer or verifier disagrees strongly with what was originally drafted.

Evaluate benchmark/test posts

The time taken for evaluating the benchmark posts (or test roles in a small organization where the next step may be to evaluate all roles) depends on the quality of role analysis and the effectiveness of the group that will form the job evaluation panel. It is best to staff the group with members of the project team who have gained experience in developing the scheme. Initially, the group will need to familiarize themselves with the methodology and procedure, and time will be taken to establish various conventions on the interpretation of factor plan or matching definitions and how information on jobs should be matched to them. As the evaluation process progresses an experienced group can refer to previous evaluations to guide their decisions, thus speeding up the process.

The speed of evaluation depends on the approach taken. Traditionally, a job evaluation panel would meet to evaluate every job. To begin with, a panel working in this way may not complete more than two or three evaluations a day. With experience they may increase this rate to seven or eight a day. Panels working in this way can easily run out of steam, so ideally they should not deliberate for more than half a day, although this may not be practical where members are being drawn from a range of locations. If the group do meet for half a day only, this means that they may only complete on average three or four evaluations in a single session. More than one panel can be used to accelerate progress, but their evaluations would have to be moderated to ensure consistency.

Many organizations have abandoned this time-intensive approach. One popular option is to get job analysts (who may be team/panel members) to evaluate the job initially. This works particularly well where the individual concerned has undertaken the job analysis and so already has a good understanding of the job. All analyst evaluation scores are entered onto a spreadsheet. The role of the evaluation team is then to review all of the evaluation results together. If a points-factor scheme is being used the review can be factor by factor. This means that the team members are not looking at the overall outcome of the initial evaluation, but looking at each factor individually. The role of the team is to look at the overall pattern of results and to see if any jobs stand out relative to each other, or to deal with any specific questions of interpretation that have come up from the initial evaluators. This may highlight issues such as:

▌ an unexpected score in a 'knowledge' or 'expertise' factor, which could indicate a score more related to the job holder's personal qualifications than to the job requirements;

▌ a score in any 'responsibility' or 'authority' factor that is the same as (or higher than) that of the line manager, which would normally be inappropriate;

▌ a factor level that is different from that awarded to the nearest relevant test job or similar, previously evaluated job, which could indicate misleading input information.

Whilst the scheme is still being developed, there is a need to identify whether the unusual pattern of results is due to the wording/levels in the scheme, in which case these should be acted on, or are genuine issues relating to the characteristics of the job concerned. Where this approach is used the analysts who conducted the evaluation should attend the meeting so that they can answer any questions about their interpretation of the role. It is important that a copy of all relevant documentation is available to the evaluation team members so that details can be checked out when necessary.

A variation on the above approach is to pair up analysts. Each evaluator evaluates the job on his or her own initially, then compares results with the other evaluator. This process can be applied whether or not the evaluators were involved in the job analysis process – involving more than one person usually provides a good test of whether the job information provided is adequate. If the two cannot agree, a third evaluator can be brought in to evaluate the role. Their evaluations are combined to form a provisional evaluation, which is then reviewed by the evaluation team. Any areas of disagreement are highlighted by the initial evaluators.

Design grade structure

It should not take too long – an elapsed time of a month or so at most – to design a grade structure, including the definition of grade or level profiles. It may take longer if the band/grade profiles are going to be used for an analytical matching process, as some time may have to be spent in reviewing the evaluation matrix and getting it approved. This is particularly the case if a decision has been made to gather all job information first, and to use this as a basis for starting to look at how many levels will be needed. However, the initial grade design may have taken place earlier in the process, so at this point the process simply involves validating the grade/banding matrix.

Analyse market rates

Prior to attaching pay ranges or scales to the grade structure to produce a pay structure, it is necessary to survey market rates. This may take several months but it can be started at an earlier stage in the project and thereby add little or nothing to the elapsed time. If the organization is quite happy with the overall pattern of salary levels, for example where it already benchmarks regularly against the external market, this step may not be needed, as it is possible to model the structure using existing salary levels and knowledge of market relativities (although the pattern of pay differentials may change). Where this is the case it is important not to embed any gender bias that may have existed in the previous structure.

Design pay structure

The design of the pay structure may take longer than designing the basic grade structure. Time will be taken to estimate the cost of implementation and to compare the costs of alternative configurations.

Evaluate and grade remaining posts

The time taken will depend on the approach taken. In a smaller project it may be decided to evaluate all the remaining test/non-benchmark posts using the full job evaluation scheme. However, using the traditional panel approach described earlier, the evaluation of 200 jobs by one panel could mean 30 to 40 meetings. Allowing for gaps between meetings because of holidays, the elapsed time could be as much as 10 to 12 months. If one of the other approaches described earlier is adopted, the time will be considerably less.

In larger projects jobs could be graded by analytical or non-analytical matching. An analytical matching team can usually match 12 or so jobs in a day if each job is matched individually. The process is far quicker if the same pre-evaluation techniques described earlier are used and if the same group are matching all roles.

Review/moderate results

It is usually advisable to review and moderate the results of panel job evaluations. Results over the period of a long project may be inconsistent because the judgement criteria used by the panel have altered over time or the composition of the panel has changed.

Introduce the new arrangements

Introducing the new arrangements means:

- assimilating employees into the new structure;

- establishing who will be 'red-circled' because they are paid more than the maximum of their new grade or 'green-circled' because they are paid less than the minimum of their new grade;

- deciding how to treat red-circled and green-circled employees in accordance with policies on protection and on phasing increases (it may be decided, for example, that increases of more than 8 per cent should be phased over two years);

- undertaking appropriate formal consultation with staff if the new pay and grading arrangements require contractual changes;

- informing employees individually of their new grade and, where applicable, their new salary and arrangements for protection or phasing increases;

- responding to appeals against the grading or evaluation.

A considerable amount of time can be spent on these activities – at least three months for a fairly large project; more for a large project or where there are many appeals.

Drawing up the timetable

The timetable should be based on analytical estimating, ie analysing the project into phased activities and estimating the time taken for each of them by reference to its scale and the resources available. However, a realistic approach to project planning means appreciating that however carefully the estimate is made it is only an *estimate*. Precision is often difficult because, depending on the size and nature of the project, a job evaluation project can involve people carrying out complex activities over a prolonged period and making difficult decisions. In most cases this is in addition to carrying out their normal work. The fact that during a project a number of policy decisions will have to be made may prolong the programme because of delays in getting a proposal considered by a board or committee, difficulties in bringing the interested parties together, or problems in reaching agreement. Discussions or negotiations with trade unions may be prolonged. There may be more appeals than anticipated.

An example of a project timetable is shown in Table 4.1. The project is to develop a computer-aided point-factor scheme in a large organization. There are 100 benchmark jobs and a total of 400 jobs to be evaluated. An analytical matching scheme based on the point-factor scheme is to be developed and applied to the 300 non-benchmark posts. All jobs are evaluated by the full panel. The estimated elapsed time in this example ranges from 52 to 104 weeks.

In estimating completion dates it is best to look at the worst case or possibly somewhere between the minimum and maximum. There is a lot of judgement involved, which is why it is best not to be committed

Table 4.1 Example project timetable

Activity	Minimum time – days	Maximum time – days	Minimum elapsed time – weeks*	Maximum elapsed time – weeks*
1 Agree deliverables	1	2	1	2
2 Design paper scheme	15	30	4	10
3 Test paper scheme	15	30	4	10
4 Computerize paper scheme	25	40	10	16
5 Test computerized scheme	20	30	8	12
6 Select benchmark jobs	1	2	1	2
7 Analyse benchmark jobs	15	20	3	5
8 Evaluate benchmark jobs	15	25	4	6
9 Design and agree grade structure	2	5	1	4
10 Grade benchmark posts	3	6	1	2
11 Conduct market survey**	12	24	3	10
12 Design pay structure	4	8	2	6
13 Agree implementation policies**	3	5	2	12
14 Estimate assimilation costs	2	4	1	2
15 Develop analytical matching	5	10	2	3
16 Evaluate and grade non-benchmark posts	20	30	6	10
17 Calculate implementation cost	2	5	1	2
18 Decide individual grades/pay	10	20	3	6
19 Inform employees generally	2	3	1	2
20 Inform individuals	5	10	1	2
21 Hear appeals	10	20	3	6
Total time	172	300	52	104

*The elapsed time allows for the fact that the work will be discontinuous and delays will occur for communication, consultation and obtaining approval.
**These activities could take pace concurrently with others and therefore do not contribute to the total time estimated for the project.

to firm completion dates. If pressed to do so by management, which is often the case, emphasize that this is an estimate and that the experience of anyone who has taken part in large-scale job evaluation projects, like the authors of this book, is that it is impossible to be certain about the timescale – many things can happen to cause delays and they frequently do, however carefully the project has been planned and managed.

A more detailed programme for the design of an analytical matching scheme is given in Appendix D.

PROJECT MANAGEMENT

Large-scale job evaluation design programmes are often complex. They can involve a range of stakeholders with different agendas. Murphy's Law may apply: 'If anything can go wrong it will.' Good project management to minimize problems is therefore essential. Even in a small organization, or where a relatively straightforward matching approach is developed, the project can be delayed if it is not managed effectively.

The fundamental requirements for a well-managed project are to have a comprehensive project plan and an effective project manager. The three most important things to control are:

1. time – achievement of project plan as programme;

2. quality – achievement of project specification;

3. cost – containment of costs within budget.

Project control is based on progress reports showing what is being achieved against the plan. The planned completion date, actual achievement and forecast completion date for each stage or operation are provided. The likelihood of delays, overruns or other complications is thus established so that corrective action can be taken in good time. Control can be achieved by the use of bar charts, as illustrated in Figure 4.2. This is a compressed version of the time estimates set out in Table 4.1 and could be used to communicate the plan (too much detail may be confusing), although a full bar chart covering all the activities listed in the timetable would be useful for detailed control purposes. There are interdependencies between activities in

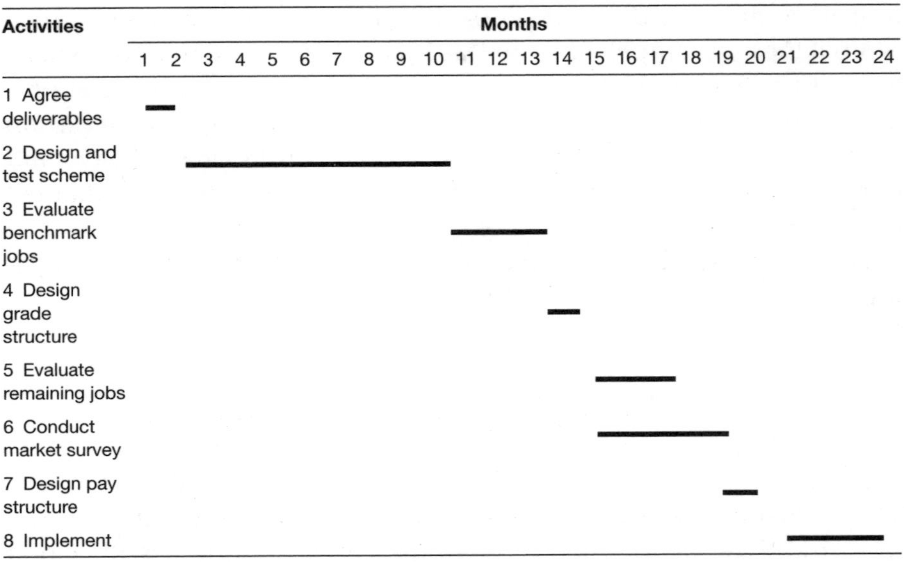

Activities	Months																							
	1	2	3	4	5	6	7	8	9	10	11	12	13	14	15	16	17	18	19	20	21	22	23	24
1 Agree deliverables	▬																							
2 Design and test scheme		▬	▬	▬	▬	▬	▬	▬	▬	▬														
3 Evaluate benchmark jobs											▬	▬	▬											
4 Design grade structure														▬										
5 Evaluate remaining jobs																▬	▬							
6 Conduct market survey															▬	▬	▬	▬						
7 Design pay structure																			▬					
8 Implement																				▬	▬	▬	▬	▬

Figure 4.2   Project plan bar chart

job evaluation projects and these could be clarified in a network, as shown in Figure 4.3.

Project management is most likely to be successful if the following steps are taken:

▌ specify objectives and deliverables;

▌ define who does what and when;

▌ define resource requirements;

▌ establish control methods – charts, network analysis, progress reports, progress (milestone) meetings;

▌ monitor progress continuously against the plan as well as at formal meetings.

COMMUNICATING TO PEOPLE ABOUT THE PROJECT

A job evaluation programme creates interest and concern amongst all those who will be affected by it. There will be expectations and

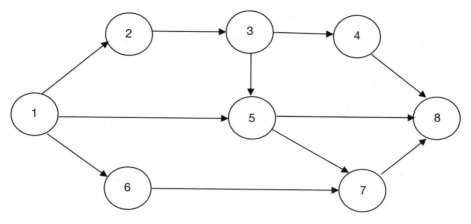

1 Agree deliverables
2 Design and test job evaluation scheme
3 Evaluate benchmark jobs
4 Evaluate remaining jobs
5 Design grade structure
6 Conduct market rate survey
7 Attach pay ranges to grade structure
8 Implement

Figure 4.3   A job evaluation project network

fears that may or may not be reasonable. In some cases staff may believe that they will get more money. In other organizations there may be concerns that the process is being used to review cost-cutting/restructuring opportunities. In practice, there are usually some winners (staff whose pay is below the minimum for their new grade and who will therefore get an increase) and some losers (staff whose pay is above the maximum for their new grade and who, although protected against any immediate reduction, may eventually 'mark time' or even lose pay when they revert to the rate for their grade at the end of the protection period). The pay of the majority of people will be unchanged. In contrast, trade unions have sometimes claimed that the aim of management is to use job evaluation to reduce pay all round.

The credibility of a new job evaluation scheme rests on how effectively it is communicated. The most widely reported problem with job evaluation reported in the 2007 e-reward survey was the lack of understanding of the scheme by managers and employees. The most common advice given to those who might be engaged in a job evaluation exercise by respondents to that survey is to communicate as much as possible. Remember that the communication programme should cover all stakeholders – senior management, front line managers, employees generally and their representatives. Where applicable, trade union officials, eg the local branch secretary, should be kept informed.

The e-reward survey respondents also stressed the importance of being specific about the business need for job evaluation. This should start at the beginning of the design process. Employees must understand the rationale so as to trust the design, roll-out and implementation processes. The same applies to the organization's leadership. As one HR manager put it, 'The business leaders should have been involved more from the outset to ensure their buy-in.'

There are key stages in a job evaluation development project when communication is essential: as the project starts, before employees are involved in job analysis, during the design stage, when the scheme design is complete, before and after the roll-out of evaluation, and before and during the implementation programme. Regular progress bulletins should be issued.

It is essential to reinforce the basic messages regularly, for example, the purpose of the project and how people will be affected (eg no one should expect to gain but no one will lose when the scheme is implemented).

Communication should cover the following matters.

Purpose

The purpose of the exercise needs to be explained. Here are some examples of the points that have been made by organizations responding to the e-reward survey:

▎ 'To provide us with a fair and equitable structure into which we can fit our reward strategy.'

▎ 'To provide felt-fair outcomes in terms of internal ranking/differentials and a link to the external market for reward comparison.'

▎ 'To ensure that the grading process is objective, transparent and consistent.'

▎ 'To develop a scheme which is easily understood and easy to manage.'

▎ 'To allow more flexibility and to accommodate the many changes in the company structure.'

▌ 'To be more relevant to new and changing roles, to be more flexible and to be more focused on individual roles and the market.'

▌ 'Introduce a scheme which is more comprehensive, addressing a wider range of staff.'

Managing expectations

Make it absolutely clear that no one should expect an increase in pay and what pay protection arrangements will apply. Implementation policies for assimilation to new pay ranges and for protecting the pay of people whose pay will be above the maximum of their new grade (red-circling), should be communicated as soon as they are agreed. The content of such policies is discussed in the next chapter.

Make it equally clear that job evaluation is not used to assess the performance of individuals (this is a common misconception). If there has been a recent reorganization it may also be necessary to address concerns about whether job evaluation is linked to further restructuring and redundancies.

Scheme features

The basis of the scheme's design and, broadly, how it operates needs to be explained. In making this explanation remember that if a scheme is being introduced for the first time it is most unlikely that more than a few people will know anything about job evaluation (other than employees who have been involved in schemes in other organizations or union representatives who may have received some training from their union). The scheme must therefore be easy to understand and jargon-free. This is why the prescription for a job evaluation scheme most frequently mentioned by practitioners – 'keep it simple' – is so important. If an existing scheme is being changed it is important to explain the benefits of the new approach.

The design process

The information provided on the design process should cover who is going to be involved in the scheme's design, how they will be involved (the composition and terms of reference of the project team), and how they can be contacted – this particularly applies to trade union and staff representatives and representatives of line managers.

The procedure for role or job analysis also needs to be explained, including the use of benchmark jobs, who will do the analysis and the methods they will use, eg questionnaires or interviews. Information should be given on how individuals will contribute to the analysis, what checks and balances are built into the process and what their direct input to the process will be.

Who is told what?

Before and during the design and roll-out process it is necessary to decide what to communicate to different stakeholders, including managers, employees generally, their representatives (where they exist) and individuals.

Managers

Managers should be briefed on their responsibilities, covering:

▌ the need for objectivity and accuracy in the provision of information on jobs, separating job content from job holder qualities;

▌ the need to allow staff members time to participate in the process and to insist that appointments, once made, are kept;

▌ their own role in managing staff expectations, answering queries and, where appropriate, approving evaluation results before these are made known to their own staff.

Employees generally

Regular and pertinent communication with staff is important at all stages throughout the development and roll-out of the job evaluation scheme. The key points are:

▌ keep restating the intention behind bringing in the new job evaluation scheme;

▌ explain the evaluation process and describe the outline programme;

▌ emphasize that job evaluation is not linked to measuring individual performance;

▌ make it clear that no specific pay decisions will be made until the evaluation programme is complete (if that is the case);

▌ stress that, for most people, pay will not increase;

▌ state assimilation arrangements, when known;

▌ state that when the evaluation and grading programme has been completed, its impact on individuals will be explained directly to them.

Staff representatives

It is helpful for all staff representatives, whether trade union or consultative committee representatives, not just those who are members of the design project team, to be briefed on the project and how they will be involved.

Methods of communication

A range of media should be used to take account of the fact that different people receive and absorb messages in different ways (visual, auditory, written). Most organizations say that face-to-face communication is the most helpful, whether in large groups or one-to-one. However, the approaches taken need to be realistic for the organization, taking into account size, location and types of staff employed.

Here are examples of what some organizations have done to make their communication more effective throughout the process:

▌ director briefings confirming their commitment to the project;

▌ use the intranet to provide information and as a forum for questions and discussion;

▌ provide a telephone helpline number, using an answerphone to collect questions;

▌ give out contact numbers and e-mail addresses of all project team members;

▌ create distinctive project information; for example special bulletins on coloured paper;

▌ brief staff regularly through team meetings, directors' meetings and any other regular briefings;

▌ run informal lunchtime sessions so that staff can ask questions about any aspect of scheme design and implementation – tie these in to take place shortly after written communication;

▌ attach information bulletins to payslips as a guaranteed way of reaching all staff;

▌ set up a network of 'champions' throughout the organization, based not on formal roles but on influencing ability; use these champions to disseminate information about the project so that it is not seen as purely an HR-driven project.

Timing

The experience of organizations that have gone through this process is that it is best to avoid giving definite completion dates if there is any chance that the timetable might deviate from the original plan. It is necessary to manage expectations carefully by only communicating those dates that are known to be achievable, and to be clear about what will, and will not, be achieved by then. A date is the one thing that everyone remembers. If a communication states that the scheme design will be completed by a certain date, employees will expect the scheme to be implemented and all jobs evaluated by that date, even if implementation is planned to follow on later.

5

Rolling-out, implementing and maintaining job evaluation

Developing a new job evaluation scheme covers not only the design and testing of the scheme itself but also the design of the grade and pay structure into which the benchmark jobs are placed. The next step is to roll-out the scheme to cover all the jobs in the organization, ie the jobs that have not been treated as benchmarks in the design stage, taking into account the principles set out below. The roll-out plan will define the jobs to be covered and the job evaluation methodology to be used; schedule the job analysis and evaluation processes; describe how additional analysts and evaluators should be trained; and provide for the review and moderation of evaluations.

To prepare for implementation, policies will need to be agreed at this stage for assimilation, protection and handling of appeals against gradings or requests for a review of the outcomes of job evaluation. These policies may usefully be formulated at an earlier stage in the programme, especially when they have to be agreed with trade unions. It is also necessary to draw up procedures for operating job evaluation. Again these may be outlined during the design stage, but the experience gained in rolling out the scheme may indicate a need to amend them. After implementation it is essential to ensure through defined operational procedures that job evaluation is properly maintained. Tips on the introduction and maintenance of job evaluation provided by participants in the 2007 e-reward survey are given at the end of the chapter.

ROLL-OUT AND IMPLEMENTATION PRINCIPLES

During roll-out and implementation:

- the quality of role analysis should be monitored to ensure that analyses produce accurate and relevant information that will inform the job evaluation process and will not be biased;

- consistency checks should be built into the implementation process;

- care is necessary to ensure that the outcomes of job evaluation do not simply replicate the existing hierarchy – it is to be expected that a job evaluation exercise will challenge present relativities;

- all those involved in role analysis and job evaluation should be thoroughly trained in the operation of the scheme and in how to avoid bias;

- there should be scope for the review of evaluations and for appeals against gradings;

- the evaluation process should take into account the diversity of the workforce, involving representation, where possible, of different types and levels of expertise, both sexes and other groups monitored for equality purposes by the organization;

- the outcomes of evaluations should be examined to ensure that sex discrimination or any other form of bias has not occurred.

ROLL-OUT

The roll-out stage involves defining the jobs to be covered and the approach to evaluation, drawing up the programme, providing training or guidance to evaluators, and directing the work of the evaluation team(s).

Define the jobs to be covered

It is necessary first to identify the remaining jobs that will be evaluated. As discussed in Chapter 4, these may be generic roles, ie roles in which the similar activities are carried out by a number of people, for example, administrative assistants or systems analysts. Alternatively, they might be individual roles carried out by one person. The same approach may be used as for the initial development of the scheme, or the opportunity may be taken to evaluate more generic roles.

However, the distinction between generic and individual roles is not always precise. It is desirable to reduce the scale of the job evaluation programme by identifying as many generic roles as possible, but it is often a matter of judgement. Individuals can become aggrieved if they feel that they are not getting the attention they deserve. This exercise often exposes the fact that there are a number of different job titles for what is essentially the same role. It therefore provides an opportunity to tidy things up, but this can be troublesome – people can be attached to their job title and resent losing it. To overcome this problem, organizations sometimes group a number of jobs into a generic role for evaluation purposes but, within reason, allow people to retain their job titles. Or they wait until the evaluation exercise is complete in order to confirm which jobs can be clustered together and use the outcomes to create more generic roles for future use.

One organization with around 600 staff started out with 185 job titles, cleaned up the list and removed obvious duplication and changes. This was sent out to divisions for review, requesting further simplification. In the process jobs were discovered that were not on the original HR list, some jobs were split because a single job title covered more than one job, and at the end of the process the number of jobs went down by only 10 jobs. However, even though the number of jobs had barely reduced, the organization was more confident in the job list it finally used, particularly as its aim was to evaluate every job. It also considered creating generic role profiles for some jobs, but realized that this would involve more elapsed time than their schedule allowed to draft the profiles and get them agreed.

Define the approach to roll-out

There are three approaches to rolling-out job evaluation across the organization. The first one is to evaluate every individual and generic job using only one type of job evaluation scheme in both the development and roll-out phase. This approach may be used in smaller organizations, when trade unions or staff associations press for a complete evaluation, or where there is an analytical matching scheme. However, it can lead to unnecessary duplication and it will be time-consuming if a point-factor scheme rather than an analytical matching scheme is used.

The next two approaches are based on a form of matching to evaluate remaining jobs after having used a point-factor scheme in the initial development phase. This may be appropriate where organizations want to retain a robust job evaluation scheme in the background for evaluating 'difficult' jobs, to enable the organization to conduct finely tuned analyses by points (eg an equal pay review) or as a defence in the event of a pay equity claim being made against it. There are two options. 1) Evaluate benchmark jobs (individual and generic, probably all of them if the latter) using a point-factor approach, design the grade structure and then 'slot' the remaining jobs into grades by a process of non-analytical matching. If the grades are defined and the matching is from job description to grade definition then this constitutes a combined approach, eg point-factor rating and non-analytical matching. 2) Use an analytical (point-factor or factor comparison) scheme to carry out the benchmark evaluations, followed by analytical matching to grade the remaining jobs (also a combined scheme).

The first approach is the most typical, but reliance on non-analytical matching may lead to equal pay problems. The second approach avoids this difficulty and is becoming increasingly popular, particularly in large-scale job evaluation roll-outs, for example in the UK National Health Service.

Draw up the roll-out programme

The time taken will clearly depend on the approach used, the number of jobs, the complexity of the organization, the resources available in the shape of job analysts and job evaluators, the availability of computer assistance, and the experience and skill of the people involved in role analysis and evaluation. The time taken may be extended through delays in obtaining management approval or because of trade union pressures.

It is usually necessary in a large project to review and moderate the panel's evaluations because, over a fairly long period or across different groups of evaluators, application of the scheme may not produce consistent results. This could take two or three months.

In a big programme it is important to keep up the momentum, particularly if the existing system is suspect. If it will take a year or more to cover all the jobs in the organization using, say, point-factor rating, then the programme should be broken down into phases of three or four months each covering a group of employees, as illustrated in Figure 5.1. Progress can then be demonstrated and announced at regular intervals. In the meantime it will be necessary to decide how to evaluate jobs. This is usually a choice between carrying on with the existing approach, running a simplified version of the existing approach, or putting a moratorium on re-gradings. In practice the latter may be difficult in a large-scale project, particularly for new jobs that need to be matched into the pay structure.

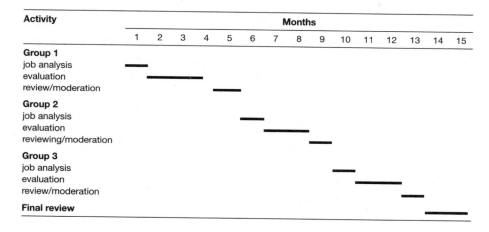

Figure 5.1 Job evaluation implementation programme

Evaluator training or guidance

The training or guidance given to the evaluators will vary according to the evaluation process adopted, and whether the process is reliant on using the team that has been involved in scheme development, or whether the group is being expanded or changed when remaining jobs are evaluated. The groups to take account of may include:

▌ interviewers/analysts who collect job information in a format for others to use;

▊ analysts or evaluation panel members who evaluate jobs using paper-based systems;

▊ analysts or facilitators who support evaluations using computer-aided systems;

▊ groups or 'panels' that are responsible for evaluating jobs or for moderating evaluation results.

Guidance on the avoidance of bias (sex or other) should be incorporated into any training, specific to the activities involved. This should minimize the risk of discrimination in the implementation of job evaluation and also demonstrate to others that all appropriate efforts are being made to avoid bias.

Job evaluation teams during roll-out

As in the initial design phase, job evaluation teams or 'panels' are commonly used during roll-out to ensure that a balanced conclusion is reached. The exception is in interactive processes such as the Gauge system, where the job holder, line manager and trained facilitator together discuss and review the input in response to a PC-based questionnaire, but even this process requires a moderating panel to review initial evaluations for consistency of interpretation.

The work of the evaluation panel(s) will vary according to the type of scheme. For example, unless evaluations are carried out initially by individual evaluators or pairs of evaluators, a point-factor scheme will require the panel to carry out the detailed and often time-consuming work of:

▊ studying the job description or role profile;

▊ establishing for each factor in the scheme the level at which it is present by comparing the information available on that aspect of the job with the level definitions in the factor plan;

▊ deciding which provides the best fit (often a judgemental process);

▊ agreeing scores for each factor according to its level;

▊ adding the factor scores to produce a total score;

▊ recording a rationale for their decision (this is useful in case there is an appeal or an equal pay claim).

The organization needs to weigh up how best to use its resources. Is it better to use people to evaluate jobs in advance of a panel review so that the panel's role is to moderate outcomes, or will the system be more credible if every job is evaluated in full by the whole panel in a committee setting?

Analytical matching requires the matching panel to study a role profile analysed in terms of predefined evaluation elements and match this to a similarly analysed level profile or benchmark role profile using predetermined matching rules or 'protocols'. Again, this can either be done in advance of the meeting, with the evaluation team looking at the overall pattern of evaluations, or the panel can match every job in full.

Membership

If a team or panel is used, its members should ideally be the same as those taking part in the evaluation of the 'test jobs' when designing the scheme development. However, depending on the approach adopted, a larger pool of potential panel members may be required to reduce the workload on individuals (evaluation meetings may well cover several days) and allow for holidays and other commitments. Any new evaluators should be trained in how evaluations take place, ideally by practising on some jobs that have already been evaluated during the design phase.

Principles

The principles governing the work of evaluation teams or panels are:

▌ No untrained person should be allowed to take part in, or influence, an evaluation.

▌ No aspect of the job holder as a person should influence any aspect of the evaluation (specifically not sex or ethnic origin). This may mean getting rid of identifying job or personal characteristics in questionnaires or job descriptions/profiles such as current grade, salary range or name.

▌ The evaluation is concerned with the normal content of the job as defined in a job description or role profile. For multiple incumbent jobs it should not be affected by the activities of any individuals that vary the standard job requirements.

▌ A full record of the scoring decisions should be kept, and, where the decision was a marginal one, the reasons why that level was determined should be noted (a rationale). This is particularly important if the panel found it difficult to reach consensus, as it may be relevant if a review of that evaluation is called for.

▌ Evaluation scores should be treated as provisional and not disclosed until they have been checked by a review panel.

▌ If the team is to evaluate every job together, all evaluators should ideally have the job analyses at least a week prior to the evaluation meeting (to provide the opportunity to clarify anything that is unclear and thus save time at the meeting itself).

Workload

The time taken to evaluate jobs will depend on the process adopted and how long it takes panel members to reach a consensus. Some jobs will be quite straightforward and may require little or no discussion if the job has been pre-evaluated and there are no queries about the resulting profile (point-factor scheme) or grade (matching scheme). Others are more complex or raise particular evaluation problems and can take a lot longer to resolve.

As evaluation teams gain experience and become familiar with the evaluation scheme and process, they can speed up their evaluations. They will have learnt more about relating job descriptions to the factor or band/grade level definitions, various 'conventions' on how particular aspects of jobs should be treated will have evolved, and there will be a data bank (recorded but also in the memory of panel members) on how levels have been evaluated in comparable jobs.

There is something to be said for limiting meetings to a half a day if that is at all possible – just to maintain the energy of the sessions. In practice, whole-day sessions might have to be arranged. Where this is the case, off-site 'away days' for panels can work very well, and can even be extended over a couple of days if it is believed that, through matching, it would be possible to evaluate all or a large proportion of the organization's jobs.

Conducting job evaluation panel meetings

The choice of the person who facilitates or chairs the evaluation process is important to the quality of the panel's decisions. The facilitator should be someone with a good overview of the whole organization or an external adviser – someone who should be seen as having no 'hidden agenda' – with the skill and personal authority to chair and facilitate the meeting in a professional manner.

The role of the facilitator or chair is to:

▌ establish the ground rules for evaluation and agree the methodology;

▌ ensure that issues about jobs are fully aired (through examination of job information and round-table discussion) before conclusions are reached;

▌ guide the team or panel through the process, probing where necessary to test whether views have been properly justified on the basis of the evidence;

▌ continually reinforce the principles that it is the job and not the performance of the person that is being evaluated, and the need to avoid sex discrimination or other bias;

▌ remind members that it is the job content as it is intended to be carried out that is evaluated, not the job as carried out by a particular job holder;

▌ stimulate reasoned debate, actively encouraging the participation of every team member;

▌ put the job to one side for further reflection or obtain more information about the point at issue, if consensus has not been reached;

▌ as a last resort, put decisions to the vote, but this is undesirable because it is divisive – consensus may be difficult to attain at first, but experience has shown that eventually it can always be achieved, although this may take time;

▌ avoid getting drawn into making decisions on behalf of the team or panel. In a small organization the facilitator may have a voice in the decision-making process, as he or she may have a direct accountability for the scheme, such as the head of HR, but in larger organizations it is more typical for the facilitator to be neutral. Where an external adviser is used, his or her role is usually to ensure impartiality and robustness of process. In this case, the individual should always be neutral, facilitating and guiding discussion, but not having a say in the final outcome.

The review or moderating group

The role of a review or moderating group is to examine the rank order of jobs resulting from the completed evaluations and to look for any results that seem out of place. In a small organization this may be the senior management team. In a larger organization it will typically be the steering group, or a second tier group reviewing results across a number of evaluation teams. In conducting this review, members must avoid the temptation to preserve previous, possibly incorrect, relativities. Ideally the group should be fairly small (say four or five members) with a good knowledge of the evaluation scheme and a good 'feel' for the organization as a whole.

The final review will involve an examination of the rank order of jobs based on their total score. However, in a large job evaluation project the moderating group may start by reviewing results from across a range of evaluation teams, so a better approach is to examine the rank order of jobs within each factor, as described in Chapter 4.

IMPLEMENTATION

Implementation involves assimilating employees to the new grade and pay structure, providing for pay protection, communicating the results to employees, and hearing appeals in accordance with an appeals procedure.

Assimilation

A policy is required on how employees should be assimilated into a new pay structure resulting from job evaluation. There are four categories of staff to be covered by the policy:

1. Those staff whose current pay and pay potential are contained within the pay range for the new grades to which their jobs are allocated.

2. Those staff whose current pay lies within the new pay range but whose pay potential is greater than the new maximum.

3. Those staff whose current pay is below the minimum for the new grade.

4. Those staff whose current pay is above the maximum for the new grade.

Current pay and pay potential both within the new pay range

The majority of employees will normally be in this category. They should not be given an increase in pay except in the special case of a pay spine on which there are fixed increments or 'pay points' (see Chapter 10), when the policy is usually to move each person's pay to the next higher pay point.

Current pay within the new pay range but pay potential higher than the new maximum

In this case, if progression to the previous maximum was based on service only, ie a scale of annual increases to the maximum that is guaranteed to those who perform effectively, then this guarantee should be honoured or bought out. If as a result of honouring a pre-existing commitment a person's pay passes the maximum for the new grade, this should be treated as a 'red circle' situation (see below).

If progression to the old maximum were not guaranteed, but was based on performance or contribution, then the new range maximum should normally be applied. Care will be needed to ensure that this does not adversely affect any specific category of staff, particularly female staff.

Current pay below the minimum for the new grade

This situation should be rectified as quickly as possible by raising the pay to the minimum of the new pay range. This should normally be the first call on any money allocated for assimilation. If the total cost of rectifying underpayments is more than the organization can afford, it may be necessary, however unpalatable, to 'green-circle' the person and phase the necessary increases, say one portion in the current year and the rest in the next year – it is undesirable to phase increases over a longer period unless the circumstances are exceptional. The simplest approach is to place a maximum on the increase that any one person may receive. This can be in absolute terms (eg maximum of £2,000) or in percentage increase terms (eg maximum of 10 per cent of current pay). Another alternative is to use an annual 'gap reduction' approach (eg pay increase of 50 per cent of the difference between current pay and range minimum or £500, whichever is the greater).

Current pay above the maximum for the new grade

This category usually includes a high proportion of people who have been in their current job a long time and who may have benefited from a lax approach to pay management in the past, or individuals who have received additional market-related payments or allowances that will no longer apply under the new pay scheme. They have to be 'red-circled' and dealt with in accordance with a protection policy.

Protection policies

Organizations have sometimes provided 'indefinite protection' to red-circled employees, ie maintaining the difference between current pay and range maximum for as long as the employee remains in the job. To differentiate them from employees paid in accordance with the pay scale, they are sometimes placed on what is called a 'personal to job holder' scale. But this is undesirable, first because it will create permanent anomalies and second, because, where there are a lot of men in this situation, it will perpetuate unacceptable sex gaps. The Equal Opportunities Commission in its *Good Practice Guide on Job Evaluation Schemes Free of Sex Bias* states that red-circling 'should not be used on such a scale that it amounts to sex discrimination'. The Equal Pay Task Force states: 'The use of red or green circling which maintains a difference in pay between men and women over more than a phase-in period of time will be difficult to justify.'

Because of these considerations, the most common approach is now to provide for red-circled employees to receive pay protection for a limited period, typically between two and four years. During this time the organization can choose to freeze the individual's salary or to give cost of living increases. The benefit to the organization of freezing salary is that the individual's pay is more likely to fall back within the grade range during the period of protection than if he or she receives a cost of living award. However, this can be regarded as unduly harsh, so many organizations still provide for the payment of 'across the board' cost of living awards during the protection period. After this period of protection, pay is reduced in accordance with the organization's new terms and conditions. This may be to the new maximum of the grade or some other point in the salary range that reflects the maximum of normal expectation (eg the salary level directly below a 'zone' created to reward exceptional performers). If a red-circled individual leaves the job, the scale of pay for the job reverts to the standard range as set up following job evaluation.

Throughout the protection period, and particularly at the start of it, every attempt should be made to resolve the red-circle cases by other means. If job holders are thought to be worth the current salary, then they may well be under-used in their existing job. Attempts should be made to resolve this by either increasing the job responsibilities so that the job will justify re-grading to a higher grade, or moving the person concerned to a higher graded job as soon as an appropriate vacancy arises.

Communicating results

All employees should be informed of the new grade and pay structure, how jobs are graded within the structure, and how pay progression takes place within grades.

Individual employees should be told the grade of their job, their rate of pay and the scope for pay progression. If they have been green-circled they should be informed of the arrangements for bringing their pay up to the minimum for their new grade. If they have been red-circled they should be told how their pay will be protected.

Consideration has also to be given to releasing the job evaluation scores for an employee's job. In principle, if the system is to be truly open and transparent, then the scores should be made known to everyone automatically or on request. If they are not disclosed it may lead to mistrust in the objectivity and fairness of the system – 'What are they trying to hide?' However, people who have not been trained in job evaluation can easily misunderstand or misinterpret such information and this level of openness may create more difficulties than it solves. When considering this issue, it should be remembered that the evaluation has been carried out by a trained panel of evaluators or reviewed by such a panel. They are the only ones who fully understand the process. If the panel includes staff representatives, as it should do, then this, coupled with a full communication programme, should help to create a climate of trust in the system.

Account should also be taken of relevant national legislation, ie The Data Protection Act and the Freedom of Information Act (which applies to public bodies in the United Kingdom). For example, in June 2007 the UK Information Commissioner declared that the guide chart profiles and scoring methodology of the Hay job evaluation scheme do not constitute a trade secret under the terms of the Act, so should be available for release to staff covered by the scheme.

Appeals procedure

It is necessary to have a published procedure for hearing appeals. The procedure should set out:

▍ the grounds upon which an appeal can be made, eg that an individual believes that he or she has been under-graded;

▍ the body that should hear the appeal, often a specially constituted appeals panel whose members should not have been involved in the original evaluation;

▍ the procedure for hearing the appeal, for example obtaining supporting evidence from the appellant, requesting a rationale from the original evaluation panel for their decision, or requesting a re-evaluation by the original panel (or by a specially formed panel);

▍ what happens if the appeals panel rejects the appeal – it is usual to make a hearing of that panel the final stage in the appeals procedure, but, typically, provision is made for individuals who are still dissatisfied to take the issue up through the standard grievance procedure.

An example of an appeals procedure in a university is given in Appendix E.

OPERATIONAL PROCEDURES

The operational procedures for job evaluation need to be defined. This can usefully be done during the design stage and modified as necessary in the light of the roll-out experience. They can be incorporated in an operating guide, which covers:

▍ the purpose of job evaluation within the organization;

▍ details of the scheme and how it functions, eg the factor plan or grade/band profiles;

▍ methods of job analysis and evaluation, including any conventions guiding the interpretation of level definitions, procedures for future job evaluations to use, which may be the same or a simplified version of the process used during scheme development;

- how results are audited or moderated, and how they will be reviewed for consistency over time;

- how the principles of equal pay for work of equal value are observed;

- how job holders are informed of the results of job evaluation and what information is provided;

- the appeals procedure;

- how managers or individual employees can request a review of a grading where a job has changed;

- the process for evaluating new jobs;

- a process for preventing unnecessary future duplication of profiles if the opportunity has been taken to create more generic role profiles – this will usually require HR to keep a library of role profiles and to have an approval process for creating new profiles;

- how the system will be maintained in the longer term.

Example of an evaluation procedure

The following is an example of the National Health Service (NHS) procedure for job evaluation using a combined point-factor and analytical matching approach. Further information on the matching procedure is given in Chapter 7.

---

1. Aims

The aims of the matching procedure are:

- to match as many jobs as possible to national evaluation profiles in the most efficient manner possible avoiding the need for many local evaluations;
- for the matching process to be carried out by a joint team and to secure outcomes acceptable to the employee and his/her line manager.

2. Matching panel(s)

- Matching should be carried out by a joint matching panel comprising both management and staff side members. It should be representative of the organization as a whole. The members will have been trained in the NHS Job Evaluation Scheme which includes an understanding of the avoidance of bias. The members will be committed to partnership working.

∎ It is important for reasons of consistency that a number of core members (typically 3 to 5) should between them attend as many panel meetings as possible.

∎ In addition the panel should include one or two people representing management and staff in the area of work under review. Their role will be to provide additional information about the post under consideration, take part in the discussion and feed the outcome back to other post holders. These representatives should be briefed about the matching process.

3. Documentation

∎ The matching process will be based on existing job descriptions for the jobs to be considered. The representatives may add local information.

4. Step by step procedure

∎ The matching panel and representatives will decide which posts are potentially covered by a profile. These should normally be a block of posts with duties substantially the same. There may, however, be some differences, including location. The post may have different titles or current grade.

∎ For each set of posts, the matching panel will complete a pro forma, summarizing the relevant job duties in the job statement section and job features under each of the factor headings. (By local agreement, this may be done in advance.)

∎ The matching panel will test the pro forma against the published profile to check for matching.

∎ Where more than one evaluation profile may match the pro forma, the matching panel will examine the posts on a factor by factor basis, comparing the information provided with each of the potential profiles. Panel members will use their evaluation and matching training and may refer to the job evaluation scheme factor level definitions to identify whether differences in information pro forma will have an effect on the profile evaluation.

∎ Copies of the profile and the completed pro forma for each set of posts will be supplied to all individuals covered by the match. Co-opted panel members will brief job holders on matching outcomes and be available to answer initial queries.

5. Resolution of queries and problems

∎ Where the matching panel is unable to identify or to agree the appropriate evaluation profile match for a block of posts, the panel may seek additional information about the post by, for example, referring specific questions to representatives, by requesting that a job analysis questionnaire be completed or by asking trained analysts to interview representative job holders.

∎ Where the matching panel agrees that a block of posts is significantly different from any of the national evaluation profiles, they should refer it for local evaluation. It is not necessary for a panel to reach an exact match. The match

should, however, be sufficiently close for the evaluation score to be in the same pay band.
▌ Possible outcomes of the procedure are:
- the matching panel confirms the match and provides an explanation for this;
- the matching panel agrees that no evaluation profile matches the new pro forma and refers the job for local evaluation.
▌ In the event that groups of staff or an individual remains unhappy with the result of matching they may request a rematch by a panel with the majority of its members different from the previous panel. Such a request must be made within three months of the notification of the original panel's decision. In order to trigger this, the post holder(s) must provide details of where they disagree with the match.
▌ The second panel will operate in the same way as the first and follow the procedure above.
▌ The second panel will:
- confirm the same match;
- confirm the match to a different profile;
- or exceptionally refer the job for local evaluation.
▌ The post holder has no right of appeal beyond the second panel. In the event that the post holder believes that the process was misapplied, they may pursue a local grievance about the process, but not against the matching and grading decision.

Another example of a job evaluation policy statement produced by a professional association is given in Appendix F.

ADVICE ON INTRODUCING JOB EVALUATION

The following advice on introducing job evaluation (JE) was given by participants in the 2007 e-reward survey:

▌ Do provide as much pay-protection as possible.

▌ Do involve line managers and unions in the evaluation process. Also use 'expert witnesses' – usually the line manager in charge of the area in which the job sits. This brings the job description to life for the committee, and enables the JE committee to raise questions/ challenge statements in the description, etc. Line managers take greater care in approving job descriptions as a result as they know they will be asked to explain the accountabilities within them to the panel.

▌ Do look at jobs submitted to the JE panel beforehand; if it doesn't look right, go back to the business before the panel meets, and work with them to achieve a win–win solution.

▌ Do expect people to be upset.

▌ Do communicate to all employees using a variety of methods; be open and honest; explain reasons/principles clearly; ensure top-down commitment to job evaluation.

▌ Do communicate at all stages of the implementation of the scheme. Have a dedicated project team to implement: ensure that those involved have been fully trained and briefed. Ensure that you have a number of key managers as ambassadors of the scheme. Have clear guidance materials.

▌ Do ensure that the job descriptions you are evaluating are well written.

▌ Do develop protocols for interpretation of factors.

▌ Don't ever fudge an evaluation score – it *always* comes back to haunt you. If there is pressure on someone's salary for any reason, increase their salary but don't fudge the job evaluation score to justify it!

▌ Don't underestimate the amount of time and effort involved in job evaluation activity.

▌ Don't create a cottage industry for evaluating roles and considering appeals.

▌ Don't present it as an HR system which HR are implementing because they know best.

▌ Don't keep it as a black art that sits within HR.

▌ Don't rush into it; staff pay and grades are too important to them.

▌ Don't leave anything open to misinterpretation; in particular ensure you clarify what happens to individuals or groups of staff (before you publish the process) when jobs are evaluated and the grade either increases or decreases.

▌ Don't underestimate the time it will take to evaluate all your jobs and the impact it will have on morale.

▌ Don't devolve the operation of the scheme to too many individuals as inconsistency of application could creep in.

- Don't underestimate the time to undertake the exercise.
- Don't underestimate the time taken to evaluate roles and how people learn to work the system.
- Don't compromise on what you intend to get out of it; don't think it is the means to solve all your problems.
- Don't underestimate the time taken to get it right.
- Fail to prepare = prepare to fail.

MAINTAINING JOB EVALUATION

The following advice on maintaining job evaluation was given by participants in the 2007 e-reward survey:

- Do ensure there is a process in place to maintain the job evaluation system in line with structural changes – it has to continually evolve with the organization, otherwise it will become obsolete very quickly.
- Do audit regularly and reflect results back to line.
- Do put the time and resources in place.
- Do review basis and rationale for use regularly – also audit evaluation outcomes on a frequent basis to ensure benchmarks are sound and the application of the scheme remains professional.
- Do audit the results to ensure consistency.
- Do make sure it's not too rigid, make sure the business buy in to it, keep it consistent and credible. Ensure that the system is regularly reviewed and users' knowledge levels are maintained.
- Don't let the communication process fall into disrepute.
- Don't forget to involve managers outside HR in the process. This gives the scheme integrity.
- Don't overlook the need for a review of job specs/role content on a regular basis – data can rapidly become outdated.
- Don't keep using a scheme that has passed its 'use-by' date; the signs that a job evaluation scheme is no longer suitable appear early and continuing to use it can infect and undermine all of your reward efforts.

6

Designing a point-factor job evaluation scheme

The steps required to design a point-factor scheme in a large organization are set out in Figure 6.1. In a small organization some of these steps may be compressed.

STEP 1. IDENTIFY AND DEFINE FACTORS

Job evaluation factors are the characteristics or key elements of jobs that are used to analyse and evaluate them in an analytical job evaluation scheme. Although many of the job evaluation factors used in different organizations capture similar job elements (this is an area where there are some enduring truths), the task of identifying and agreeing factors can be challenging.

Factor areas

When the main job dimensions have been identified, they need to be sorted into clusters in order to identify the main factor headings. An analysis of job evaluation factors shows that they typically fall into six main areas:

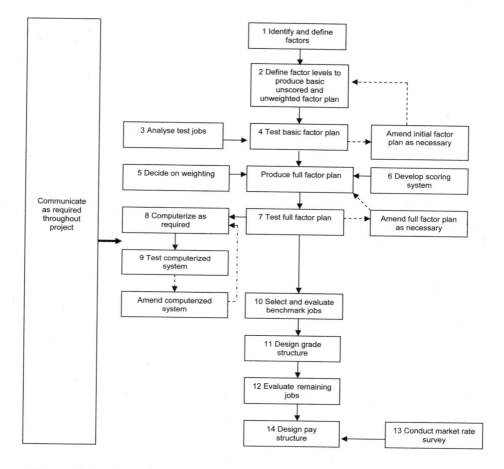

Figure 6.1 Point-factor scheme design sequence

1. The combination of the skills, knowledge and expertise that the employee needs to do the job.

2. The thinking challenges of the job, for example planning, analysis, decision making and problem solving.

3. Interpersonal skills, including communication and relationship-building skills.

4. The responsibilities that the job has for resources, eg human, financial or physical resources.

5. The kinds of impact that the role has, either on internal operational effectiveness or on the external customer or environment.

6. The environmental, emotional or physical demands that are made in a job, for example difficult working conditions, involvement in dealing with challenging behaviour, pressures on those with caring responsibilities, or operational dexterity.

Within these six areas there are many different ways in which jobs can be described. This will depend on the extent to which the organization wants to express jobs in terms of responsibility or the effects of the job on the organization, or in terms of the 'inputs' that a job requires, ie what combination of applied knowledge, skills or behaviours (competencies). For example, most organizations include a factor relating to communication skills in their scheme. However, one organization may define this as the interpersonal skills needed to build relationships; another might place emphasis on the level and type of internal or external contacts that the job is required to have; whereas another might focus on core verbal and aural communication skills required at different levels. Factors are a vehicle for communicating values – what is important to the organization – so there is no 'right' answer in selecting and defining factors, subject to reasonableness tests discussed later in the chapter.

Guidelines for selecting factors

The guidelines for selecting factors are:

▌ The factors must be capable of identifying relevant and important differences between jobs that will support the creation of a rank order of the jobs to be covered by the scheme.

▌ The factors should between them measure all significant job features and should be of broadly comparable scope.

▌ The factors should reflect the values of the organization.

▌ They should apply equally well to different types of work, including specialists and generalists, lower level and higher level jobs, and not be biased in favour of one sex or group.

▌ The whole range of jobs to be evaluated at all levels should be covered without favouring men or women, people belonging to a particular racial group, different age groups or any particular job or occupation.

▌ The scheme should fairly measure features of female-dominated jobs as well as male-dominated jobs.

▌ The choice should not lead to discrimination on the grounds of sex, race, disability, religion, age or for any other reason. Experience should not be included as a factor because it could be discriminatory either on the grounds of sex or age. The same principle applies to education or qualifications as stand-alone factors.

▌ Job features frequently found in jobs carried out mainly by one sex, for example manual dexterity, interpersonal skills and 'caring' responsibilities, should not be omitted. However, if such features are included, it is important that the scheme captures the range of skills across all jobs, including those that might be dominated by another sex.

▌ Double counting should be avoided, ie each factor must be independent of every other factor – the more factors (or sub-factors) in the plan, the higher the probability that double counting will take place.

▌ Elision or compression of more than one significant job feature under a single factor heading should be avoided. If important factors are compressed with others it means that they could be undervalued.

▌ The factor definitions should be clear, relevant and understandable, and written in a way that is meaningful to those who will use the scheme.

▌ The factors should be acceptable to those who will be covered by the scheme.

Most frequently used factors

The e-reward 2007 survey established that the factors most frequently used by the respondents with analytical schemes were:

▌ knowledge and skills;

▌ responsibility;

▌ problem solving;

▌ decision making;

- people management;
- relationships/contacts;
- working conditions;
- mental effort;
- impact;
- creativity.

The following sources of information and approaches to support the development of factors are available.

Reviewing internal strategy/business documents

Looking through existing written materials such as organization or human resources strategy documents can give an insight into the current values and language.

Reviewing people-related frameworks or processes

In the past, job evaluation criteria were not necessarily linked to other human resources processes or frameworks. However, many organizations have now accepted the need to adopt a more coherent approach by applying the organization's values and language across related processes. Reviewing existing job descriptions may be a place to start.

The most obvious potential link is with an organization's competency framework, as many of the concepts reflected in competencies are similar to job evaluation criteria, albeit expressed in behavioural or skills-based language. The extent to which a link can be made with an existing competency framework will depend on how the competency framework has been defined. It will be easier to do where the competencies are skills related to job requirements, eg business acumen (job-centric), rather than person-oriented, eg tenacity (person-centric). The desirability of achieving a degree of linkage was a finding from the e-reward survey, and was one of the main reasons for companies favouring a tailor-made scheme.

Interviews with line managers and other stakeholders

Discussions with key managers can help to get an early perspective on the senior management priorities for the scheme. This group is most likely to have a view about the future demands on the organization and what work will be valued. Early senior manager involvement can also help to dispel myths and misconceptions about job evaluation, and will support the overall communication process – particularly if the managers concerned are those who will later be responsible for approving the scheme.

Focus groups

Structured meetings with employees can be a good way of understanding what aspects of jobs are currently valued and what people think are the most important. Such meetings can also contribute to achieving better involvement and communication. Because employees may be unfamiliar with job evaluation concepts, the agenda will normally need to cover an overview of what job evaluation is, the rationale for introducing job evaluation, what factors are, and what makes a 'good' factor. Views can be explored on possible factors. Focus groups can also be used to obtain the views of employees about how the scheme should be communicated.

Focus groups can be particularly useful for organizations with geographically or functionally diverse constituencies or for developing sector-wide schemes. In developing the UK further education scheme, focus groups were run in about a dozen colleges around the country. They were selected to represent different types of institution as well as geographic diversity. The focus groups generated a long list of possible factor headings, which showed a high degree of consistency across the institutions. This input was clustered into 10 main groups, which became the factors.

Consideration should also be given to whether input from other stakeholders is helpful. Where a scheme is to be jointly agreed with trade unions, their representatives should be involved at an early stage. Staff consultative groups can also be consulted. A voluntary organization may want to include volunteers in focus groups, or to obtain the views of key trustees.

Project team input

The project team can explore possible factors in a number of ways, for example:

▮ Open discussion – drawing on the inputs that are available to the team from other sources.

▮ Selecting a number of jobs/roles and exploring the differences between them – what makes one 'bigger' or 'smaller' than another. This can be done informally or through a process such as whole job ranking or paired comparison.

▮ Using an existing database or list of common factor headings; posting these on a flipchart and drawing out and clustering the job dimensions that seem most relevant to the organization; if a consultant is being used, this exercise is likely to use headings from their factor database.

STEP 2. DEFINE FACTOR LEVELS TO PRODUCE THE BASIC FACTOR PLAN

The factor plan is the key job evaluation document. It guides evaluators in making decisions about the levels of demand and responsibility present in a job. The basic factor plan defines the levels within each of the selected factors. No points are allocated to factors and their levels at this stage.

A decision has to be made on the number of levels (often four, five, six or seven), which has to reflect the range of responsibilities and demands in the jobs covered by the scheme.

The starting point can be an analysis of what would characterize the highest or lowest level for each factor and how these should be described. For example, the highest level in a judgement and decision-making factor could be defined as: 'Deals with widely differing problems calling for extreme clarity of thought in assessing conflicting information and balancing the risks associated with possible solutions. Additionally, one of the main requirements of the role may be to develop fundamentally new strategies and approaches.' The lowest level could be defined as: 'The work is well defined and relatively few new situations are encountered. The causes of problems are readily identifiable and can be dealt with easily.'

It might then be decided that there should be three levels between the highest and lowest level on the basis that this truly reflects the graduation in responsibilities or demands. The outcome would then be the definition of the factor and each of the five levels illustrated in Table 6.1. This process is repeated for each factor.

Table 6.1 Example of factor level definitions

Judgement and decision making: The requirement to exercise judgement in making decisions and solving problems, including the degree to which the work involves choice of action or creativity.

1	The work is well defined and relatively few new situations are encountered. The causes of problems are readily identifiable and can be dealt with easily.
2	Evaluation of information is required to deal with occasional new problems and situations and to decide on a course of action from known alternatives. Occasionally required to participate in the modification of existing procedures and practices.
3	Exercises discriminating judgement in dealing with relatively new or unusual problems where a wide range of information has to be considered and the courses of action are not obvious. May fairly often be involved in devising new solutions.
4	Frequently exercises independent judgement when faced with unusual problems and situations where no policy guidelines or precedents are available. May also frequently be responsible for devising new strategies and approaches that require the use of imagination and ingenuity.
5	Deals with widely differing problems calling for extreme clarity of thought in assessing conflicting information and balancing the risks associated with possible solutions. Additionally, one of the main requirements of the role may be to develop fundamentally new strategies and approaches.

The following guidelines should be used in defining levels:

▍ Each level should be defined as clearly as possible to help evaluators make 'best fit' decisions.

▍ The levels should cover the whole range of demands in this factor that are likely to arise in the jobs with which the evaluation scheme is concerned.

▍ The link between the content of level definitions should be related specifically to the definition of the factor concerned and should not overlap with other factors.

▍ There should be uniform progression in the definitions level by level, from the lowest to the highest level. There should be no gaps or undefined intermediate levels that might lead to evaluators finding it difficult to be confident about the allocation of a level of demand. Some schemes have undefined interim levels. This is only likely to work where there are clear steps in demand between the defined levels and where there are protocols on how to use the undefined levels.

▌ The factor levels should represent clear and recognizable steps in demand.

▌ The levels should be defined in absolute, not relative terms. So far as possible any dimensions should be defined. They should not rely upon a succession of undefined comparatives, eg small, medium and large.

▌ Each level definition should stand on its own. Level definitions should not be defined by reference to a lower or higher level, ie it is insufficient to define a level in words to the effect that it is a higher (or lower) version of an adjacent level.

Job evaluation was described earlier in this book as a subjective process carried out within an objective framework. The factor plan provides the framework, but interpreting factor level definitions and relating them to a role profile requires judgement. There is a limit to the number of words that can be included in a factor level definition (too many confuse rather than clarify) and the words themselves cannot always convey accurate meanings. For example, level 3 of the planning and organization factor in the NHS job evaluation scheme refers to 'planning and organization of a number of complex activities'. But this does not tell the evaluator how many activities justify a level 3 rating or what constitutes a 'complex' activity. What has to happen is that, as evaluators gain experience in interpreting the level definitions, they record conventions or protocols that help to achieve consistent evaluations by providing guidance on what these or similar words mean, preferably with quantitative examples illustrated by reference to benchmark jobs that have already been evaluated. One of the main purposes of testing in the design programme is to identify where conventions are necessary and ensure that they are made available to evaluators. But this process of developing conventions continues when the benchmark jobs are evaluated, which means that in a large job evaluation project evaluators may have to revisit the conclusions reached in earlier stages of the programme and re-evaluate them in the light of the conventions.

STEP 3. ANALYSE TEST JOBS

A small representative sample of test jobs should be identified. The proportion depends on the size and complexity of the organization, but in a large organization it may be up to 10–15 per cent of the jobs to be covered. These are then analysed in terms of the factors as described.

STEP 4. TEST BASIC FACTOR PLAN

No one ever gets the definitions of factors and their levels right first time. At the initial drafting stage a useful test is to cut up the factor plan by level and factor and to ask the project team, or another team not involved in the initial design work, to sort the independent statements back into the factors and levels as originally drafted. This 'jig-saw' test provides a good test of the wording, as each statement is looked at individually in a way that does not happen if the plan is always reviewed as a complete document. Even if a team have already worked through two or three drafts of the plan, they are likely to come up with some changes or queries about relativities between statements.

The draft definitions must then be tested on actual jobs. The aim of this initial test is to check on the extent to which:

▌ the factors are appropriate;

▌ the factors cover all aspects of the jobs to be evaluated;

▌ the factors are non-discriminatory;

▌ the factors avoid double counting and are not compressed unduly;

▌ level definitions are worded clearly, graduated properly and cover the whole range of demands applicable to the jobs to be evaluated so that they provide good guidance on the allocation of factor levels to evaluators and thus enable consistent evaluations to be made.

The test can also begin the process of establishing conventions.

A more comprehensive test should be carried out later when the full factor plan with scoring systems and weightings has been devised.

STEP 5. DECIDE ON THE FACTOR WEIGHTING

Weighting is the process of attaching more importance to some factors than others. An unweighted or equally weighted scheme is one in which the factors are treated as being equally important and the maximum number of points is the same for each of them. Nineteen per cent of the respondents to the 2007 e-reward survey had unweighted schemes. If it is believed that weighting is desirable there are two approaches: 1) *explicit weighting* by increasing the maximum points available for what are regarded as more important factors (53 per cent of the e-reward respondents had explicitly weighted schemes); 2) *implicit weighting*, which was used by 28 per cent of the respondents to the e-reward 2007 survey. The latter takes place when some factors have more levels than others but the same scoring progression per level exists as in the other factors. The factors with more levels would have more points available to them and would have therefore been implicitly weighted. For example, in a seven-factor scheme with the same pattern of score progression per level in each factor, but with two factors with more levels than the others, the factors with more levels will have been weighted. Sometimes this is referred to as an 'unweighted scheme', but this is not the case because decisions on the number of factors and levels within them and the scoring progression used may in effect 'weight' the scheme.

The number and choice of factors may also implicitly weight a scheme. If two factors that would normally be treated as being of equal importance are compressed into one and the scoring has not been increased proportionately, then implicit weighting of that combined factor has taken place, ie it is undervalued in terms of its significance.

There should be a rationale for the weighting system, eg relative value of factors to the organization, agreed relative values – it should not just give the answers people want. Explicit weighting accords with the belief that some factors are more important than others. Implicit weighting is more likely to take place when there are a large number of factors – 10 or more – and the impact of explicitly weighting any factors is less (unless the weighting is so disproportionate that the non-weighted factors become immaterial). Implicitly or equally weighted schemes are also common in small organizations where there is no desire to have a complicated scoring formula.

There is no single 'right' approach to developing factor weights. The main approaches are:

▌ Using the predetermined weighting built into a proprietary scheme.

▌ Statistical analyses; typically this refers to multiple linear regression analysis that is used to predict what the 'best' combination of weights will be to replicate a reference ranking. Less commonly it involves analysing stakeholder views to tease out the most important factors.

▌ Using judgement, which may involve open discussion or is based on agreed guiding principles (eg no factor will have a weighting of less than 5 per cent or more than 30 per cent).

The benefits and risks of the various approaches are summarized in Table 6.2.

It is worth noting that the statistical approach carries a specific risk with respect to equal value. The most common statistical approach to generating weightings is through multiple regression analysis. This is used to compute a set of weighting coefficients by objective mathematical means. The analysis seeks to find the weighting combination that will most closely replicate a predetermined reference rank order of jobs. The reference ranking might be based on external market benchmarking of the test jobs, or an internally derived reference ranking such as a 'felt-fair', or by another ranking method such as paired comparison. However, unless the reference ranking has itself been developed using an objective process, the regression analysis may simply reproduce the existing hierarchy, thus reinforcing inequalities or preconceptions. The use of market data is particularly suspect in this respect, as pay discrimination in favour of male-dominated roles may already be embedded in the market.

Decisions on explicit weighting are often made by job evaluation project teams using a judgmental approach. Arguments are based on opinions and feelings. For example, it is often held that knowledge and skills or expertise are more important than anything else and must therefore be weighted. A typical method is to ask each member of the team to distribute 100 points amongst the factors. The distributions are then reproduced by the facilitator on a flipchart that does not reveal their source. The team then discusses the suggested weightings and comes to a conclusion. Averaging the weightings should be avoided if possible. It is far better to reach a decision through consensus after a debate. This process is totally unscientific. It is essential, therefore, to make the initial weightings provisional and test them using the full weighted factor plan.

Table 6.2 Different methods of weighting

Approach	Benefits	Risks
Consultancy developed	• Tried and tested across many organizations • Enables comparability across organizations	• May place value on factors that are different from the organization's own values • May be perceived as a 'black box' approach if not understood internally • Lack of transparency and ownership
Statistical analyses	• Can be a useful kick-start to the decision-making process • Appears to be 'objective'	• Can yield unhelpful results, eg negative coefficients for factors that are most applicable to lower level jobs • Has an equal value risk because it relies on potentially biased reference ranking • May be difficult to know when to stop
Judgemental	• Reflects the values of the organization • Can be as simple or complex as required to meet needs	• Can be unfocused if there are no guiding principles • May end up biased in favour of one group if the process turns into a negotiation. For example, in one international development bank, the weighting debate became a negotiation between the economists, who argued for a high weighting on knowledge and expertise, and the investment bankers, who argued for the highest weighting on financial impact.
Implicit	• Easy to understand • Easy to calculate • Avoids protracted discussions about weighting that may only marginally affect the overall rank order	• May not reflect relative importance of a factor that is particularly significant, eg analytical skills in a research-based organization

One of the authors has used all types of approaches to developing weightings and scoring and has found that if the factors are well thought through in the first place, and if the factors have the same or a similar number of levels, a good starting place is to test out an implicit weighting first. If this seems to be producing an unacceptable pattern of results, further testing can be undertaken using explicit weighting. However, unless the scheme is to be weighted in favour of a factor that applies strongly to a specific area of work, the remodelling of weightings is likely to yield fairly small changes in rank order as all jobs will be affected to the same degree by the re-weighting. The initial choice of factors is far more significant in determining the relative score of jobs.

STEP 6. DEVELOP SCORING SYSTEM

The aim is to design a point-factor scheme that will operate fairly and consistently to produce a rank order of jobs, based on the total points score for each job. Each level in the factor plan has to be allocated a points value so that there is a scoring progression from the lowest to the highest level.

A decision needs to be made on how to set the scoring progression within each factor. There are two methods. 'Arithmetic' or linear progression assumes that there are consistent step differences between factor levels, eg a four level factor might be scored 1, 2, 3, 4. Alternatively, geometric progression assumes that there are increasingly larger score differences at each successive level in the hierarchy to reflect progressive increases in responsibility. Thus the levels may be scored 1, 2, 4, 8 rather than 1, 2, 3, 4. This increases the scoring differentiation between higher level jobs.

The rank order produced by either of these methods is unlikely to differ much, but senior managers sometimes like to think that there should be larger gaps between levels at their end of the scale and that the greater 'distance' between scores is proportionate to an increasing gap between job requirements at the top end of the factor levels. It can also indicate clearer breaks between grades when it comes to designing the structure, as described below.

It is best to allocate a single finite score for each level because giving a choice from a range of scores can complicate evaluations. If it is decided that there should be some choice, this should be as simple as possible, for example low, standard and high. If this approach is used, protocols should be developed to explain what each step change means and it should be subject to thorough testing to ensure consistency.

The outcome of stages 5 and 6 is a draft fully scored and weighted factor plan, which is tested in Step 7.

STEP 7. TEST THE FULL FACTOR PLAN

The full factor plan is tested on the same jobs used in the initial test of the draft factors. Further jobs may be added to extend the range of the test. Each test job is evaluated and scored by the project team and then ranked according to the total score. The project team then considers the extent to which it is believed the rank order is valid in the sense that the evaluations correctly indicate relative job value. There is no single, simple test which will establish the validity of a factor plan. The methods available are as follows:

▌ *Reference ranking* – the team compares the ranking produced by the job evaluation with the rank order produced by a ranking exercise. The technique of paired comparison (see Chapter 2) may be used to guide the ranking process.

▌ *Hierarchy comparisons* – the rank order produced by the test is compared with the existing organizational hierarchy and any obvious discrepancies are investigated. However, care must be taken not to assume that the existing hierarchy is the correct one.

▌ *External market test* – compare the internal rank order with that existing in comparable jobs elsewhere. But this may reflect pay differentials between job families, rather than internal measures of job worth. It may also replicate existing inequities between male and female jobs.

▌ *The 'felt-fair' test* – the rank order produced by the test is compared with what the job evaluation panel 'feels' is the fair and there-fore appropriate ranking, and discrepancies are identified. This is dangerous because it is liable simply to reproduce existing prejudices. Inevitably, however, a 'felt-fair' approach will be adopted by some of those reviewing the test. It is therefore necessary to be particularly alert to the possibility of pre-judgements affecting opinions and to challenge any apparent move in that direction. The first three tests can be used for this purpose.

STEP 8. CONVERT THE PAPER SCHEME TO A COMPUTER-AIDED SCHEME

The steps set out above will produce a paper-based scheme, which is the most common approach. Converting the paper scheme to a computer-aided scheme can offer a number of advantages including greater consistency, speed and the elimination of much of the paperwork.

Computer-aided schemes use software provided by suppliers, but if the job evaluation scheme is bespoke it will typically be derived from the paper-based scheme devised by the methods set out above. If a computer-aided scheme is adopted, the job evaluation project team or panel will not be required to spend time carrying out detailed paper evaluations, but it is necessary to set up a review panel that can validate and agree the outcomes of the computer-aided process. A grading outcome is only as good as the job information that has been entered on the system, and hard lessons have been learnt by organizations that have ended up with a 'fully automated' scheme but unacceptable outcomes.

STEP 9. TEST THE COMPUTER-AIDED SCHEME

If the computer-aided scheme has been derived from a paper-based scheme, it is necessary to test it on the same jobs to establish that similar results will be produced.

STEP 10. SELECT AND EVALUATE BENCHMARK JOBS

Benchmark jobs are a sample of typical jobs representing the different occupations and levels in the organization and can also be used to represent jobs held mainly by women or members of particular racial groups, where applicable. When evaluated, the benchmark jobs provide the basis for designing the grade structure. The jobs used for tests can become benchmark jobs, but it is often advisable to extend the number to provide a satisfactory basis for grading. The proportion of distinct jobs varies according to the complexity and size of the organization. Even in a simple structure it will be 10 per cent or more and it could be much higher in some complex organizations (30 per cent or more). In a small organization this stage may involve the evaluation of all jobs, rather than a benchmark sample.

As described in Chapter 5, there is a choice of evaluation approach. Either the panel evaluates all jobs together, or jobs are evaluated by an analyst or sub-group of evaluators (pairs or more), and the full panel is then used to review the initial evaluations. There is a choice of three methods of evaluation by the panel.

Factor by factor

The panel takes each factor in turn and evaluates all jobs in respect of that factor, ie whole jobs are not evaluated in turn. This is the best method, but is only likely to work where jobs have been pre-evaluated prior to the panel review and where the panel then reviews the overall results for each factor one at a time.

A factor by factor approach rather than a job by job approach means that panel members are less likely to make decisions on total scores based on *a priori* judgements about the relative value of the whole jobs, which they might find it hard to change. Instead, they are looking at responses for that factor in relation to responses for other jobs. They are more likely to focus on 'read-across' analytical judgements about the level of particular factors and it will be easier for them to refer for guidance to previous evaluations of the same factor in other benchmark jobs. It also takes less time than other methods because it is possible to concentrate on factor evaluations that are questionable relative to the levels given to other jobs.

When there are variations in factor evaluations, individual panel members are asked to give reasons for their conclusions. The facilitator or chair has to be careful not to allow them to be pressurized to change their views. If panel members have been properly trained and if there is a carefully designed, tested and understood factor plan and good information about the job, the extent to which evaluations vary is usually fairly limited, which enables consensus to be achieved more easily.

Whole jobs disclosed

Each panel member evaluates whole jobs factor by factor and then informs the panel of his or her conclusions. The facilitator records their separate views and then initiates a discussion with the objective of achieving consensus on the rating for each factor and therefore the overall score. This can be time-consuming because panel members may be influenced by pre-formed judgements and, having made up their mind, find it difficult to shift their ground. Again, time is saved if individual or pairs of panel members evaluate the jobs prior to the panel meeting, and the responses are collated on a spreadsheet. It also helps if the collated responses can be reviewed by panel members prior to the group meeting, as it will give time for them to consider their response in the light of any areas of difference.

Whole jobs undisclosed

This is a variation of the second approach where the whole panel is involved in evaluating each job. Each panel member evaluates whole jobs factor by factor but does not communicate his or her views formally to other members of the panel. Instead, the panel as a whole discusses and agrees the evaluation of each factor in turn to produce a total job evaluation score. This speeds up the evaluation and consensus can be easier to achieve because panel members are not put in the position of having to defend their prior judgements against all comers. However, there is the danger of the weaker members of the panel allowing themselves to be swayed by strongly expressed majority views. This approach therefore only works with good facilitation, which ensures that the discussion is not dominated by one or two powerful members and that all members have their say. Where the whole panel is evaluating jobs, some organizations start with the whole job disclosed method and, when panel members (and the facilitator) become more experienced, move on to the whole job undisclosed method.

STEP 11. DESIGN GRADE STRUCTURE

A point-factor job evaluation scheme often provides the basis for the design of a grade structure that contains a sequence or hierarchy of grades, bands or levels into which groups of jobs that are broadly comparable in value are placed. Grade structure design is dealt with in Chapter 11. As mentioned earlier, depending on the size of the organization this may be based either on a set of benchmark jobs or all the remaining jobs.

STEP 12. ROLL-OUT EVALUATION TO REMAINING JOBS

If a reasonable sample of benchmark posts has been used, the remaining jobs can be evaluated by a process of matching (preferably analytical) rather than evaluating each job in full. In small organizations, where all jobs are evaluated in Step 10, this step is not required.

STEP 13. CONDUCT MARKET RATE SURVEY

Information on market rates for all or a selection of the benchmark jobs is required as the basis for the design of a pay structure (see Chapter 11). This step may not be required if the organization already has good benchmark data through regular external pay benchmarking, or if it is confident that existing pay levels provide a sound starting point for pay structure design.

STEP 14. DESIGN PAY STRUCTURE

Pay ranges are attached to the grade structure by reference to the external market and current actual salaries. Account is taken of the external market to ensure that rates of pay are competitive. The cost of implementation may be estimated at this stage, although the final costs will not be known until all jobs are evaluated. Costs arise because, while it is the usual policy not immediately to reduce any-one's pay if they are over-graded, those who are under-graded will have their pay brought up to the minimum of their new grade. The scale of cost depends on the number of anomalies (ie under-gradings) in existence before the job evaluation exercise and the type of structure that is being introduced. In the UK higher education sector, the cost of moving all staff onto a new incremental structure with 3 per cent in-crements was typically around 1 per cent to move everyone onto their new incremental point and an additional 2–3 per cent for bringing under-graded staff up to the new minimum. The total of 3–4 per cent is not untypical of an incremental structure. If there are no incremental points and if grades are broad, the cost will be lower, although limiting the number of grades (eg broad-banding as described in Chapter 11) can create equal pay problems.

7

Designing a matching job evaluation scheme

Matching is the process of comparing a role profile with a hierarchy of grade/level profiles or one or more benchmark jobs to establish which provides the best fit. It can either be developed to support an underpinning point-factor scheme or in its own right as a simpler or more transparent alternative to a point-factor scheme.

A distinction was made in Chapter 2 between analytical and non-analytical role matching. A fully analytical role matching scheme will specifically analyse grades/levels and roles under common factor headings or elements, and use these headings as the basis for comparison. A non-analytical scheme will involve making 'whole job' comparisons, ie the grades and jobs will not have been defined in terms of specific factors. The latter is essentially a job classification approach (see Chapter 2). As also mentioned in that chapter, the distinction between analytical and non-analytical matching is not always precise and the term 'matching' is frequently used to cover both methods.

The steps required to develop a matching scheme are set out below.

STEP 1. IDENTIFY AND DEFINE MATCHING ELEMENTS

The factors can be those used in a point-factor scheme if a combined approach is adopted. This might be a pre-existing scheme (whether proprietary or bespoke), or a point-factor scheme that has been developed as part of the project. If the latter is the case, the matching criteria should reproduce the point-factor scheme factors, although it may be possible to combine sub-factors or any factors that are highly correlated (eg freedom to act and decision making). If analytical matching is to be used as a stand-alone approach, the decisions on the elements can be made as described above. Whether or not matching is analytical will depend on the extent to which the elements represent discrete job dimensions (and then whether jobs are analysed separately according to each of these dimensions).

In a classification scheme the hierarchy of grade definitions could consist of overall statements such as the following:

Grade 1 – the work involves standard routines such as maintaining straight-forward record systems or operating simple office equipment. Close supervision is exercised or the work is easily controlled by self-checking. Tasks are clearly defined and the choice of action is within narrow limits. Contacts are limited to routine exchanges of information with colleagues.

This example does in fact describe the job under a number of headings covering skill requirements, responsibility and contacts with others. These could be expanded to form an analytical grade definition or profile that would facilitate the use of analytical matching if jobs were described under the same headings and compared, factor by factor. Thus job classification becomes more analytical.

STEP 2. DECIDE ON GRADE STRUCTURE

The grade structure may have already been designed following the initial benchmarking exercise when developing a point-factor scheme. If not, decisions on the structure should be made as suggested in Chapter 11. These will initially determine whether the structure should be a single one covering all jobs, or whether it should be a career or job grade and pay structure (see Chapter 11). A decision will also have to be made on the provisional number of grades or levels (this number may be amended when the grade definition process takes place). This can be done at the outset based on an *a priori* decision that is made empirically by reference to the existing hierarchy or a belief that the present number of grades should be reduced to a more manageable number, say from 14 to 8. A less judgemental approach is to base the decision on a ranking of benchmark posts, possibly using paired comparisons, and an analysis of the clustering of jobs based on the identification of common characteristics. The ranked jobs are then divided into grades according to views on the number of the distinct levels of responsibility that need to be differentiated in terms of pay and, possibly, benefits provision.

Another approach is to get the project team to sort benchmark job descriptions, role profiles or questionnaire responses into levels, with the criteria for allocating jobs to different levels being discussed as part of the process. The outcomes from the discussion and the number of levels arrived at through the process can be built into the matching definitions, while information about which jobs fall into each level can be discarded pending a more thorough matching process. Whichever approach is used the number of levels may be amended at a later stage if it is shown to be inappropriate.

STEP 3. DEFINE PROFILES

Role matching involves the use of two types of profiles: grade, level or career band profiles and benchmark role profiles against which individual profiles for the role to be graded are matched.

Grade or level profiles

Where there is no pre-existing point-factor or analytical proprietary scheme the grade or level profiles will need to be developed from scratch based on the criteria decided upon in Step 1. Otherwise they should be based on the existing factors or a selection of them. The easiest way of producing definitions is simply to draw up the grade profiles on the basis of assumptions about the characteristics of any jobs that would be placed in the various levels. An alternative approach is to select benchmark jobs covering all levels, analyse and rank them, allocate them to grades on a judgemental (felt-fair) basis and then prepare grade profiles by reference to the analyses of the benchmark jobs. However, where there is a pre-existing point-factor or analytical proprietary scheme the most robust method is to refer to the analyses of benchmark jobs that have already been graded and distil these to produce a generic definition. This is done by reviewing the job evaluation scores for each grade, and creating a description for each level that reflects the typical pattern of responses for that grade. In job and career family structures, generic profiles may be supplemented by levels of technical skills and accountability.

The career band profiles used by Friends Provident Insurance are shown in Table 7.1.

Table 7.1 Friends Provident career band profiles

Career Band A *Job example: clerical and administrative staff*	
Technical knowledge/ business experience and qualifications	Developing a knowledge of one or more key areas within the function or business unit, together with an understanding of the systems utilized. Ensures that technical information is appropriately presented and correct
Problem solving	Solves problems by following well-defined procedures and precedents. Will consult with more experienced colleagues on more difficult or novel situations.
Leadership	Takes responsibility for management of own workload, delivering against performance standards and individual/team objectives.
Communication/ influence	Communicates information clearly and concisely, applying standards of common courtesy to all contacts.
Career Band B *Job example: customer services consultant*	
Technical knowledge/ business experience and qualifications	Demonstrates a good understanding of a range of non-standard processes, procedures and systems to be utilized in carrying out responsibilities. Is likely to have two or more years' relevant experience working within the function or business unit or have gained relevant experience elsewhere. May be starting to study for specific technical exams, eg FPC or ACII.
Problem solving	Works within procedures and precedents determining solutions from a number of appropriate alternatives.
Leadership	Offers guidance and technical support to less experienced members of the team.
Communication/ influence	Applies developed communication skills in effectively handling more challenging contacts.

Table 7.1 (continued)

Career Band C *Job example: customer services team leader*

Technical knowledge/ business experience and qualifications	Fully conversant with the procedures, policies and systems applied within the function or business unit, having gained relevant experience over a period of five or more years. Demonstrates a comprehensive understanding of one or more well-defined areas for which they will provide technical leadership. Is developing an understanding of the relationship between different subject areas/ business units. Is likely to have gained a qualification in a technical subject in a relevant discipline.
Problem solving	Applies specialist knowledge of own area in making judgements based on the analysis of factual information in straightforward situations.
Leadership	Plans and coordinates the work of the team and/or provides technical leadership, eg through delivery of on-the-job training, quality audits or application of developed specialist skills and knowledge.
Communication/ influence	Explains technical information clearly and effectively, adopting a style of communication to fit differing levels of audience understanding. Is able to persuade colleagues and gain commitment to new ideas or approaches by expressing own views confidently and logically.

Career Band D *Job examples: customer services team manager, analyst, programmer*

Technical knowledge/ business experience and qualifications	Is able to apply and consolidate specialist skills and knowledge gained over a period of eight or more years' relevant experience to ensure essential procedures are followed and standards maintained. Demonstrates an understanding of the relationship between different subject areas and applies this knowledge in delivering cross-functional support, projects or advice.

As a professional entrant to the business, will be developing professional skills through exam success and be increasing their contribution to the business. |
Problem solving	Uses analytical skills and evaluative judgement, based on the analysis of factual and qualitative information to solve problems of a non-routine or more complex nature. Will be guided by precedents.
Leadership	In a team management role will be handling staff management issues including recruitment, resource management, training, coaching and performance management, and playing a leading role in determining salary recommendations for team members. Alternatively, will be a technical specialist with well-developed technical skills and specialist knowledge.
Communication/ influence	Demonstrates strong verbal and written communication skills in influencing the outcome of decisions. Involves appropriate contacts in developing the final solution.

Table 7.2 Grade profiles

Factor	Grade 1	Grade 2	Grade 3
Decisions	Post requires little freedom to act, work is carried out within clearly defined rules or procedures and advice is available if required. Decisions have limited and short-term effect on employees beyond immediate colleagues or on the public. Effects of decisions would be quickly known and readily amended if necessary	Contacts with employees of other departments or occasionally receiving enquiries from outside the authority as first contact. Contacts beyond the organization's employees would be within limited terms of reference and generally be restricted to situations where information is readily available	Contacts which are generally not contentious but where the need or potential outcome may not be straightforward, or where the circumstances call for an element of tact or sensitivity. Contacts at this level would include interviewing to establish details or service needs, the supply of straightforward advice and initiating action to provide assistance. Contacts within the organization would require the provision of advice or guidance on matters that are less well established
Knowledge and skills	Ability to undertake work, consistent with a basic knowledge and skills requirement, which involves a limited range of tasks that can be carried out after initial induction	Ability to undertake work, consistent with a comparatively basic knowledge and skills requirement, which encompasses a range of tasks involving application of readily understood rules	Ability to undertake work concerning more involved tasks confined to one function or area of activity which requires a good standard or practical knowledge and skills in that area of activity
Work context	Work where the programme of tasks is not normally interrupted	Work subject to interruption to programme of tasks but not involving any significant change to the programme	Work subject to changing problems or circumstances or demand

Table 7.2 *(continued)*

Factor	Grade 4	Grade 5	Grade 6
Decisions	Decisions that lead to the setting of working standards in the provision of operational services or changes in important procedures or service practice	Decisions involve independent action within precise policy frameworks	Decisions made within broad policy frameworks which have a profound impact on the organization's policies and activities across a number of departments or on large numbers of people or on organizations in receipt of the organization's services
Knowledge and skills	Ability to undertake work on a variety of advanced tasks confined to one function or area of activity that requires detailed knowledge and skills in a specialist discipline	Undertake work of a highly complex and diverse nature that requires advanced/ high level knowledge and skills in a range of specialist disciplines	Possess highly developed specialist knowledge across a range of work procedures and practices underpinned by theoretical knowledge and relevant practical experience
Work context	Work subject to frequently changing circumstances	Work is highly complex and frequently involves the resolution of conflicting priorities	Work demands are largely unpredictable; may be involved in crisis management on issues deeply affecting the organization

An example of grade profiles set out under job evaluation headings for a six-level structure developed for a large not-for-profit organization is given in Table 7.2.

In a career or job family structure, ie one in which there are separate structures for 'families' of jobs as described in Chapter 11, separate profiles may be made for each family, as in the example from a large charity in Table 7.3.

Benchmark role profiles

As mentioned earlier, roles can also be matched to benchmark role profiles. Benchmark profiles are set out under the analytical factor

Table 7.2 Grade profiles *(continued)*

Factor	Grade 1	Grade 2	Grade 3
Supervisory responsibility	Little or no supervisory responsibility other than helping/inducting less experienced staff in the work of the group	Minor supervisory responsibility, eg in the absence of Section Head allocation of work and checking for quality and quantity	Occasional supervision of staff temporarily assigned or shared supervision of permanent staff
Creativity	Work with very limited opportunity for creative work or innovatory thinking	Work largely regulated by laid-down procedures, but needing occasional creative skills	Creativity is a feature of the job but exercised within the general framework of recognized procedures
Contacts	Contacts and exchanges information within the organization beyond the immediate associates, but usually within the post's own department. Exchange usually on non-contentious and well-established matters	Contacts with employees of other departments or occasionally receiving enquiries from outside the authority as first contact. Contacts beyond the organization's employees would be within limited terms of reference and generally be restricted to situations where information is readily available	Contacts which are generally not contentious but where the need or potential outcome may not be straightforward, or where the circumstances call for an element of tact or sensitivity. Contacts at this level would include interviewing to establish details or service needs, the supply of straightforward advice and initiating action to provide assistance. Contacts within the organization would require the provision of advice or guidance on matters that are less well established

headings or a distilled version of them and may refer to the job evaluation level established when the role was evaluated, as in the example given in Table 7.4 of a profile prepared by the NHS as part of its Agenda for Change programme. In the relevant job information section a summary of the job evaluation level description is given (in bold) and the job level is quoted.

Table 7.2   *(continued)*

Factor	Grade 4	Grade 5	Grade 6
Supervisory responsibility	Supervision of staff carrying out tasks in one identifiable area of work	Supervision or coordination and planning of the work of groups of staff carrying out work of a diverse nature	Plan and organize a large department or highly significant area of activity and/or manage a portfolio of important short- and long-term projects to meet both internal and external requirements
Creativity	Creativity is essential to the job and needs to be regularly exercised within general guidelines	Work that requires creative input in a number of diverse subjects and range of expertise where the frequent opportunity and need for imaginative thinking is not limited by defined policies	Carry out work in unprecedented situations frequently involving innovatory response on diverse subjects which have extensive policy or service implications. Make a major contribution to high profile reviews of key organization policies
Contacts	Contacts that deal with situations where the content and outcome are not straightforward. Contacts within the authority with staff on matters that are not well established and where some authority in the provision of services is required	Contacts regularly dealing with a range of complex and contentious matters where the outcome will have substantial implications for the contact or the organization's service provision. Though the post operates within broad policy guidelines, the handling of contacts would demand a consistently high degree of discretion, sensitivity and advocacy	Contacts advising the organization on high level complex matters with profound implications for the person or the organization contacted or that require a responsibility to act on behalf of the organization and commit the organization to a course of action involving substantial impact on resources. It would be expected that the expert guidance would be accepted and only ever overruled as a result of a change in policies

Table 7.3 Career family level profiles

Level	Role	Key accountabilities	Key competencies
8	HR Director	• Contribute to development of business strategy • Develop HR strategies aligned to business strategy • Exercise overall direction of all HR activities required to support achievement of business goals • Oversee human capital management projects	Knowledge of: • the business, its strategy and its drivers • HRM/HCM at a strategic level Ability to • articulate a vision and set a leadership agenda • contribute to business strategic planning on equal terms with other directors • develop and implement HR strategies that are aligned to the business strategy and integrated with one another
7	Head of HR	• Prepare and implement plans to support achievement of HR strategic goals • Act as Deputy to HR Director • Coordinate the provision of HR services through departmental managers and HR business partners • Direct human capital management projects	Knowledge of: • the business, its strategy and its drivers • HRM/HCM at the level of a Fellow, CIPD Ability to: • develop and implement strategic plans for the function • manage a diverse range of activities • plan and coordinate the work of senior HR managers
6	Learning and Development Manager	• Contribute to the development of the leaning and development strategy • Identify learning needs and plan blended learning and development programmes to meet them • Deliver major programmes • Direct the activities of learning and development consultants	Knowledge of: • current thinking and good practice in learning and development • advanced concepts and techniques in the field (Fellow, CIPD) Ability to: • analyse key factors affecting activities in the function • coordinate and direct complex HRD programmes
5	Assistant Head of Talent Management	• Contribute to the preparation of human capital plans • Assist in preparing management succession plans • Coordinate performance management activities • Analyse human capital data and prepare reports	Knowledge of: • techniques of human resource and management succession planning • HRM at the level of Member, CIPD with at least 6 years' experience Ability to: • analyse business plans and draw conclusions on talent management requirements • carry out the analysis and diagnosis of people issues and propose practical solutions

Table 7.3 *(continued)*

Level	Role	Key accountabilities	Key competencies
4	HR Business Partner	• Contribute to the effective management of the division • Ensure the division has the skilled people it requires • Work alongside line managers and provide help and advice on HR issues • Deliver HR services required by the division	Knowledge of: • HRM techniques at the level of Member, CIPD with at least 4 years' experience • business imperatives in the division • corporate HR policies and practices Ability to: • provide efficient and cost-effective services in each HR area • promote the empowerment of line managers to make HR decisions but provide guidance as required. • anticipate requirements and set up and operate appropriate services
3	Reward Analyst	• Maintain information systems on pay and benefits • Assist in the conduct and analysis of market surveys • Maintain databank of information on market rates • Prepare role profiles for job evaluation purposes	Knowledge of: • the labour market and sources of market data • reward management techniques at the level of the CIPD Certificate in Reward Management Ability to: • carry out numerical and statistical analysis • use IT systems, software and spreadsheets • conduct role analyses
2	HR Assistant (recruitment)	• Place job advertisements • Arrange interviews • Deal with routine correspondence to applicants including standard offer letters • Ensure records created for new employees	Knowledge of: • HR techniques relevant to recruitment (studying for CIPD) Ability to: • select appropriate media • administer fairly complex procedures
1	Administrative Assistant	• Provide word processing services • Maintain records • Operate office machinery • Deal with routine queries	Knowledge of: • Microsoft Office – Word, Excel, PowerPoint Ability to: • word process all types of documents, including reports and complex tabulations • prepare PowerPoint presentations • administer standard procedures

Table 7.4 Example of NHS role profile

Job title	Payroll Manager	
Job statement	1 Manage a payroll department 2 Interpret statutory regulations and NHS terms and conditions of employment 3 Deal with payroll and tax issues	

Factor	Relevant job information	JE level
Communication & relationship skills	**Providing and receiving complex, sensitive or contentious information where persuasive skills are required, gain agreement or cooperation** Persuade staff to comply with new practices and procedures; reassure staff; communicate complex information	4
Knowledge, training & experience	**Understanding of a range of work procedures and practices, requiring an intermediate level of theoretical knowledge** Knowledge of legislation and employment conditions, financial procedures, computer software	4
Analytical & judgemental skills	**Judgements involving a range of facts or situations, which require analysis or comparison of a range of options** Analyse and resolve complex financial issues	3
Planning and organizational skills	**Planning and organization of a number of complex activities, which require the formulation and adjustment of plans** Long-term planning within a structured framework; plan the departmental programme; plan for tax and legislative changes	3
Physical skills	**Standard keyboard skills** Inputting payroll information into computer	2
Responsibility for patient/ client care	**Provide information**	1
Responsibility for policy/ service department	**Implements policies for own area and proposes policy or service changes which implement beyond own area** Implements policies for own department, proposes changes to general financial policies	3
Responsibility for financial & physical resources	**Budget holder for department** Holds the budget for the payroll department	4(a)
Responsibility for human resources	**Responsible as line manager for a department** Manages the payroll department	4(a)
Responsibility for information resources	**Responsible for the management of information systems** Manages the implementation of new payroll systems	6

Table 7.4 *(continued)*

Job title	Payroll Manager	
Responsibility for research & development	**Undertakes surveys or audits as necessary to own work**	1
Freedom to act	**Guided by principles and broad occupational policies or regulations** Initiate action within broad professional policies	4
Physical effort	**Combination of sitting, standing and walking**	1
Mental effort	**Frequent requirement for concentration, predictable work pattern** Processing financial information	2(a)
Emotional effort	**Exposure to distressing or emotional circumstances is rare**	1
Working conditions	**Occasional exposure to unpleasant working conditions** Dealing with staff whose wages have not been paid	2(a)
JE Score/band	**JE score 383**	**Band 5**

An example of a generic role profile for a lecturer used in higher education for matching is shown in Table 7.5.

STEP 4. DEVELOP MATCHING PROCEDURE

Matching will be role profile to benchmark profile, or role profile to grade profile, or both. It is necessary to decide who does the matching, how they should do it (the matching protocol in a large exercise) and the documentation to be made available.

Matching is usually carried out by a matching panel. This may include union representatives as well as line managers, as in a National Health Service (NHS) Trust hospital where there is usually one panel for the whole organization, or it may be a group of line managers facilitated by HR as in the Peabody Trust, a large housing association. In a small organization or in a self-contained project, matching can take place over a short time span, using a single panel.

In the Peabody Trust, separate panels for different functions or job families were established with no more than three or four managers in each panel. Using their knowledge of the jobs and with the right documentation and guidance from HR, their task was completed

Table 7.5 Example of a generic role profile for a higher education lecturer

Elements	Role analysis
1 Teaching and learning support	• Plan, design and deliver a number of modules within subject area. • Deliver at undergraduate and/or postgraduate levels across a range of modules. • Use appropriate teaching, learning support and assessment methods. • Supervise projects, field trips and, where appropriate, placements. • Supervise postgraduate students. • Identify areas where current course provision is in need of revision or improvement. • Contribute to the planning, design and development of course objectives and material. • Ensure in conjunction with colleagues that modules complement other courses taken by students. • Set, mark and assess course work and examinations and provide feedback to students.
2 Research and scholarship	• Develop research objectives and proposals, obtain funding and design research projects. • Conduct individual and collaborative research projects, lead small research teams or play a major part in research teams. • Identify sources of funding and contribute to the process of securing funds. • Extend, transform and apply knowledge acquired through scholarly activities. • Write and referee journal articles, or write or contribute to textbooks and make presentations at national and international conferences.
3 Communication	• Communicate straightforward through to complex information to a variety of audiences, including students, peers and external contacts. • Use high-level presentation skills and a range of media.
4 Liaison and networking	• Liaise with colleagues in other departments and/or institutions on professional matters. • Participate in departmental and other committee meetings. • Join external networks to foster collaboration and share information and ideas. • May represent the department at external meetings.
5 Managing people	• Lead the delivery of teaching in a module or programme: plan the timetable, allocate teaching responsibilities, and monitor the delivery of programmes to ensure that they achieve learning objectives and are meeting quality standards. • Lead small research teams. • Act as mentor to more junior lecturers. • Appraise staff and advise them on their personal development.

Table 7.5   *(continued)*

Elements	Role analysis
6 Teamwork	• Attend and actively participate in regular team meetings at which course development and delivery issues are discussed. • Collaborate with colleagues to identify and respond to students' needs.
7 Pastoral care	• Use listening, interpersonal and pastoral care skills to deal with sensitive issues concerning students and provide support. • Refer students as appropriate to services providing further help. • Act as personal tutor.
8 Initiative, problem solving and decision making	• Identify the need for developing the content or structure of a course and put proposals together in conjunction with colleagues on how this should be achieved. • Develop creative ideas as a result of research and scholarship. • Deal with admission queries and problems concerning student performance. • Sole responsibility to decide how to deliver own modules and assess students.
9 Planning and managing resources	• As module leader or tutor, liaise with colleagues on content and method of delivery. • May plan and implement consultancy projects to generate income for the institution.
10 Emotional demands	• Work under pressure to deliver results.
11 Work environment	• Work in a stable environment or a laboratory or workshop.
12 Expertise	• Possess in-depth knowledge of the subject. • Possess the required levels of expertise in teaching and research. • Update skills and knowledge continuously. • Understand equal opportunity issues as they impact upon the delivery of teaching and collegiate working.

remarkably quickly (15 to 20 posts in half a day). The results of the different panels were reviewed by the senior management team advised by HR to ensure consistency. The whole exercise for 700 staff was completed within a month.

In a large and devolved project there is a need for prescriptive guidance on the procedures to be followed and especially on what constitutes an acceptable match. Guidelines may be produced as formal protocols that specify:

▌ what constitutes a perfect profile match, ie where all the elements in the role profile match all the elements in the grade or benchmark role profile;

▌ the number of matches required of individual elements to indicate that a profile match is justified, for example six out of 10, but it is usual to restrict the mismatches allowed to fairly small variations – if there are any large ones, the match would be invalidated;

▌ any elements that must match for there to be a profile match; for example, it may be decided that there must be a match for an element covering knowledge and skills;

▌ the procedure for grading if there has been a mismatch; this may specify a full evaluation of the role if the matching process is underpinned by a point-factor or proprietary analytical scheme.

The NHS protocol requires that, in order to determine the appropriate level, matching panels should record the profile level in the profile level column of the matching form, and the proposed level for the job in the job level column, referring to the job evaluation scheme factor levels only when the job evaluation levels do not appear to match the profile level(s). Where the job level is the same as the profile level or within the profile range, evaluators are required to mark M (for match) in the match column. Where it is one level higher or lower than the profile level or range, they mark V (for variation) in the match column. Where the job level is more than one level higher or lower than the profile level or range, they mark NM (no match). The possible outcomes are:

▌ If all factor levels are within the range specified on the profile, this is a perfect profile match.

▌ If most factor levels match but there are a small number of variations, there may still be a band match if *all* the following conditions apply:

   – the variations are of *not more* than one level above or below the profile level or range, *and*

   – the variations do *not* relate to the Knowledge or Freedom to Act factors; variations in these factors are indicative of a different profile and/or band, *and*

- the variations do not apply to more than *five* factors; multiple variations are indicative of a different profile or the need for a local evaluation, *and*

- the score variations do not take the job over a grade boundary,

- if there are any NM variations in the Match column, there is no match.

In a smaller project these guidelines may be developed as the matching process takes place, although it is useful from the outset to come to at least a provisional agreement on what would constitute a good match (this can be refined with experience).

A matching approach adopted in a medium sized charity started with the independent analysis of each role, element by element, by two project team members (one from HR and one from the line) who allocated it provisionally to a band. The procedure was then as follows:

▍ The team members compared outcomes and sought to reconcile differences: if there were significant differences that called into question the initial band allocation, a third team member was called in for another opinion. These results were entered on a spreadsheet, highlighting outstanding queries. If the evaluators needed more information, the HR team member went back to the line manager and job holder, as appropriate.

▍ In a two-day meeting the whole project team looked at the outcomes across all jobs in provisional band order, addressing questions that had arisen in the initial evaluations and by reviewing job relativities.

▍ If there were still any question about the banding for a role, team members were asked to consider whether the overall profile of the role resembled more closely the jobs allocated to the same band, or one of the profiles on either side of the band. If a decision could not be reached, it was invariably because there was insufficient supporting evidence. Where this was the case HR went back to the manager or job holder for clarification before the team finalized their evaluation.

▍ The senior management team reviewed all evaluations, with the power to question but not change evaluation outcomes.

STEP 5. TEST THE MATCHING PROCEDURE

In a large job evaluation project where there are a number of panels it is essential to test the grade profiles and the matching protocol by preparing a representative set of individual role profiles or questionnaire responses using the same format of factors and then matching the latter to the former. Any difficulties in doing this and achieving a sensible result, or any problems with the matching rules, will indicate what changes need to be made to the grade profiles.

STEP 6. PREPARE INDIVIDUAL ROLE PROFILES FOR MATCHING

Where matching is from role profile to benchmark role profile, individual role profiles should be prepared in the same format as the benchmark profiles, taking into account any lessons learnt from the test.

STEP 7. TRAIN MATCHING PANEL

The panel should be trained in the matching process and the use of the guidelines or protocols using real examples. It is essential to carry out this training thoroughly as the process is likely to be completely unfamiliar to the panel members, except in a small organization where the project team may have been involved throughout the development process. Training is needed even where the scheme is non-analytical and the matching process is on a whole job basis, as panel members will still need to be reminded about the basic principles of job evaluation, including the need to match the job not the person, and how to avoid potential bias for sex, race, disability or age.

STEP 8. CONDUCT MATCHING

The panel conducts matching in accordance with the protocol. If matching cannot be agreed the panel may request further information or refer the job to be evaluated by the basic job evaluation scheme, where matching is underpinned by a factor plan.

8

Market pricing

There are two senses in which the term 'market pricing' is used. First, it can denote a method of directly pricing jobs on the basis of external relativities with no regard to internal relativities (this is sometimes called 'extreme market pricing'). Second, the term is used more generally to describe the process of analysing and tracking market rates to inform the design of pay structures and to ensure that the rates of pay for individual jobs are competitive in terms of the 'market stance' adopted by the organization, ie where it wants to position its levels of pay in relation to market rates. In this chapter we focus on the first use of the term as a method of valuing roles on the basis of their market rate or price without using any form of job evaluation to assess internal relativities, ie extreme market pricing. We call the second use of the term 'market rate analysis' and discuss its application to the design and maintenance of pay structures in Chapter 11.

Our description of extreme market pricing in this chapter describes its rationale, uses, process and limitations and the methods used to obtain the information required on market rates. This explanation of market rate analysis also serves to define the approach used when obtaining the information required to develop competitive pay structures in association with job evaluation. Further guidance on conducting market surveys is provided in the e-reward guide (2005).

THE RATIONALE FOR MARKET PRICING

The rationale for market pricing can be expressed in the adage, 'A job is worth what the market says it is worth.' The only thing that counts is to be competitive, and this governs the design of pay structures and the rates for individual jobs. Relativities within the organization reflect relativities in the marketplace. Market pricing means that the organization does not need to bother with job evaluation. As Zingheim and Schuster (2002) remark: 'The history of pay involves entitlement disguised as a nearly singular emphasis on internal equity'; the future as they see it 'depends on our ability to develop and implement a base salary system... that is anchored in the market place'.

USE OF MARKET PRICING

Organizations that adopt a market pricing approach can be described as 'market-driven', and 16 per cent of the respondents to the 2007 e-reward job evaluation survey stated that they were in this category. Market pricing can be used generally in the design of graded pay structures. Specifically it is used to determine the rates of pay for jobs in a spot rate or individual job range system. A 'spot rate' is a rate for a job or an individual that is not fitted into a grade or band in a conventional grade structure and does not allow any scope for pay progression. An 'individual job range' is in effect a spot rate in which there is a defined range for pay progression.

Market pricing can also provide the basis for fixing rates of pay in a broad-banded structure (see Chapter 11) and for informing the design of market groups in a job family structure (see also Chapter 11).

THE PROCESS OF MARKET PRICING

The detailed process of market pricing will vary according to the use to which it is put. In general, however, it involves the following steps:

1. Determine approach to structuring pay – a formal grade structure or spot rates/individual job ranges.

2. If a grade structure, decide whether it is to be narrow-graded, broad-graded, broad-banded, a career family or a job family, and define its likely features.

3. If a spot rate or individual job range system, decide which approach and how it will operate.

4. Identify and analyse benchmark jobs for which market rate data will be collected.

5. Identify or develop sources of information on market rates.

6. Obtain, analyse and interpret market rate data.

7. Use market rate data to design pay structure, to fix individual base pay rates or to determine market supplements.

8. Track market data to indicate when changes are required to pay scales, individual rates or market supplements.

The design of pay structures is dealt with in Chapter 11. Methods of collecting and analysing market rate data are described later in this chapter.

LIMITATIONS OF MARKET PRICING

The effectiveness of market pricing depends on getting the right data – accurate information on the rates for jobs in the marketplace that can be matched with comparable jobs within the organization. The problem with achieving this ideal state is the nebulous nature of the concept of a market rate.

Establishing what the market rate for a job is can be a matter of judgement rather than certainty. All too many managers and senior executives – and, indeed, many employees – commonly believe that it is not only possible, but relatively easy, to establish a 'correct' rate for any given job, in any industry, in any location, for any age or experience level, preferably to the nearest pound. But as a report by online pay database CubikSurvey.com (2005) explained, accurate market rate information may be difficult to obtain:

> The expectation is that reward specialists, and the surveys they provide, can wave a magic wand and come up with the only right answer. This rather overlooks the complexity of remuneration issues. It is rare that two companies, even within the same industry and location, are managed in identical ways. Different corporate values, perceptions of the contribution of each job to the effectiveness of the organization, and the experience and performance of the individuals holding the jobs all impact on the remuneration paid to people in apparently similar positions.

Ultimately those differences are reflected in the market. There is always a choice of rates. No survey is able, despite the claims of some surveyors, to provide a single 'right' rate of pay for any position, or range of positions. This is because different organizations have different policies as to what they need to pay. Employees in effect have their own market rate, depending on their expertise and ability and the degree to which their talents are unique. This individual 'market worth' varies widely and is often as much a matter of perception as of fact. When making comparisons between internal and external rates for jobs the aim is to compare like with like. But it may be difficult or even impossible to obtain precise matches between jobs in the organization and jobs elsewhere. 'Like' jobs may not exist. The comparisons may be approximate, with the result that the range between the highest and lowest levels of pay for a job as established by an individual survey can be as much as 50 per cent or more. Different surveys will produce different results depending on the sample of organizations covered, the quality of matching and the timing of the survey.

The translation of salary market data into an acceptable company pay structure or competitive pay levels for individuals is a process based on intuition, judgement and compromise. Advocates of market pricing assert that it obviates the need for spurious attempts to validate formal job evaluation. They claim that market rates are ascertainable facts not subject to the judgements present in traditional approaches. However, this claim is specious; judgements have to be made about market rate data just as they have to be made in any type of role valuation. Market pricing cannot guarantee valid results.

Market pricing means striking a balance between the competing merits of the different sources of data and extracting what may be called a 'derived market rate'. However, the judgements will be more accurate if they are based on the systematic analysis of valid and reliable data gained from reputable published surveys, established 'pay clubs' (organizations that exchange pay information), or well-conceived surveys conducted by the organization.

Many people believe that a further limitation to market pricing is that it ignores principles of internal equity. They claim that a pay structure based on market pricing will distort internal relativities and lead to unequal pay. The counter-argument is that pay structures cannot ignore external relativities and the use of such devices as market supplements will unavoidably create internal inequities. When market supplements are used, at least the basic structure has been designed in accordance with the principle of establishing comparable worth and supplements can be identified as such and objectively justified. Moreover, it is generally recognized that reliance on market pricing is likely to reproduce within the organization existing inequities between the pay of men and women in the marketplace.

THE VALIDITY AND RELIABILITY OF MARKET RATE DATA

As has already been mentioned, market pricing depends on good market data, the validity and reliability of which depends on three factors:

1. *Job matching* – the extent to which good job matching between internal and external jobs has taken place.

2. *Sample frame* – the degree to which the sample of organizations from which the data have been collected is fully representative of the organizations with which comparisons need to be made in such terms as sector, technology or type of business, size and location.

3. *Timing* – the extent to which the information is up-to-date or can be updated reliably. By their very nature, published surveys, upon which many people rely, can soon become out of date. This can happen the moment they are produced – pay levels may have changed and people may have moved in or out since the date of the survey. While it is not possible to overcome this completely, as data must be gathered and analysed, surveys that aim to have as short a time as possible between data collection and the publication of results are likely to be of more use than those with longer lead times. Estimates can be made of likely movements since the survey took place, but they are mainly guesswork.

Job matching

Inadequate job matching is a major cause of inaccuracies in the data collected by market analysis. So far as possible the aim is to match the jobs within the organization and those outside (the comparators) so that like is being compared with like. It is essential to avoid crude and misleading comparisons based on job titles alone or vague descriptions of job content. It is first necessary to ensure that a broad match is achieved between the organization and the types of organizations used as comparators in terms of sector, industry classification, size and location.

The next step is to match jobs within the organizations concerned. The various methods in ascending order of accuracy are:

1. *Job title:* this can be misleading. Job titles by themselves give no indication of the range of duties or the level of responsibility and are sometimes used to convey additional status to employees or their customers unrelated to the real level of work done.

2. *Brief description of duties and level or zone of responsibility:* national surveys frequently restrict their job-matching definitions to a two- or three-line description of duties and an indication of levels of responsibility in rank order. The latter is often limited to a one-line definition for each level or zone in a hierarchy. This approach provides some guidance on job matching, which reduces major discrepancies, but it still leaves considerable scope for discretion and can therefore provide only generalized comparisons.

3. *Capsule job descriptions:* club or specialist 'bespoke' surveys frequently use capsule job descriptions that define main responsibilities and duties in about 100 to 200 words. To increase the refinement of comparisons, modifying statements may be made indicating where responsibilities are higher or lower than the norm. Capsule job descriptions considerably increase the accuracy of comparisons as long as they are based on a careful analysis of actual jobs and include modifying statements. But they are not always capable of dealing with specialist jobs and the accuracy of comparisons in relation to levels of responsibility may be limited, even when modifiers are used.

4. *Full role profiles,* including a factor analysis of the levels of responsibility involved, may be used in special surveys when direct comparisons are made between jobs in different organizations. They can be more accurate on a one-for-one basis but their use is limited because of the time and labour involved in preparing them. A further limitation is that comparator organizations may not have available, or be prepared to make available, their own full role profiles for comparison.

5. Job *evaluation:* can be used in support of a capsule job description or a role profile to provide a more accurate measure of relative job

size. A common method of evaluation is necessary. An increasing number of international and UK consultancies now claim to be able to make this link, either through a point-factor scheme or a matching approach, even though they do not necessarily restrict survey participation only to those organizations that are prepared to conduct a full evaluation process. This approach will further increase the accuracy of comparisons but the degree of accuracy will depend on the quality of the job evaluation process.

THE PROCESS OF MARKET ANALYSIS

The process of market analysis consists of the following steps:

1. Decide on the jobs for which market rate data will be collected.

2. Identify potential sources of market rate data and select the most appropriate ones.

3. Analyse and interpret the data from the various sources.

Decide on benchmark jobs

The survey should aim to collect data on a representative sample of benchmark jobs that will be used to provide guidance on the design of a pay structure (see Chapter 11) or as a basis for market pricing. The jobs selected should be ones for which it is likely that market data will be available. There are usually some jobs that are unique to the organization and for which comparisons cannot be made. When conducting a market pricing exercise it is necessary to make a judgement on the positioning of these jobs in the structure on the basis of comparisons with the benchmark jobs. A points-factor evaluation scheme, if available, helps to make these comparisons more accurate.

Sources of market data

There is a wide variety of sources of varying quality and it is advisable to select more than one to ensure that a spread of information is obtained. Because it is unlikely that precise job matching, a perfect sample, and coincidence of timing will be achieved, it is best to obtain data from more than one source. Ultimately, a judgement has to be made about market levels of pay and this will be helped if a range

Table 8.1 Analysis of data sources

Source	Brief description	Advantages	Disadvantages
Online data	Access data from general surveys	Quick, easy, can be tailored	May not provide all the information required
General national published surveys	Available for purchase – provide an overall picture of pay levels for different occupations in national and regional labour markets	Wide coverage, readily available, continuity allows trend analyses over time, expert providers	Risk of imprecise job matching, insufficiently specific, quickly out of date
Local published surveys	Available for purchase – provide an overall picture of pay levels for different occupations in the local labour market	Focus on local labour market especially for administrative staff and manual workers	Risk of imprecise job matching, insufficiently specific, quickly out of date, providers may not have expertise in pay surveys
Sector surveys	Available for purchase – provide data on a sector such as charities	Focus on a sector where pay levels may differ from national rates, deal with particular categories in depth	Risk of imprecise job matching, insufficiently specific, quickly out of date
Industrial/occupational surveys	Surveys, often conducted by employer and trade associations on jobs in an industry or specific jobs	Focus on an industry, deal with particular categories in depth; quality of job matching may be better than general or sector surveys	Job matching may still not be entirely precise; quickly out of date
Management consultants' databases	Pay data obtained from the databases maintained by management consultants	Based on well-researched and matched data. Often highly tailored to specific market segments	Only obtainable from specific consultants and often confidential to participants. Can be expensive

Source	Brief description	Advantages	Disadvantages
Special surveys	Surveys specially conducted by an organization	Focused, reasonably good job matching, control of participants, control of analysis methodology	Takes time and trouble, may be difficult to get participation, sample size may therefore be inadequate. May not be repeated, therefore difficult to use for ongoing pay management
Pay clubs	Groups of employers who regularly exchange data on pay levels	Focused, precise job matching, control of participants, control of analysis methodology, regular data, trends data, more information may be available on benefits and pay policies	Sample size may be too small, involve a considerable amount of administration, may be difficult to maintain enthusiasm of participants
Published data in journals	Data on settlements and pay levels available from IDS or IRS, and on national trends in earnings from the New Earnings Survey	Readily accessible	Mainly about settlements and trends, little specific well-matched information on pay levels for individual jobs
Analysis of recruitment data	Pay data derived from analysis of pay levels required to recruit staff	Immediate data	Data random and can be misleading because of small sample. Can be distorted if applicants inflate their salary history or if data geared to recruitment salaries
Job advertisements	Pay data obtained from job advertisements	Readily accessible, highly visible (to employees as well as employers), up to date. Data can be quite specific for public and voluntary sector roles	Job matching very imprecise, pay information may be misleading
Other market intelligence	Pay data obtained from informal contacts or networks	Provide good background	Imprecise, not regularly available

of information is available that enables a view to be taken on what should be regarded as 'the market rate' for internal use. This is more convincing if it has been derived from a number of sources. It will also provide the objective justification for any market premium that might create unequal pay. In choosing data sources it is important to take account of how easily replicable the analysis will be in future years. Trends can only be identified if a consistent set of sources are used, and if those sources are reasonably stable.

Published surveys, which are readily accessible and are based on a large sample, can be used to back up individual or club surveys. If the information can be obtained online, so much the better, but it has to be relevant to the needs of the organization and particular attention should always be paid to the range of data and the quality of job matching. General market data can be supplemented by specialist surveys covering particular jobs. Should the quality of job matching be important, an individual survey can be conducted or a salary club can be joined if there is room.

Market intelligence and published data from journals and associated sources should always be used as back-up material and for information on going rates and trends. They can provide invaluable help with updating.

Although the analysis of job advertisements has its dangers, it can be used as further backup or to give an instant snapshot of current rates, but it is risky to rely on this source alone.

Published surveys are of widely varying content, presentation and quality and are sometimes expensive. When selecting a published survey use the following guidelines:

▌ Does it cover relevant jobs in similar organizations?

▌ Does it provide the information on pay and benefits required?

▌ Are there enough participants to provide acceptable comparisons?

▌ So far as can be judged, is the survey conducted properly in terms of its sampling techniques and the quality of job matching?

▌ Is the survey reasonably up to date?

▌ Are the results well presented?

▌ Does it provide value for money?

As a starting point to identifying a relevant survey, look at the regular reviews included in publications from Incomes Data Services (IDS) and IRS. Pay analysts IDS also publish a directory that brings together information on virtually every available survey of salaries and benefits produced in the United Kingdom, providing an unmatched guide to data sources. It currently lists some 290 surveys of salaries and benefits from 76 UK survey producers, covering national surveys, local surveys, benefit surveys and international surveys, and gives details of employee groups and jobs covered by each survey, sample size, date of the survey data and the length and price of the report. Subscribers to the directory can also access it online and search for data by job title, type of benefit, sector, UK region or overseas region. Contact www.salarysurveys.info.

The features of the main sources and their advantages and disadvantages are listed in Table 8.1.

Interpret and present market data

Data need to be interpreted by reference to the details provided from each source and by assessments of their reliability, accuracy and relevance. If data have been obtained from a number of sources these will also have to be interpreted to produce a derived market rate that will be used as the basis of comparison.

REFERENCES

CubikSurvey.com (2005) *Market Rate Survey Report*, Cubik, London
e-reward (2005) *Guide to Market Rate Analysis*, e-reward.co.uk, Stockport
Zingheim, P K and Schuster, J R (2002) Pay changes going forward, *Compensation & Benefits Review*, **34** (4), pp 48–53

9

Consultants' schemes

The e-reward 2007 survey established that a high proportion (60 per cent) of respondents with job evaluation used consultants' 'ready-made' schemes in their complete form, while a further 20 per cent used modified (hybrid) versions. However, this figure should be regarded with some caution because of the possibility that the sample was biased in favour of organizations that are more likely to use such schemes. The e-reward 2003 survey found that fewer respondents (37 per cent) had full schemes and 26 per cent were using modified schemes.

In this chapter the features of a number of the main schemes are summarized, developments in the approaches adopted by consultancies are reviewed, and a checklist is provided on the points to consider when selecting a scheme (guidance on whether to develop a tailor-made scheme or use a 'proprietary brand' was given in Chapter 3). At the end of the chapter there are case studies illustrating the use of consultants' schemes.

SUMMARY OF CONSULTANTS' SCHEMES

The features of a number of the schemes offered by consultants are set out in Table 9.1.

Table 9.1 Summary of consultants' schemes

Consultant	Main features of proprietary scheme	Factors/job dimensions of proprietary scheme
Deloitte & Touche	Company size and complexity system provides a consistent basis for supporting executive reward strategy work; geared to executive roles but can be extended further. Framework can be extended to broader range of roles and by 14 more detailed competency-based factors covering knowledge, skill, intellect, communication, physical and environmental aspects	Financial size Human capital size Internationality
DLA MCG	Points-factor or competency-based development of point-factor scheme that is linked to performance and progression through behavioural competencies	Library of 30 potential factors; typically using 8 to 12; weightings are agreed with client
ER Consultants	Proprietary scheme is 'Decision Band method' (DBM): in most cases is not a point-factor scheme, but can use a point-factor approach when appropriate to client needs. The scheme can be tailored on request	The scheme places roles into one of six decision-making bands, then further classified into coordinating or non-coordinating based on effort and supervisory responsibilities. Jobs then divided into sub-grades based on complexity, difficulty and skills required

Hay	Guide Chart Profile Method; can be used for all groups of staff but most commonly used for managerial positions. On request the factor definitions can be revised to address specific issues, or method can be used to underpin job family structures	The scheme combines judgements against three factors, with total of eight sub-elements to give total job size:
		1. Know-how
		  – depth and range of technical know-how
		  – breadth of managerial know-how
		  – human relations skills
		2. Problem solving
		  – thinking environment
		  – thinking challenge
		3. Accountability
		  – freedom to act
		  – area of impact
		  – nature of impact
		There is a guide chart for scoring each factor and sub-element.

Hewitt Bacon & Woodrow	Fixed factor approach or bespoke point-factor or classification schemes	Typically bespoke to client, but can be linked to factors in total compensation measurement tool (TCM)

Table 9.1 Summary of consultants' schemes *(continued)*

Consultant	Main features of proprietary scheme	Factors/job dimensions of proprietary scheme
Inbucon	IJE© is re-branding of Inbucon's proprietary point-factor scheme. The scheme can be tailored on request	Knowledge, skills and experience Problem solving Decision making Operational responsibilities Communication Working environment Each factor has two sub-factors forming a two-dimensional matrix for scoring
Link HR Systems	Offers 'Universal JE scheme' and tailored solutions. Also licenses software to other consultancies	Responsibility Knowledge Mental skills Communication Working environment
Logosoft (UK)	'Reward Manager' system is derived from Institute of Administrative Management's Office JE scheme. The approach is tailored to fit each client	Scheme contains over 3,000 pre-graded job elements and industry-specific elements can be added. Overall points score and grade generated through combination of 'time spent' allocation, and other job elements including competencies and 'hard measures' for supervisory/management jobs. Can use all or some of 36 Management Charter Initiative competencies
Mercer Human Resource Consulting	'International Position Evaluation' (IPE) plus bespoke schemes, both point-factor and classification schemes: schemes based on IPE can be linked to the Mercer Total Remuneration Survey Database	Four main factors, split into sub-factors, with optional risk factor: Impact – Organization – Impact – Contribution Communication – Communication – Frame Innovation – Innovation – Complexity Knowledge – Knowledge – Team – Breadth Risk – Risk – Environment
Pilat HR Solutions	Computerized point-factor scheme using 'Gauge' interactive software based on decision tree (ie questions asked for evaluation	Seven factors, each with two sub-factors: Knowledge and experience Problem solving

Table 9.1 *(continued)*

Consultant	Main features of proprietary scheme	Factors/job dimensions of proprietary scheme
	purposes are based on responses to previous questions). 'Gauge' can be used to accommodate existing or newly designed scheme	Planning and organization Job focus Business impact Interpersonal skills Work skills and conditions
Pricewaterhouse Coopers	Most job evaluation is based on the Monks point-factor, competency-based job evaluation 'six factor' system. Results can be compared with Monks pay database. PWC also offers work level profiling tool that can be used as job evaluation or for organization design profiling. It assumes that there are up to seven levels of added value in an organization and uses an interactive software tool to allocate jobs to levels	Six factor scheme: Knowledge Specialist skills People skills Customer service/external impact Decision making Creative thinking Optional: Physical environment/ emotional demands Work profiling tool: has one core accountability factor. Optional factors for more precise levelling are: Resource complexity Problem solving Change Internal collaboration External Interaction Timeframe
Towers Perrin	Career map method maps out steps in individual's career. There are six standard steps that roles can be classified into: associate/ developing, career, advanced career, expert and master; number of levels used will vary by family. Levels map across to survey database. Bespoke and fixed point-factor schemes also available	Career map competency dimensions: Technical expertise Client/business orientation Creating and delivering solutions Working relationships
Watson Wyatt	'Global Grading System'(GGS) is proprietary point-factor scheme, linked to pay database. Three stage process: 1. size the business (turnover, employees, diversity/ complexity) to set parameters for evaluations and grade ceiling (from maximum of 25 grades); 2. Place roles into managerial or professional/technical career ladder and one of six bands; 3. evaluate each role against seven factors, using questions tailored to career path and band. Results map across to global database	Functional knowledge Business expertise Leadership Problem solving Nature of impact Area of impact Interpersonal skills

DEVELOPMENTS IN THE APPROACH USED BY CONSULTANCIES

The major consultancy firms have adapted their products over recent years to reflect changes in demand as well as, in some cases, streamlining their approach to make their package more affordable (and profitable). Developments are taking place in scheme design and in computer-aided job evaluation.

Scheme design

In the 1990s when observers and practitioners (particularly in the United States) were commentating that 'traditional' job evaluation was in decline, many consultancy firms focused on providing tailor-made schemes. This development was affected by the belief that organizations were tending to reject some of the organizational constructs implied in traditional job evaluation schemes. The pendulum has since swung back and most of the major consultancies are using or developing a standard point-factor scheme as well as a matching scheme as an alternative. In some cases the standard scheme is all that is offered, in other cases it is used as a basic framework which can be varied to a certain extent.

Traditionally, if a standardized scheme were offered it tended either to be a point-factor scheme or, in the case of Hay Group, a factor comparison scheme. Some of the major consultancies now offer a simpler approach to valuing roles. For example, Towers Perrin's career pathways approach is based on classification according to career steps ('career mapping'), whereas Watson Wyatt's Global Grading System (GGS) involves an initial classification based on the size and complexity of the organization, then classification into bands and a career pathway, before evaluating roles using a point-factor scheme.

Starting from a standardized scheme gives a framework from which organizations can choose to adapt, if there are compelling reasons for doing so. For example, the UK universities that use the Hay system worked together with Hay Group to adapt the scheme's language to suit the particular nuances of work in an academic and research environment.

Another move for Hay Group has been away from reliance on the Guide Chart to using a descriptive matrix of level/type of role. This move reflects organizations' desire for a simpler process, although a points score can still be attached if needed. Geoff Nethersell of Hay Group says that the advantage of this approach is that it avoids job evaluation jargon (eg words like 'heterogeneous'), and can be linked to a framework for talent management, but it may not be equal-value proof.

For some time the Hay scheme has been the market leader by a considerable margin (it was used by 58 per cent of the respondents to the e-reward 2007 survey with a consultancy scheme). One of the competitive features of the Hay offering is that it has a pay database linked directly to its job evaluation scheme. To break down this competitive advantage, large consultancies such as Mercers, Towers Perrin and Watson Wyatt have developed an integrated approach and others are in the process of doing so. Where this is the case they also offer data access to other organizations that do not use their full job evaluation system by using a simplified matching process.

Computer-aided evaluation

With the advent of more sophisticated software to support the job evaluation process, there is probably more variety in the approach today than ever before. Opposition to job by job panel evaluations and the need to write lengthy job descriptions has led the consultancies to offer a range of solutions.

At the simplest level, software is used to support manual evaluations as a record-keeping tool and calculator of scores. At the most sophisticated end of the range, interactive systems allow direct entry of questionnaire responses and adapt the questions asked in response to the initial information entered (eg, Watson Wyatt's GGS, PWC's work levels profiler and Pilat's Gauge systems).

SELECTING A PROVIDER

In considering which provider to choose, it is important to be clear about what kind of support is needed. There is a wide range of technical capability amongst job evaluation consultants and system providers. Some companies have a long history of supporting computer-aided applications and may have a systems rather than a job evaluation background. Others have a strong consulting capability, but still offer only basic technology support (eg through spreadsheet applications).

Where an organization is aiming to computerize an existing system or has good job evaluation skills in-house, consultancies with computer expertise in this field may be a good option. However, if the level of in-house knowledge about job evaluation is limited, the prime focus ought to be on engaging the consultant that is strong in job evaluation design. Although GIGO (garbage in – garbage out) is an old adage, it is worth remembering that the information that comes out of a software application is only as good as what has gone into it. The quality of the information about jobs that is processed by the computer is crucial.

Other points to consider when making a choice are:

▌ How scaleable is the system? What is the maximum number of records that it can hold? What are the maximum number of users – in total and using the system simultaneously?

▌ What level of technology support is available? Where is it provided from, and over what hours (particularly relevant in global applications)? What elements of support are 'free' and what has to be paid for?

▌ What are the financial arrangements? Is software bought or leased? If bought, what are the annual maintenance fees after the initial purchase price? Does the price include written user documentation, or is all user support online?

▌ What links are there to other management information systems? Can direct transfers of data be made, or how good is the import/export capability?

▌ What expectations does the consultancy have about the level of technological understanding required by potential users of the system? If the provider says the system is 'user-friendly', can they demonstrate this?

▌ What training is provided and how is this costed? What follow-up training and support is given – automatically or at cost?

▌ Are upgrades provided automatically as part of a licence arrangement or do they have to be paid for?

▌ Can you get references from or arrange site visits to active users of the system?

CASE STUDIES

The following case studies prepared by e-reward in 2007 illustrate how schemes provided by consultants have been implemented in Age Concern England, T-Mobile (UK) and Lloyds TSB Asset Finance Division.

Age Concern England

Employee nos (UK): 500 plus 300 shop-based staff
Location: throughout the UK
Business activities: charitable, working with and for older people

Background and pay structure

In 2003 Age Concern England started to use Hay Group's job evaluation methodology to underpin the construction of a new contribution-related pay system for its 500 general charity staff. The organization had previously used Hay to benchmark salaries and wanted to continue the relationship through the adoption of the Hay JE methodology. The jobs of the paid shop staff (mostly managers and deputy managers) have not been evaluated since their pay arrangements are kept quite separate from those for the other employees.

The former pay structure had 13 grades and up to eight service-related annual increments, though as most staff had less than five years' service, few ever reached the top of their grades. There was also some grade drift, which had been a problem with the few staff who reached the top of their grade under the old system. The organization wanted a structure that would enable it to reward individual contribution and, once all the evaluations had been carried out, to use the scores to draw up six broad bands to replace the 13 existing grades, with progression through the bands based on performance.

Each of the new broad bands consists of three zones: one for newly recruited and developing staff (80–95 per cent of the mid-point), one for fully competent staff (95–105 per cent) and one for staff making an exceptional contribution (105–120 per cent of the mid-point).

When the new pay structure was first implemented, mid-points were set with reference to Hay medians for the public and not-for-profit sectors, but Remuneration Economics data for large charities is used currently, together with data gleaned from recruitment agency websites.

Job evaluation process

Age Concern recognizes the T&G ACTS, and the union representatives were initially hostile to Hay, associating it with management jobs and the private sector. A joint management–union steering group was set up to address this, and there was also some 'tinkering' with the Hay language to make it more palatable to the workforce. The union sits on evaluation panels where, says Austen Cooper, Age Concern's reward and systems manager, managers and union reps work together without any factionalism.

Job descriptions were written up in a Hay format and all 250 posts were evaluated by the HR department with advice from Hay Group. Once the points scores had been arrived at, the six broad pay bands were constructed, where the breaks between scores were obvious, also with advice from Hay Group. Once someone was placed in a grade, evaluation scores faded into the background. For example, if two jobs came out with similar scores but one person supervised the other, the more senior role was placed higher in the band. Individuals were informed only of their grade, not their points score, although panel members are aware of individual scores. Similarly, where an individual is promoted, he or she will be moved up the band, regardless of points scores.

When the new structure was implemented, most staff were assimilated on their existing salaries, although everyone in post for at least three years at the date of implementation of the new pay arrangements was placed at the minimum (95 per cent of the mid-point) of the fully competent zone. The only staff placed in the exceptional contribution (EC) zone with salaries up to 120 per cent of the mid-point, were those with long service where this is the appropriate assimilation point. Some were above it, in the EC+ zone.

A joint management–union panel consisting of two managers, two union representatives and the HR manager handled appeals. As time went by, the size of the panel fell to three – one manager, one union representative and the HR manager, and the panel now meets on an ad hoc basis. To save time, the HR manager alone evaluates new jobs where no one is in post, and finds that it takes between half an hour and an hour per job. When a job changes, a small joint panel re-evaluates it. In general, new jobs are tailored to fit into a specific grade, with HR advising managers how jobs need to be constructed.

Communication

The details of the job evaluation arrangements were communicated at the same time as the new contribution-related pay and progression structure. All communication was joint, with the management–union steering group putting out statements throughout the initial evaluation process. Everyone received a letter informing them about their new grade. People mostly relied on the unions to raise questions about the job evaluation process, says Austen Cooper, though there were a few tricky departmental away days when barbed questions were asked about the new arrangements.

Hay Group provided good training for managers and union representatives involved in the evaluation process, which helped them to work together effectively and to support the implementation of the new pay structure.

The organization is very satisfied with its current job evaluation scheme and has no plans to change it, describing it as 'a reputable scheme which suits our business'. The scheme is not linked to performance appraisal or competencies, but it is being used for career planning. Where the gap between two jobs is so great that no one could be promoted from one to the other, an intermediary job (a step up) is being constructed.

Advice

Age Concern advises organizations thinking of introducing or changing their job evaluation arrangements to consult and inform staff as to what job evaluation will do, what the process entails, and what the benefits are. Austen Cooper also emphasizes the importance of having sufficient time and resources available to set up good systems to hold details of each job description and how the job was evaluated, and to ensure the smooth introduction of new arrangements. He also advises organizations to be on the look out for manipulation of the evaluation process and its outcomes. 'Don't assume that managers will back you on this and unions won't', he says. And finally, 'Don't forget about sore-thumbing (reviewing a result that sticks out like a sore thumb as a doubtful evaluation) and have an appeals process to ensure that disgruntled managers and staff can air their grievances and get them considered quickly and fairly.'

T-Mobile (UK)

Employee nos (UK): 6,500
Location: UK-wide
Business activities: Mobile network operator

Background

T-Mobile brought in job evaluation in 2005 to gain a greater depth of granularity of roles within its five broad bands. It held a 'beauty contest' and picked Watson Wyatt's Global Grading System (GGS; see below), which enabled it both to differentiate between roles and to refine benchmarking against the market. GGS was chosen partly with the intention of building competency frameworks, and the company is currently establishing career development frameworks that link competencies with GGS levels.

Watson Wyatt's Global Grading System

The Watson Wyatt Global Grading System (GGS) enables organizations to compare roles across functions, business units and countries. Once the global grade has been calculated for a role, pay levels can be benchmarked against the market, using Watson Wyatt's international pay and benefits database.

The first step in the GGS process is to measure the size and complexity of the organization by reference to:

▍ annual sales turnover;
▍ number of employees;
▍ market complexity (local/international/global);
▍ product/service diversification.

Each job is then banded according to the nature of the contribution it makes in one of two defined career paths – managerial or technical/professional.

Finally, the global grade is determined by evaluating the job against seven factors:

1. functional knowledge;
2. business expertise;
3. leadership;
4. problem solving;
5. nature of impact;
6. area of impact;
7. interpersonal skills.

Job evaluation process

Once the consultancy and JE scheme had been selected, the company's reward team was trained in the GGS methodology (see Table 9.2 and Chapter 12 for details). It began work by collecting role profiles of jobs in bands D, E and X, and evaluated some 70 per cent of the roles. It also selected benchmark roles in bands A, B and C from across the rest of the organization (some 20 per cent of jobs), and is evaluating these too. The remaining jobs are being slotted into the structure using analytical matching. There is no job evaluation panel; the governance for the process is provided by the reward team in conjunction with HR business partners and senior managers from across the business.

Table 9.2 Broad bands and GGS scores at T-Mobile

Job examples	Band	GGS score
CEO and the most senior roles	X	17–20
Managers responsible for functional and business strategy	E	15–16
Senior professionals and middle managers	D	13–14
Professionals, middle managers, senior supervisory	C	11–12
Supervisory and professionals	B	9–10
Technicians and administrative staff	A	7–8

Once role profiles have been interpreted, the factors that drive the job evaluation outcome are keyed into the grading tool, and the system calculates the final grade. This has the advantage of speeding up the evaluation process, provides more consistency, and means there is less paperwork. The process is fast and flexible and these qualities help because roles often have to be re-graded when they either change or organization restructuring occurs. On the downside, however, T-Mobile has found that it has had to spend more time moderating computer-generated evaluations than it expected.

In the first instance, the job evaluation exercise enabled the company to segment the existing five broad bands – A to E – into GGS scores. This has provided a level of granularity within the current broad bands, which has helped to determine differences in role sizes and relativities.

One of the initial applications is to use the outcomes for external pay benchmarking purposes. Further applications may include reviewing bonus targets, and linking to competencies via career development frameworks.

Communication

Reward workshops were run for 60 or so senior managers. Job evaluation was explained and the Watson Wyatt methodology was set out. Managers assisted with the job evaluation and this was critical to gain their 'buy-in' at the start of the process. These workshops were intended to provide transparency to senior management and also to avoid the problem that so often arises when managers, who do not understand the process, complain about jobs getting the 'wrong' scores.

Maintenance

In the last two years there has been a good deal of reorganization within the businesses, so roles have required reassessment. There are ongoing changes whereby a manager will inform his or her HR business partner that a job has changed. The role will then be submitted to the reward team for re-evaluation. Robert Cross, a reward manager at T-Mobile, says that they are frequently challenged, but the system is robust and there is generally little difficulty in dealing with the challenge. The role may not have been fully understood or the challenger may not understand the JE methodology. Once the reward team has investigated, the challenger is usually satisfied with the outcome of the process.

Problems

Setting up the job evaluation system has been a huge project, and all the work has had to be done on top of normal workloads, while maintenance is a continuing and heavy commitment.

Advice

Some dos identified by T-Mobile are:

▌ determine at the start why you want to use JE;

▌ limit the number of roles that are evaluated – select a framework of benchmarks;

▌ communicate across the business how the system works and why it is being introduced;

▌ ensure that there is a governance process whereby the JE outcomes are agreed with all parts of the business and signed off by the heads of each business;

▌ ensure there is a process in place to maintain the JE system in line with structural changes – it has to continually evolve with the organization, otherwise it will become obsolete very quickly.

Lloyds TSB Asset Finance Division

Employee nos (UK): 7,000
Location: throughout the UK
Business activities: Finance

Background and pay structure

Lloyds TSB Asset Finance Division (AFD) started to use Hay Group's job evaluation methodology in 1999. This was principally to ensure that the organization was implementing equal pay for work of equal value, but also to support a new broadband pay structure, introduced when Lloyds Bowmaker merged with United Dominions Trust in 1999 to form Lloyds UDT. Before this, Lloyds Bowmaker had used a JE scheme called 'W D Scott'. This was kept a 'black art' in HR, and Janine Sparks, head of reward, had concerns that it could be challenged in terms of equal pay. 'Hay has been tested in the courts and has come out squeaky clean as far as I am aware, and this is what we needed.'

Lloyds TSB Asset Finance has around 30 job families, with pay for jobs in each family benchmarked against specialist surveys. Pay for jobs with the same points scores therefore vary according to their job family. Once the jobs had been evaluated, the six broad bands were constructed to define benefit breaks. The company looked at the market to determine at which Hay score various benefits are typically offered. Levels within each band are determined by the Hay 'know-how' score. Every job is carefully benchmarked against the external labour market, and jobs in external databases are benchmarked back to Lloyds TSB AFD jobs

Job evaluation process

Currently, the evaluation panel meets for half a day around once a month. If a job comes through that is similar to another job, it will just be benchmarked against that job, but every new job is evaluated fully. The panel consists of three people – a line manager, a union representative and an HR manager. If the job being evaluated is outside the bargaining unit, which covers jobs up to 450 Hay points (junior managers), the head of reward replaces the union representative on the panel.

A job profile covering two sides of A4 and an organization chart are submitted to the panel. This is vetted by HR beforehand. Someone from the department submitting the job is asked to bring the job to life as an 'expert witness'. The panel can ask questions and challenge the witness. This person then goes away and the panel evaluates the job in private – an exercise that generally takes around half an hour per job.

The company is going through a stable period at the moment, but there have been times, such as during the last major restructuring, when hundreds of jobs have had to be re-evaluated and there has been insufficient time to do them all. However, the result is that all the 500 jobs have been examined at one time or another. The system now 'runs like clockwork', Janine Sparks says. It is respected by line managers and the unions, who see it as a fair and open process, and generalist HR staff like the efficiency of the arrangements, which result in jobs being evaluated quickly.

Communication

There was a great deal of communication when the new pay structure was introduced, and job evaluation was explained alongside the new pay arrangements. However, people were more concerned about the broad bands than how job evaluation works. Communicating the new pay scheme took place soon after the merger, so staff were preoccupied with a range of issues. Although the trade unions were not enthusiastic about Hay, they did welcome their involvement in the evaluation process. They have been trained in the Hay methodology and sit on evaluation committees as equal partners when jobs within the bargaining unit are being evaluated.

It is really important to consult with the business and explain what is being measured and what job evaluation is all about – this will help to dispel some of the myths, Janine believes, and she also suggests that an organization should involve as many stakeholders as possible.

Other uses for JE

Lloyds TSB Asset Finance is also using Hay to build career paths. It has a number of business units across the UK and there may be several business units in a single location. Each business unit has a separate 'head of', which has resulted in a 'silo' mentality, with people not moving between business units. The company is using Hay points to help identify and encourage potential moves. A marketing job worth x Hay points will be advertised in the hope that others doing marketing jobs with similar Hay scores will apply. Individuals are thereby encouraged to develop their jobs within the organization, rather than feeling they have to leave to do so.

Advice

'Look at jobs submitted to the JE panel beforehand, and if it doesn't look right go back to the business before the panel meets, and work with them to achieve a win–win solution', says Janine Sparks. 'And make sure you involve line managers and unions in the evaluation process and use "expert witnesses", usually the line manager in charge of the area in which the job sits. This brings the job description to life for the committee and enables it to raise questions or challenge statements in the job description. This has the added advantage that line managers take more care when approving job descriptions if they know they will be asked to explain the accountabilities within them to the panel.'

'Don't,' Janine advises, 'ever fudge an evaluation score – it always comes back to haunt you. If there is pressure on someone's salary for any reason, increase it, but don't fudge the job evaluation score to justify it.'

Part 3

Applications of Role Valuation

10

Equal pay

Role valuation is concerned with equity. The concept of equity as described by Adams (1965) is that people will be better motivated if they are treated equitably and demotivated if they are treated inequitably. Equity is about people's perceptions of how they are being treated in relation to others. To be dealt with equitably is to be treated fairly in comparison with another group of people (a reference group) or a relevant other person. Equity involves feelings and perceptions, and it is always a comparative process. Formal job evaluation aims to provide a systematic basis for making such comparisons. As Elliott (1991) wrote: 'Discrimination arises when equals are treated unequally', and job evaluation provides a means of avoiding discrimination or revealing when discrimination has taken place.

Job evaluation has particular significance when it refers to the achievement of equal pay for work of equal value between women and men – the main focus of this chapter. But the approaches to achieving equal pay the chapter covers are also applicable to other forms of potential pay discrimination including between people of different races, religions and age, and those with disabilities and those without.

The gap between the pay of men and women is created by a number of factors in addition to direct discrimination between the base pay rates of men and women for like jobs. The causes of inequality also include other aspects of sex discrimination such as the fact that women tend to be clustered towards the bottom of organizational hierarchies and pay ranges, while men tend to be clustered towards the top. The UK Equal Pay Task Force (2001) expressed the view that pay discrimination only contributes to between 25 and 50 per cent of the pay gap. To reduce the pay gap it is therefore necessary to address issues concerning equal opportunity, pay progression systems, and fixing rates of pay on appointment or promotion. It is equally important to prevent direct pay discrimination. Job evaluation has a major part to play in this by establishing when jobs are equal in value and should therefore be paid equally, and by underpinning equal pay reviews designed to analyse the size of pay gaps and assist in the diagnosis of their causes.

The role of job evaluation in achieving equal pay is carried out in many countries within the framework of equal pay legislation. The first part of this chapter therefore summarizes the international regulatory framework. The second part outlines the equal pay legislation of a selection of major countries. The next four parts deal respectively with how to avoid discrimination in job evaluation, defending an equal pay claim in the United Kingdom, managing the risk of an equal pay claim, and conducting an equal pay review.

THE REGULATORY FRAMEWORK

The regulatory framework consists of the Equal Remuneration Convention of the International Labour Office (ILO) and the EU equal pay legislation.

The Equal Remuneration Convention

Article 2 of the 1951 ILO's Equal Remuneration Convention states that:

> Each member shall, by means appropriate to the methods in operation for determining rates of remuneration, promote and, in so far as is consistent with such methods, ensure the application to all workers of the principle of equal remuneration for men and women workers for work of equal value.

One hundred and sixty-three countries have ratified this convention, including Albania, Kazakhstan and the United Kingdom, but not the United States.

Europe – Treaty of Rome and Equal Pay Directive

Article 119 of the EC founding Treaty of Rome of 1957 (now subsumed and expanded as Article 142 of the Treaty of Maastricht) stated that men and women should receive equal pay for equal work – in order to achieve what is often described as a 'level playing field' in terms of wages. Article 119 was extended by the Equal Pay Directive of 1975, which stated that:

▌ men and women should receive equal pay for work of equal value;

▌ job classification systems (which is Euro-English for any formal grading system and thus encompasses job evaluation schemes) should be fair and non-discriminatory;

▌ EC member states should take steps to implement the equal pay principle.

EQUAL PAY LEGISLATION

Many countries have introduced equal pay legislation, with varying degrees of effectiveness. However, even in those that have well-established laws the gap between the pay of men and women remains high, although it has been reduced over the years. The degree to which pay is unequal between men and women is measured by the pay gap. In the United Kingdom in 2006 this was 17.2 per cent for full-time employees. The UK Equal Opportunities Commission has estimated that the average woman working full time will lose out to the amount of £330,000 over the course of her working life. In the United States the pay gap in 2005 was 23 per cent. In France, in spite of strong legislation since the early 1970s, the pay gap in 2005 was 25 per cent. In Sweden, however, a country with perhaps the most effective equal pay legislation in Europe if not the world, the pay gap in 2001 was only 4.8 per cent, which arises more from factors related to occupation, age and education than pay differentials for equal work. Summaries of the legislation in a selection of countries follow.

Equal pay legislation in the United Kingdom

The 1970 Equal Pay Act

This Act effectively outlawed separate women's rates of pay by introducing an implied equality clause into all contracts of employment.

It also provided two grounds on which an applicant could take a claim to an industrial (now employment) tribunal for equal pay with a comparator of the opposite sex: 1) 'like work', meaning the same or very similar work; 2) 'work rated as equivalent' under a job evaluation 'study'.

The Equal Pay (Amendment) Regulations, 1983

These Regulations were introduced to conform to the European Directive. They provide that women are entitled to the same pay as men (and vice versa) where the work is of equal value 'in terms of the demands made on a worker under various headings, for instance, effort, skill, decision'.

This removed the barrier built into the Act that had prevented women claiming equal pay where they were employed in women's jobs and no men were employed in the same work. Now any woman could claim equal pay with any man and vice versa, subject to the rules about being in the same employment. Equal value claims can be brought even if there are no job evaluation arrangements, although the existence of a non-discriminatory analytical job evaluation scheme that has been applied properly to indicate that the jobs in question are not of equal value can be a defence in an equal value case.

The amendment also provided for the assignment of 'independent experts' by employment tribunals to assess equality of value between claimant and comparator under such headings as effort, skill and decision without regard to the cost or the industrial relations consequences of a successful claim.

Employment Act 2002

One of the biggest barriers to bringing equal pay claims has been a lack of access to information regarding other peoples' pay. The Equal Pay (Questions and Replies) Order 2003 of the Employment Act 2002 provided for an equal pay questionnaire, which can be used by employees to request information from their employer about whether their remuneration is equal to that of named colleagues. Unions may also lodge these forms on behalf of their members. The questionnaire includes:

1. A statement of why the individual (the complainant) thinks he or she is not receiving equal pay, followed by a statement of who he or she believes the comparators are. A comparator is the person the complainant is comparing him- or herself with. A complainant

can compare him- or herself with a predecessor or successor in the job. The comparator must be in the same employment as the complainant.

2. Factual questions to ascertain whether the complainant is receiving less pay than his or her comparator and, if so, the reason why.

3. A question asking whether the employer (the respondent) agrees or disagrees (with reasons) that the complainant is being paid less than the comparator.

4. A question asking whether the employer agrees or disagrees (with reasons) that the complainant and the comparator are doing equal work.

5. Space for the complainant's own questions.

The employer is asked to respond within eight weeks but is not required to reply to the complainant's questions. But if, without reasonable excuse, the employer fails to reply within eight weeks or replies in 'an evasive or ambiguous way', the employment tribunal may conclude that a respondent did not provide a proper explanation for a difference in pay because there was no genuine reason for the difference.

The Gender Equality Duty 2007

The Gender Equality Duty is a statutory duty that came into force in April 2007. It places the legal responsibility on public authorities in England, Scotland and Wales to promote gender equality and eliminate sex discrimination and to demonstrate that they treat men and women fairly.

Case law

A number of leading cases in the United Kingdom provide guidance on how the equal pay legislation should be applied. The key areas covered are:

▌ *Use of job evaluation as a defence in an equal pay claim* – the Court of Appeal ruled that a job evaluation system can provide a defence only if it is analytical in nature. The employer must demonstrate the absence of sex bias in the job evaluation scheme, and jobs will be held to be covered by a job evaluation scheme only if they have been fully evaluated using the scheme's factors (*Bromley v. Quick,* 1988).

▮ *The basis of comparison* – a comparison of each term of the contract considered in isolation is required. The applicant was therefore entitled to the same rates of basic and overtime pay as the comparator even though the other terms of her contract were more favourable (*Hayward v. Cammell Laird,* 1988).

▮ *The definition of pay* – occupational pensions under a contracted-out pensions scheme constitute 'pay' and so must be offered to men and women on equal terms (*Barber v. Guardian Royal Exchange Assurance Group,* 1990).

▮ *Market forces* – the state of the employment market, which may lead an employer to increase the pay of a particular job in order to attract candidates, may constitute a justified ground for a difference in pay. But tribunals will want clear evidence that a market forces defence is based on objectively justified grounds, bearing in mind that the labour market generally discriminates against women. They may view with suspicion evidence gleaned only from published surveys, which they may hold to be inherently discriminatory because they simply represent the status quo (*Enderby v. Frenchay Health Authority, 1993*).

▮ *Red-circling* – if an employee's pay is not reduced, ie is 'protected', following a re-grading exercise when his or her pay falls above the maximum for their new grade (red-circling), the protection should not last indefinitely, (*Snoxell v. Vauxhall Motors Ltd,* 1977).

▮ *Transparency* – in what is usually referred to in abbreviated form as the 'Danfoss' case, the European Court of Justice in 1989 ruled that when an undertaking applies to a pay system that is characterized by a total lack of transparency, the burden of proof is on the employer to show that pay practice is not discriminatory where a female worker has established, by comparison with a relatively large number of employees, that the average pay of female workers is lower than that of male workers.

▮ *Pay related to experience* – in *Crossley v. ACAS* (1999) the applicant claimed that she was doing work of equal value to the comparator but earned significantly less due to the fact that the ACAS pay scales required many years experience to reach the top of the pay band. It was argued that this discriminated against women, who are more likely to have shorter periods of service. Although the tribunal accepted that there was a period during which the job was being learnt, it agreed the period in this case was too long. In *Cadman v. the Health and Safety Executive* (2006) the European Court ruled that pay could be related to service but might have to be objectively justified by demonstrating that longer service results in skills necessary to do a higher job. This means that employers can be challenged by women if the latter can provide evidence that longer service does not lead to better performance.

▌ *Objective justification of the material factor defence* – employers have a defence against an equal pay claim if the difference in pay is genuinely due to a material factor that is not a difference in sex. The Employment Appeals Tribunal in the case of *Sharp v. Caledonia Group Services* (2006) ruled that employers using this defence must 'objectively justify' it in all cases. This means showing that the pay disparity:

- is unrelated to sex;
- relates to a real need of the employer;
- was appropriate to achieving the objective pursued;
- was necessary to that end and is proportionate.

In other words, the difference must be sensible and necessary rather than merely genuinely due to a material factor.

Equal pay legislation in Europe

All the original members of the Common Market have introduced equal pay legislation conforming to the requirements of the Equal Pay Directive. However, Sweden, a country not in the European Union, has introduced stronger legislation. Since 1994 private and public employers with at least 10 employees have been required to conduct annual equal pay surveys. Finland adopted similar legislation in 2005.

Equal pay legislation in the United States

The Equal Pay Act (1963) and the Civil Rights Act (1964) require employers to pay all employees equally for equal work, regardless of their sex. The courts have ruled that two jobs are equal for the purposes of the Equal Pay Act when they both require equal levels of skill, effort and responsibility and are performed under similar conditions. However, if the employer can show that the disparity has a legitimate basis – for example, that the higher earner has more seniority or more experience – the claim will be defeated. The Act provides for liquidated (fixed and limited) damages and back pay awards. The number of Equal Pay Act complaints is declining. In 2006 they were the lowest for 10 years, a 24 per cent decline since 1997. According to the National Women's Law Center this is because the Bush Administration has undermined enforcement tools.

In his State of the Union address in 1999, President Clinton said: 'Let's make sure that women and men get equal pay for equal work by strengthening enforcement of the equal-pay laws.' *The National Review* (a right wing journal) dismissed this as a 'loony idea ... designed to bring employers to their knees'. Undaunted, President Clinton introduced a $27 million Equal Pay Initiative in 2001 to help the Equal Employment Opportunity Commission and the Department of Labor fight wage discrimination, but the Bush administration terminated it in 2002. As far back as 1999 Congress debated but rejected 'The Paycheck Fairness Act', designed to strengthen equal pay law and increase penalties. This has been resurrected in 2007, sponsored by Senator Hilary Clinton, but even if passed by Congress could well be vetoed by President Bush.

Equal pay legislation in Canada

The pay equity legislation in Canada provides a mandatory approach to eliminate sex discrimination in pay. This applies to both the public and private sectors in Ontario and Quebec and to the public sector in other jurisdictions. The legislation requires employers covered by the law to achieve pay equity within the prescribed time periods. Where there is a union, it participates actively in the process. Employers and unions are obliged to follow prescribed steps to evaluate the employment of predominately female groups versus the employment of predominately male groups.

Equal pay legislation in Australia

As reported by the Australian Human Rights and Equal Opportunity Commission, Australian women workers were granted equal pay in 1969 in line with the provisions of the ILO's convention, and 30 years later it is rare, but not unheard of, for women to be paid a lower base wage than men doing the same jobs. But there is still inequality in a complex pay situation. For example, job evaluation processes may undervalue female-dominated occupations and therefore set lower pay rates compared with male-dominated jobs, or part-time workers may not be paid the same as full-timers doing the same jobs on a pro-rata basis.

AVOIDING DISCRIMINATION IN JOB EVALUATION

Job evaluation schemes can be discriminatory in two ways: first, in the methodology incorporated in the scheme's design (design discrimination) and second because of the process used in evaluating jobs (process discrimination). The main points on avoiding discrimination in design or process made by the Equal Opportunities Commission in its *Good Practice Guide – Job evaluation schemes free of sex bias* (2003), the European Commission, Employment & Social Affairs (1996) and in case law are set out below.

Avoiding design discrimination

To avoid design discrimination:

▌ the scheme should be analytical;

▌ the scheme should be appropriate for the jobs it is intended to cover – it should incorporate all the important and relevant differentiating characteristics of those jobs;

▌ the scheme should be designed and operated to measure fairly all significant features of jobs typically carried out by women as well as of those generally carried out by men;

▌ the factors should operate fairly;

▌ the factor and level definitions should be exact and detailed descriptions should be provided for each factor;

▌ the factors should cover all important job demands – a scheme will be discriminatory if it fails to include or properly take into account a demand such as caring that is an important element in the jobs carried out by women – the exclusion of an important factor will result in it being undervalued compared with other jobs;

▌ knowledge and skills factors should measure what is actually required for the job (not recruitment level or what the current job holder has), measure all forms of knowledge and skills, not just occupational knowledge, measure actual knowledge (qualifications as indicators, not determinants) and avoid measuring years of experience;

▌ the factor levels should represent clear and recognizable steps in demand and be defined in absolute, not relative terms, ie they should define the differences in terms of what is done at each level, not in terms such as small, bigger, big;

▌ there should be no double counting of factors;

▌ factors that are characteristic of jobs largely held by one sex should not unjustifiably have a greater number of levels than the number of levels in factors mainly held by the other sex;

▌ factors that are characteristic of male-dominated jobs should not have a wider dispersion of scores than factors that are characteristic of female-dominated jobs;

▌ there should be a rationale for the scoring and weighting system; it should not just give the answer people want;

▌ the method of scoring for each factor should be reasonably similar;

▌ variation between points should reflect real differences in demand;

▌ the weighting system should not favour men or women.

Process discrimination

To avoid process discrimination:

▌ job analysts, facilitators and evaluators should be trained on how to avoid bias;

▌ job evaluation panels should include fair proportions of both men and women;

▌ the selection of grade boundaries should be objectively based on the evidence provided by job evaluation, irrespective of the sex of the job holders;

▌ job descriptions should contain information about the jobs in terms of each of the job evaluation factors – traditional organizational job descriptions should not be used because evaluators are likely to use their own experience or make assumptions when assessing jobs against factors for which information may not be provided;

▌ the outcome of a new job evaluation scheme should be monitored to check for sex bias; other things being equal, it is to be expected that a new job evaluation scheme will result in some upward movement of female-dominated jobs as historical pay discrimination is eliminated, particularly those that show typical features of work carried out by women, relative to other jobs;

▌ existing schemes should be kept up to date and reviewed to ensure that sex discrimination has not crept in;

▌ evaluation outcomes should be properly recorded with reasons, consistency should be checked by factors and by whole jobs, and the outcome should be revised if there is good reason, such as faulty job information.

If after carrying out the investigation it is established that there is no risk of an equal pay claim or the risk is negligible, this by no means absolves an organization from fulfilling its moral responsibility to provide equal pay for work of equal value and from taking whatever steps are necessary to fulfil that responsibility. Ideally this should be through an analytical non-discriminatory job evaluation scheme and the use of equal pay reviews to identify equal pay problems.

DEFENDING AN EQUAL PAY CLAIM IN THE UNITED KINGDOM

The two most common grounds for defending a claim in the United Kingdom are 1) that the work is not equal, and 2) that even if it is equal, there is a genuine material factor that justifies the difference in pay. Employers cannot defend equal value cases on the grounds of the cost of implementation or the effect a decision could have on industrial relations, and part-time working per se cannot provide a defence to a claim. A tribunal can ask an independent expert to analyse the jobs and report on whether or not they are of equal value.

Proving that the work is not equal through the job evaluation study defence

The onus is on the employer to prove that the complainant is not carrying out like work, work rated as equivalent, or work of equal value when compared with the comparator. If the employer invokes job evaluation to provide support to a claim that the jobs are not equal (the job evaluation study defence), the scheme must be analytical, unbiased and applied in a non-discriminatory way. The 'job evaluation study defence' applies only where applicant and comparator jobs are covered by the same job evaluation scheme.

'Analytical' means that the scheme must analyse and compare jobs by reference to factors such as, in the words of the UK Equal Pay Regulations, 'effort, skill, decision'. Slotting jobs on a whole job comparison basis is not acceptable as a defence. The legislation and case law does not specify that a point-factor or a scored factor comparison scheme should be used, but even if an 'analytical matching' process is followed a tribunal may need to be convinced that this is analytical within the meaning of the Act and has not led to biased decisions.

The genuine material factor defence

UK law provides for a case to be made by the employer that there is a 'genuine material factor' creating the difference between the pay of the applicant and the comparator that can be objectively justified. A genuine material factor could be the level of performance or length of service of the comparator, which means that he or she is paid at a higher level than the applicant in the pay range for a job, or it could be the need to respond to market rate pressures. This only applies if the basis for deciding on additions to pay and the process of doing so are not discriminatory. The Crossley case referred to above is an example of where a tribunal found that length of service criteria could be discriminatory if they meant that women are paid less than men and find it hard to catch up. In the Cadman case, also referred to earlier, it was ruled that pay could be related to service but might have to be objectively justified by demonstrating that longer service results in skills necessary to do a higher job.

Pay differences because of market supplements can be treated as genuine material factors as long as they are 'objectively justified'. In the case of a claim that market pressures justify unequal pay, the tribunal will need to be convinced that this was not simply a matter of opinion and that adequate evidence from a number of sources was available. In such cases, the tribunal will also require proof that the recruitment and retention of the people required by the organization was difficult because pay levels were uncompetitive.

MANAGING THE RISK OF EQUAL PAY CLAIMS

Some organizations in low-risk situations may be convinced that they are doing enough about ensuring equal pay without introducing job evaluation. Others have decided that because their business imperatives are pressing they are prepared to accept a measure of risk in their policy on equal pay. Some, regrettably, may not care. But if there is medium or high risk, then action needs to be taken to minimize it. Successful equal pay claims can be hugely expensive, especially in UK public sector organizations with powerful and active trade unions. Equal pay risk management may therefore involve using a non-discriminatory job evaluation scheme, following the prescriptions for avoiding discrimination set out above and conducting equal pay reviews as described in the last section of this chapter.

The 2007 e-reward survey of job evaluation established that only 52 per cent of respondents had an analytical job evaluation scheme, and the 2007 CIPD reward survey found that only 20 per cent of participants had carried out an equal pay review. Clearly many organizations have decided that the risk of a claim is negligible. However, it is unwise simply to assume that there is little or no risk and it is advisable to carry out a risk assessment so that the organization is aware of the scale of the risk, if any. It can then decide whether or not to have a formal job evaluation scheme and if so, whether or not it should be analytical.

Conducting a risk assessment

Equal pay risk assessment involves considering two factors: 1) the risk of having to defend an equal pay claim, and 2) the risk of a claim being successful.

Assessing the risk of a claim means first analysing the extent to which there is unequal pay, and if it does exist, diagnosing the cause(s). For example, these could be any of the following:

▍ different base rates of pay for work of equal value;

▍ disproportionate distribution of men or women at the upper or lower part of a pay range or an incremental scale, bearing in mind that this is a major cause of unequal pay;

▍ men or women placed at higher points in the scale on appointment or promotion;

▍ men or women receive higher merit or performance pay awards or benefit more from accelerated increments;

▍ market supplements applied differentially to men or women;

▍ 'red or green circling' applied in a way that results in pay discrimination between men and women doing work of equal value or like work;

▍ a discriminating job evaluation scheme in terms of factors or weightings, or the job evaluation scheme is applied in a discriminatory way.

The best way to make this assessment is to carry out a formal equal pay review as described at the end of this chapter. If an organization is unwilling or unable to take this step, it should at least carry out an analysis of the pay of men and women carrying out like work to identify the existence and cause of any unjustified differences.

Secondly, assessing the risk of a claim means considering the possibility of an individual initiating action on his or her own, or trade unions taking action on behalf of their members. Individual actions may come out of the blue, but the individual may have raised an equal pay grievance formally or informally and line managers should understand that they must report this immediately to HR or senior management. In the United Kingdom a clear indication of trouble brewing is when an employee under the Employment Act 2002 submits an equal pay questionnaire to request information about whether their remuneration is equal to that of colleagues. Although trade unions are most likely to lodge questionnaires on behalf of their members, individuals can still do so independently by obtaining advice from the EOC (available on its website, www.eoc.org.uk). The likelihood of trade union action will clearly be higher when there is a strong union with high penetration in the organization, which is often the case in the public sector. But any union member can seek help from her or his union. Even if the union is not recognized for negotiating purposes it can still provide support. It is well worthwhile to keep track of developments in claims in the organization's own sector by reference to the employer's organization, or for the Civil Service, the Cabinet Office Personnel Management Division. Reference can also be made to the IRS and IDS publications, which report on employment legislation cases.

A schedule for the analysis of risks is shown in Table 10.1.

Table 10.1 Equal pay claim risk analysis schedule

Area of risk	Risk assessment			
	nil	low	medium	high
1. Of an equal pay claim				
2. Of being unable successfully to defend a claim by use of the job evaluation defence				
3. Of being unable successfully to defend a claim by use of the material factor defence				
4. Of being unable successfully to defend the claim because there is no formal job evaluation scheme				

EQUAL PAY REVIEWS AND JOB EVALUATION

Equal pay reviews establish whether any sex-related pay inequities have arisen, analyse the nature of any inequities, diagnose their cause or causes and determine what action is required to deal with them. In the United Kingdom they are mandatory in civil service departments and agencies.

Equal pay reviews take place in three stages:

1. *Analysis*: the collection and analysis of relevant data to identify any sex gaps.

2. *Diagnosis*: the process of reviewing sex gaps, understanding why they have occurred and what remedial action might be required if the differences cannot be objectively justified.

3. *Action*: agreeing and implementing an action plan that eliminates any inequalities.

Job evaluation can play a major part in the analysis stage.

Analysis options

The analysis options are:

▌ *Like work* – this means identifying jobs anywhere in the organization where the work is the same or broadly similar. When there is no job evaluation this is the only type of equal work comparison that can readily be made. Although this should be a straightforward comparison, there are potential pitfalls, such as over-reliance on unrepresentative job titles. If existing job titles are not a good guide, it might be necessary to re-categorize jobs to arrive at who is doing 'like work'.

▌ *Work rated as equivalent* – this means work that has been rated as equivalent using the organization's own analytical job evaluation scheme. Clearly analyses can only be readily applied where the organization has a job evaluation scheme that covers the whole organization.

▌ *Work of equal value* – this is the 'catch all' in equal pay legislation. It means that an equal pay claim can be brought by any employee where he or she believes that his or her job is of equal worth to any other role in the organization that is occupied by someone of the opposite sex. As with the 'work rated as equivalent' test, the only organizations that can readily conduct analyses under this heading are those with an organization-wide job evaluation scheme that enables different types of jobs to be compared using criteria that apply equally across the organization.

Using job evaluation

If job evaluation is used on an organization-wide basis it is possible to conduct pay gap analyses that meet all three equal work categories. This can be done by conducting both a 'like work' and an organization-wide comparison between the pay for men and women in the same grade irrespective of their occupational groups. This is because where organizations use analytical job evaluation, different types of jobs on the same grade defined in terms of a range of job evaluation scores, will generally be regarded as being of 'equal worth', thus enabling a pay gap analysis that covers all employees in the same grade.

However, this is unlikely to be a satisfactory assessment of equal worth where bands or grades are so broad that they include jobs with a wide range of responsibilities and skills. Where this is the case, it may be necessary to split the grades/bands into narrower groups. This can be done fairly easily using a point-factor scheme's total job scores, but will not be so straightforward where other job evaluation techniques have been used (eg classification), without some adaptation to the scheme or alternative approach to deriving additional levels. Of course, the type of job evaluation approach used also impacts on the perceived robustness of the equal worth comparison in the first place.

Where more than one job evaluation scheme is used, a careful check should be made as part of the equal pay review on whether the schemes are creating equivalent outcomes. For example, if a different scheme is used for the most senior roles in an organization, a check should be made on the boundary between the two schemes, preferably evaluating a sample of jobs on both sides of the boundary.

REFERENCES

Adams, J (1965) Injustice in social exchange, in ed L Berkowitz, *Advances in Experimental Psychology*, Academic Press, New York

Elliott, R F (1991) *Labor Economics*, McGraw-Hill, Maidenhead

Equal Opportunities Commission (2003) *Good Practice Guide – Job evaluation schemes free of sex bias*, EOC, Manchester

Equal Pay Task Force (2001) *Just Pay*, Report of the Equal Pay Task Force to the Equal Opportunities Commission, EOC, Manchester

European Commission, Employment & Social Affairs (1996) *A Code of Practice on the Implementation of Equal Pay for Work of Equal Value for Men And Women*, EC, Luxembourg

11

Developing grade and pay structures

The outcome of a job evaluation exercise is usually a new or revised grade and pay structure. The purpose of this chapter is to describe how job evaluation can be used to initiate or contribute to the design process for the various types of grade and pay structures. The chapter starts with definitions of grade and pay structures. It then describes how job evaluation is used in the design process – generally and for particular structures. Equal value considerations are dealt with at the end of the chapter.

GRADE AND PAY STRUCTURES

Grade and pay structures provide a logically designed framework within which an organization's pay policies can be implemented. They enable the organization to determine where jobs should be placed in a hierarchy, define pay levels and the scope for pay progression, and provide the basis upon which relativities can be managed, equal pay achieved and the processes of monitoring and controlling the implementation of pay practices can take place. A grade and pay structure can also serve as a medium through which the organization communicates the career and pay opportunities available to employees.

GRADE STRUCTURES

A grade structure consists of a sequence or hierarchy of grades, bands or levels into which groups of jobs that are broadly comparable in size are placed. There may be a single structure that is defined by the number of grades or bands it contains. Alternatively, the structure may be divided into a number of career or job families consisting of groups of jobs where the essential nature and purpose of the work are similar but the work is carried out at different levels.

The main types of graded structures are:

▮ *Narrow-graded structures* – which consist of a sequence of narrow grades (generally 10 or more). They are sometimes called 'multi-graded structures'.

▮ *Broad-graded structures* – which have fewer grades (generally six to nine).

▮ *Broad-banded structures* – which consist of a limited number of grades or bands (often four or five). Structures with six or more grades are often described as broad-banded even when their characteristics are typical of broad-grade structures.

▮ *Career family structures* – which consist of a number of families (groups of jobs with similar characteristics) each divided typically into six to eight levels. The levels are described in terms of key responsibilities and knowledge, skill and competence requirements, and therefore define career progression routes within and between career families. There is a common grade and pay structure across all the career families.

▮ *Job family structures* – which are similar to career families except that pay levels in each family may differ to reflect market rate considerations (this is sometimes referred to as 'market grouping'). The structure is as much concerned with market rate relativities as mapping careers. The number of levels in families may also vary.

▮ *Combined structures* – in which broad bands are superimposed on career/job families or broad bands are divided into families.

▮ *Pay spines* – consisting of a series of incremental 'pay points' extending from the lowest to the highest paid jobs covered by the structure.

Some organizations do not have a graded structure at all for any jobs or for certain jobs such as directors. Instead they use 'spot rates' or 'individual job ranges'. A spot rate is the pay for a job or an individual that is not fitted into a grade or band in a conventional grade structure and does not allow any scope for pay progression. An individual job range is in effect a spot rate in which there is a defined range for pay progression.

Grades, bands or levels may be defined in one or other of the following ways or a combination of them:

▌ by means of a range of job evaluation points – jobs are allocated to a grade, band or level if their job evaluation scores fall within a range or bracket of points;

▌ in words that describe the characteristics of the work carried out in the jobs positioned in each grade or level – these grade, band or level definitions, often called 'profiles', may set out the key activities and the competencies or knowledge and skills required at different points in the hierarchy;

▌ by reference to benchmark jobs or roles that have already been placed in the grade, band or job family level.

PAY STRUCTURES

A grade structure becomes a pay structure when pay ranges, brackets or scales are attached to each grade, band or level. In some broad-banded structures, reference points defining the rate for the job or pay zones defining the scope for pay progression may be placed within the bands.

Pay structures are defined by the number of grades they contain and, especially in narrow- or broad-graded structures, the span or width of the pay ranges attached to each grade. Span is the scope the grade provides for pay progression and is usually measured as the difference between the lowest point in the range and the highest point in the range as a percentage of the lowest point. Thus a range of £20,000 to £30,000 would have a span of 50 per cent.

Pay structures define the different levels of pay for jobs or groups of jobs by reference to their relative internal value as determined by job evaluation, to external relativities as established by market rate surveys and, sometimes, to negotiated rates for jobs. They provide scope for pay progression in accordance with performance, competence, contribution or service.

THE USE OF JOB EVALUATION IN DEVELOPING A GRADE STRUCTURE AND GRADING JOBS

There are three ways in which job evaluation can be used generally to develop a grade structure and grade jobs:

1. by dividing the rank order produced by an analytical job evaluation exercise into grades or bands;

2. by validating a 'matching' process following the design of a career or job family structure; or

3. through the use of a non-analytical job classification scheme, which might, however, be validated by the use of an analytical job evaluation scheme.

Grading following an analytical job evaluation exercise

An analytical job evaluation exercise will produce a rank order of jobs according to their job evaluation scores. A decision then has to be made on where the boundaries that will define grades should be placed in the rank order. So far as possible, boundaries should divide groups or clusters of jobs that are significantly different in size, so that all the jobs placed in a grade are clearly larger than the jobs placed in the next lower grade and smaller than the jobs in the next higher grade.

Fixing grade boundaries is one of the most critical aspects of grade structure design following an analytical job evaluation exercise. It requires judgement – the process is not scientific and it is rare to find a situation where there is one right and obvious answer. In theory, grade boundaries could be determined by deciding on the number of grades in advance and then dividing the rank order into equal parts. But this would mean drawing grade boundary lines arbitrarily and the result could be the separation of groups of jobs that should properly be placed in the same grade.

The best approach is to analyse the rank order to identify any significant gaps in the points scores between adjacent jobs. These natural breaks in points scores will then constitute the boundaries between clusters of jobs that can be allocated to adjacent grades. A distinct gap between the highest rated job in one grade and the lowest rated job in the grade above will help to justify the allocation of jobs between grades. It will therefore reduce boundary problems leading to dissatisfaction with gradings when the distinction is less well defined. Provisionally, it may be decided in advance when designing a conventional graded structure that a certain number of grades is required, but the gap analysis will confirm the number of grades that is appropriate, taking into account the natural divisions between jobs in the rank order. However, the existence of a number of natural breaks cannot be guaranteed, which means that judgement has to be exercised as to where boundaries should be drawn when the scores between adjacent jobs are close.

In cases where there are no obvious natural breaks the guidelines that should be considered when deciding on boundaries are as follows:

▌ jobs with common features as indicated by the job evaluation factors are grouped together so that a distinction can be made between the characteristics of the jobs in different grades – it should be possible to demonstrate that the jobs grouped into one grade resemble each other more than they resemble jobs placed in adjacent grades;

▌ the grade hierarchy should take account of the organizational hierarchy, ie jobs in which the job holder reports to a higher level job holder should be placed in a lower grade, although this principle should not be followed slavishly when an organization is over-hierarchical with, perhaps, a series of one-over-one reporting relationships;

▌ the boundaries should not be placed between jobs mainly carried out by men and jobs mainly carried out by women;

▌ ideally the boundaries should not be placed immediately above jobs in which large numbers of people are employed, or if they are there needs to be a convincing reason why the boundaries are placed as they are;

▌ the grade width in terms of job evaluation points should represent a significant step in demand as indicated by the job evaluation scheme – there is no need for each grade to have the same number of points, but if there are significant differences between grades the reasons for creating such differences may be subject to question.

The same approach can be used when designing broad-banded or broad-graded structures, although it is more likely that the number of bands or grades will have been determined beforehand. The aim will still be to achieve clear distinctions between the jobs clustered in successive bands. This may be easier because there will be fewer boundary lines to draw, but unless they can be defined by reference to significant gaps the decision may still be judgemental.

The role of job evaluation in the design of career or job family structures

The design of a career family structure can be based on job evaluation by the grading process described above following the use of an analytical job evaluation scheme to produce a rank order of jobs. Alternatively, analytical job evaluation can be used in the design of either career or job families to validate prior decisions on grades and levels and the allocation of jobs to levels by matching role profiles to level definitions.

When the design of a career family structure follows an analytical job evaluation exercise, the grades or levels determined by reference to the rank order produced by job evaluation are in effect sliced up into families. Career ladders are devised by defining the levels for each family in terms of the key activities carried out and the knowledge and skills required. Each level is also defined by reference to a range of job evaluation points. Benchmark jobs are allocated to levels according to their point scores, but once the design has been confirmed many organizations allocate jobs to levels simply by matching role profiles with level definitions or profiles, although job evaluation scores can always be consulted to validate the allocation and to check that equal value considerations have been met.

When the design of a career or job family structure is based on *a priori* decisions on the number and definition of levels without reference to job evaluation scores, the first step is to select benchmark roles, which may be generic, and prepare role profiles defining the key activities carried out and the knowledge and skills required. The role profiles are then 'matched' with the level definitions or profiles to determine the allocation of the roles to levels. The role profiles may readily match one level, but they often fit parts of one level definition and parts of another. In this case judgement is required to achieve the best general fit. It should be noted that unless 'matching' is done on an analytical basis, ie against a defined set of factors, it may lead to pay discrimination and would not provide a defence in an equal pay claim.

Grade structure design based upon job classification

The non-analytical job classification method of job evaluation starts with a definition of the number and characteristics of the grades into which jobs will be placed. These *a priori* decisions are made without reference to job evaluation scores, as is sometimes the case when designing career or job family structures. There are therefore no problems in defining grade boundaries, as can occur when the structure is derived from the rank order produced by an analytical evaluation exercise.

When the grade definitions have been produced, jobs are slotted into the grades. This should ideally be carried out by means of a matching process that is analytical to the degree that it specifically compares the characteristics of whole jobs with the characteristics set out in the grade definitions.

Job classification is the simplest method of grade design, but when there is no analytical base, grading decisions may be arbitrary and inequitable and no reliable defence will be available in the event of an equal pay claim. The solution to these problems adopted by some organizations is to use an analytical point-factor scheme to validate the gradings and check on internal equity.

DEVELOPING PAY STRUCTURES

Pay structures other than broad-banded structures are devised by attaching pay ranges to each grade or level. All jobs placed in a particular grade will be paid within the range for that grade and will progress through the range on the basis of service, performance, competence or contribution. Progression within a range may be limited by thresholds that can only be crossed if defined levels of performance and competence have been achieved. The pay ranges are determined by reference to the existing rates of pay for the jobs allocated to each grade and their market rates. An analysis of market rates forms part of the pay structure design programme, but in practice it may not always be possible to get reliable information for all the jobs, especially those for which good external matches are difficult to make.

Broad-banded structures may or may not have bands with defined pay ranges, but in either case they may include pay zones for jobs or clusters of jobs within a band.

Designing pay structures other than broad-banded structures

The following steps are required:

1. List the jobs placed within each grade on the basis of job evaluation (these might be limited to benchmark jobs that have been evaluated, but there must be an adequate number of them if a proper basis for the design is to be provided).

2. Establish the actual rates of pay of the job holders.

3. For each grade, set out the range of pay for job holders and calculate their average or median rate of pay (the pay practice point). It is helpful to plot this pay practice data as illustrated in Figure 11.1, which shows pay in each grade against job evaluation scores and includes a pay practice trend line.

4. Obtain information on the market rates for benchmark jobs where available. If possible this should indicate the median rate and the upper and lower quartiles.

5. Agree policy on how the organization's pay levels should relate to market rates – its 'market stance'. This could be at the median, or above the median if it is believed that pay levels should be more competitive.

6. Calculate the average market rates for the benchmark jobs in each grade according to pay stance policy, eg the median rates. This produces the range market reference point.

7. Compare the practice and market reference points in each range and decide on the range reference point. This usually becomes the mid-point of the pay range for the grade and is regarded as the competitive rate for a fully competent job holder in that grade. This is a judgemental process that takes into account the difference between the practice and policy points, the perceived need to be more competitive if policy rates are higher, and the likely costs of increasing rates.

8. Examine the pay differentials between reference points in adjacent grades. These should provide scope to recognize increases in job size, and, so far as possible, variations between differentials should be kept to a minimum. If differentials are too close – less than 10 per cent – many jobs become borderline cases, which can result in a proliferation of appeals and arguments about grading. Large differentials below senior management level of more than 25 per cent can create problems for marginal or borderline cases because of the amount at stake. Experience has shown that in most organizations with conventional grade structures a differential of between 15 and 20 per cent is appropriate, except, perhaps, at the highest levels.

9. Decide on the range of pay around the reference point. A conventional arrangement is to allow 20 per cent on either side; thus if the reference point is 100 per cent, the range is from 80 per cent to 120 per cent. The range can, however, vary in accordance with policy on the scope for progression, and if a given range of pay has to be covered by the structure, the fewer the grades the wider the ranges.

10. Decide on the extent, if any, to which pay ranges should overlap. Overlap recognizes that an experienced job holder at the top of a range may be making a greater contribution than an inexperienced job holder at the lower end of the range above. Large overlaps of more than 10 per cent can create equal pay problems where, for example, men are clustered at the top of their grades and women are more likely to be found at the lower end.

11. Review the impact of the above pay range decisions on the pay of existing staff. Establish the number of staff whose present rate of pay is above or below the pay range for the grade into which their jobs have been placed, and the extent of the difference between the rate of pay of those below the minimum and the lowest point of that pay range. Calculate the costs of bringing them up to the minimum. Software such as the pay modellers produced by Link and Pilat can be used for this purpose.

12. When the above steps have been completed it may be necessary to review the decisions made on the grade structure and pay reference points and ranges. Iteration is almost always necessary to obtain a satisfactory result that conforms to the criteria for grade and pay structures mentioned earlier and minimizes the

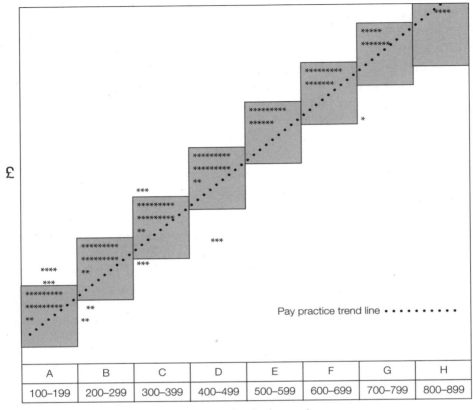

Scattergram of evaluations and pay

Figure 11.1 Scattergram of evaluations and pay

cost of implementation. Alternatives can be modelled using the software mentioned above.

Broad-banded pay structures

The definition of bands and the allocation of jobs into bands in a broad-banded structure may be based on job evaluation. The most common approach to the definition of pay levels within bands is to insert reference points indicating the rates for individual jobs or clusters of jobs. These reference points are aligned to market rates and may be surrounded by pay ranges to form a zone. If an organization is 'market-driven', that is, it attaches prime importance to market rate relativities, broad-banding is said to allow for greater flexibility in responding to market rate pressures than more conventional structures. It is also claimed by supporters of broad-banding that it provides for role flexibility. In a zoned band, movement to a higher zone can take place when it is evident that the role an individual is carrying out matches the role carried out by people in the higher zone, or if specific competencies or performance criteria are met. It is not dependent on the evaluation score of their job, and re-evaluations are not required unless matching is difficult or there are equal pay considerations. Zones of the type described above are not usually defined as a hierarchy within a band. In some broad-banded structures, there is scope for creating a special zone for individuals whose role has enlarged significantly but not enough to justify allocation to a higher zone in the band.

This feature of broad-banded structures means that their design is mainly dependent on decisions concerning reference points and zones (the range of the latter is often smaller than the typical range in a conventional structure, usually 10 per cent on either side of the reference point). The flexibility resulting from their use and the fact that, overall, the span of pay covered by a broad band is much wider, means that few anomalies are created and the cost of implementation will therefore be much lower. This is an argument for broad-banding that is seldom revealed in public. However, if broad bands include performance or competency defined zones, any straight move across on assimilation into the new band without reference to these criteria may create a mismatch between those assimilated initially and those that are allocated to zones using the more rigorous new criteria at a later date.

The various types of flexibility provided by broad-banding have made it an attractive proposition to many organizations. Generally, however, it has been found that broad-banded structures are harder to manage than narrower graded structures, in spite of the original claim that they would be easier – they make considerable demands on line managers as well as HR. Instead of relying on the structure and system to provide the answer, managers need to be capable of making decisions on market data and performance. Broad-banding can build employee expectations of significant pay opportunities that are doomed in many cases if proper control of the system is maintained. It can be difficult to explain to people how broad-banding works and how they will be affected, and decisions on movements within bands can be harder to justify objectively than in other types of grade and pay structures. Employees may be concerned by the apparent lack of structure and precision. Above all, they create formidable equal pay problems, as described below.

EQUAL VALUE CONSIDERATIONS

The design process should minimize the risk of discrimination for any of the following reasons:

▍ the grade boundary lines in a multi-graded structure are based purely on judgements that may simply reinforce existing inequities;

▍ generic role profiles take insufficient account of significant differences between male and female roles;

▍ an analytical job evaluation scheme is not used to define grades or allocate jobs to grades – whole jobs are slotted into a graded, broad-banded or career/job family structure by a process of internal benchmarking, which could simply perpetuate existing discrimination;

▍ benchmark jobs do not fairly represent the distribution of male and female jobs;

▍ market-related pay levels and differentials reproduce marketplace sex discrimination and do not take account of internal relativities;

▍ pay ranges are so broad that there is scope for pay inequity within the grade or band unless there are specific measures to ensure that everybody will normally reach at least a specific reference point in the range within a certain timescale.

12

International job evaluation

In this chapter two aspects of international job evaluation are covered: first, the considerations that affect the degree to which job evaluation is standardized in international firms, and second, the approaches adopted in a number of different countries. The chapter ends with case studies on the development and use of job evaluation internationally.

STANDARDIZATION OF JOB EVALUATION PRACTICES INTERNATIONALLY

International businesses have to consider whether the achievement of corporate best fit in job evaluation practices requires taking into account the extent to which this is compatible with, or overrides local best fit.

Recent research by the CIPD (Perkins, 2006) suggests that the shift is towards greater standardization of reward policies across multi-national operations. Perkins comments that companies have to consider the extent to which organizational imperatives override local cultural or external environment considerations, and environmental considerations are beyond the reach of the organization to override, eg trade unions, collective agreements and legislation.

Where non-domestic subsidiaries are regarded as of limited importance, or as relatively autonomous operations, he comments that the focus of international human resource management has been on appointments at senior level and expatriate management. However, his research suggests that the corporate will is winning out: organizations are 'limiting room for manoeuvre below the corporate level'. There are a number of reasons advanced by Perkins for this:

▌ 'Increasingly tight corporate governance standards appear to have strengthened corporate management resolve to offer new monitoring structures to coordinate what people do more prescriptively across multinational networks'.

▌ There is a requirement for greater accessibility of information for reporting purposes, for financial management and to assess and manage risk exposure.

▌ Outsourcing and off-shoring have also raised 'new issues for organizations seeking to invest reward and recognition budgets', in a way that meets Westernized governance standards.

The CIPD study reveals what may be seen as mixed messages about the extent to which reward practices generally are corporately or locally determined. Results of a 2005 survey conducted as part of the research (covering 63 responses from members of the CIPD's international reward forum) gave the following responses:

▌ Asked whether the priority is to integrate the reward system with corporate strategy for the multinational, 84 per cent said that this was their preferred approach.

▌ In response to a question about whether they tended to adapt their reward system to the local host context, 62 per cent claimed it as a priority.

▌ Asked about whether a globally integrated approach would be preferred, 78 per cent of the respondents said 'Yes'.

Perkins feels that although the results could indicate indecision amongst reward practitioners, they might illustrate a pragmatic and sometimes opportunistic response to the challenge of developing an organization-wide approach.

This is supported by Bloom *et al* (2003), who indicated that although managers claimed to be acting strategically, they tended to act as 'pragmatic experimentalists', adapting the detail of reward systems to fit the constraints encountered in local situations, whilst remaining as constant as possible to corporate policies.

The conclusion that companies are moving increasingly to a standardized approach to reward is backed up by the major international reward consultancies with respect to job evaluation. They have commented, without exception, that more companies are taking a global approach to job evaluation.

Further confirmation of a preference for standardization was provided by the 2007 e-reward survey, which found that 65 per cent of the international organizations in the sample adopted the same approach to job evaluation worldwide. The reasons given by organizations for this policy include:

▋ 'To ensure consistency.'

▋ 'Our overseas bases are relatively small, so we try to follow the same approach where possible.'

▋ 'We aim for global consistency – whether we truly achieve it is another thing!'

The reasons given by organizations that have not standardized their approach include:

▋ 'There are different cultures/market forces.'

▋ 'To date there has been no global HR infrastructure to deliver or maintain such an approach.'

▋ 'Some countries in which we operate are heavily unionized – eg Sweden; in these situations a union negotiation approach is taken locally.'

As David Conroy of Mercer consultancy commented, although some international companies are now taking an interest in aligning total remuneration opportunities around the world at senior level, in practice there may be considerable challenges in achieving this.

There is evidence that organizations are adopting different approaches to how far down global reward policies are applied based on a combination of organizational philosophy, culture and pragmatism. This difference is reflected in our case studies, with Anglo American focusing on the top management cadre across the group, while ABC Limited has adopted a top to bottom approach. However, even where the focus is on the management cadre, local operations are often encouraged and supported in making use of the scheme further down. This approach has the benefit of reducing organizational cost and effort in introducing job evaluation, while allowing local operations the flexibility when fixing pay levels to respond to the local marketplace as they feel fit. In addition, regulatory issues that do not impact on global implementation are left for local resolution.

Job evaluation is likely to work most effectively globally where there are common business models and organization structure. As Jim Crawley of Towers Perrin points out: 'Without that, it can be almost impossible to effectively bring in job evaluation – it would be meaningless.'

Characteristics of job evaluation schemes in international companies

To what extent do cultural or legal factors come into play in determining the characteristics of the job evaluation scheme? Amongst the companies and consultancies that we have spoken to, the answer appears to be typically, 'Not a lot'. Certainly, the international reward consultancies have not suggested that there is any need to adapt the fundamentals of scheme design across borders. However, there are some differences in what is important in different countries. For example, in some parts of the world, such as Japan or Latin America, it is important to recognize the existence of a strong emphasis on seniority. Even so, a Latin American management consultant fed back that the increasingly competitive external market, and the need to be able to compare within and across companies, was driving more organizations to adopt job evaluation to give more structure to these internal and external comparisons.

It appears that there are two different marketplaces: 1) organizations that operate mainly within national borders and are therefore more likely to reflect local culture and practice in terms of job evaluation characteristics, grading and pay design; and 2) organizations operating globally that are more likely to follow conventional Western European and US norms. This difference of emphasis needs to be considered when deciding on the approach to a job evaluation scheme and designing the grade and pay structure.

However, even where the same company scheme is applied worldwide there might be scope for interpreting it differently across countries. For example, in a country where seniority is highly valued, there might be an expectation that seniority correlates with higher levels of applied knowledge and skills or decision making. However, the extent to which this type of local interpretation differs from the devolved operation of a large job evaluation scheme in a single country can be questioned where the local operating environment may give rise to different interpretations. If the aim is to achieve international comparability, then there is a need for high-level moderation across countries. This is little different from the need to moderate cross-organizationally in a large-scale devolved scheme.

APPROACHES TO ROLE VALUATION IN DIFFERENT COUNTRIES

The success of the Hay system in Europe, the Americas and parts of Asia Pacific has meant that across the world many organizations apply similar job evaluation concepts, despite nuances of interpretation or application to meet different local operating conditions and legislative, trade union or regulatory environments. Of all countries, the United States is the most noteworthy, because, as in other areas of business practice, what they do at home and in their international operations tends to impact across practices elsewhere. The rest of this section focuses on North America and the Americas.

United States

Consultants and practitioners have detected traces of a shift away from the extreme market pricing model described in Chapter 8, which has been the dominant approach to managing relativities in the United States for the last couple of decades. Although the emphasis is still on market pricing, some commentators suggest that the tide may have turned as organizations realize that in throwing out their old grade structures they have lost some of their capability to describe careers within their organization.

In the opinion of Gayle Spear, Towers Perrin worldwide leader in their Career Map methodology, job evaluation techniques and language are still generally regarded as old-fashioned and companies do not recognize job evaluation as something they want. However, a number of forces are leading organizations to look at how they describe levels of work. These include the introduction of major technology systems, for HR and broader reporting/analytical purposes that require levels to be applied to all jobs in these systems – whilst not creating an appetite for full job evaluation; and global organizations are tending to develop a single approach across countries of operation, although their main purpose is often talent/career management rather than pure job evaluation for grading purposes and pay for its own sake. This focus on career mapping is reflected in the Towers Perrin approach, which is based on career levels by job family.

The result is that Towers Perrin is increasingly engaging with organizations through heads of learning and development or talent management, which in turn may lead to a combined approach – levels from career maps may be linked to benefits and to job family pay ranges. If used for talent management alone, Spear comments that levelling is more likely to be restricted to more senior people.

A shift in emphasis was also picked up by Hewitt consultancy in an internal survey of the Americas that they conducted on behalf of the authors as research for this book in May 2007. The results are summarized below.

North America

The demand for job evaluation has evolved over time. During the 1990s there was a shift from factor-based evaluation including point-factor to 'rank to market' approaches in general. The shift from multi-grade systems to broad bands also introduced a number of classification type approaches for slotting jobs into bands, with the market driving the development of a specific market reference point.

There has been some renewed interest in factor-based approaches lately in North America, including point-factor. This is partly because organizations are more global, and while market values for jobs differ around the world, they still need a single hierarchy from top to bottom, and a common method of levelling (job evaluation) helps to define that hierarchy. Although a major return to factor-based evaluation may not occur, there may be some increase because organizations find that it is expensive and time-consuming to gather and prepare market data, and internally focused job evaluation presents an alternative.

The main drivers for changing or introducing job evaluation now are that the old system is obsolete, organizations want to revise the number of levels they have and they believe that they need a more objective process for slotting jobs.

The most common approaches to job evaluation/levelling are, in order of popularity:

1. 'Rank to market', ie market pricing.

2. Whole job slotting.

3. Point-factor rating.

4. Other approaches such as job classification and factor comparison.

Argentina

Over the last few years, in Argentina the demand for job evaluation increased to a degree, especially in companies with an HR department. The main reasons for introducing a job evaluation scheme is its use as a tool to help companies rank all the positions in an objective way, link pay to position and design a pay structure.

Brazil

The main type of scheme used is point-factor rating. There is a trend towards levelling in the form of defining which competences are needed for a position, and which are needed to go up a level.

The specific cultural, legal and external factors that need to be considered in Brazil are:

- seniority is always important;

- there are regional pay differences across the country;

- there is equal pay legislation, so large salary differences between men and women can lead to law suits.

Chile

The demand for job evaluation has increased, because more companies want to compare their jobs with companies in the same industry that have different structures (because of different business strategies) and with similar sized companies in other industries.

The reasons for organizations wanting to change or introduce an evaluation system are pay/grade structure design, career management and the need for an impartial system to assign a pay level for a specific job. The main approach to job evaluation in Chile is point-factor rating.

Mexico

Job evaluation is common in Mexico, for the purpose of developing salary structures. There is some shift in practice as some corporations are moving to a banded approach and requiring locals to change their approach accordingly. Point-factor job evaluation is the most common approach.

Venezuela

The most common method of evaluation is point-factor rating. The demand in Venezuela for job evaluation/levelling has stayed about the same. The reason is that multinational companies have had their methodology for many years and owing to current economic conditions there are no new investments and operations that require sophisticated job evaluation. The trend is likely to continue. The reasons for changing existing systems include:

▮ seeking less complex methodologies;

▮ introducing a new HR system/platform such as PeopleSoft or SAP;

▮ guaranteeing homogeneous methodology across the company over different locations;

▮ developing a new salary structure due to merger, acquisitions or new facilities;

▮ introducing a formal mechanism to provide for internal equity and making appropriate market comparisons;

▮ supporting HR practices and compensation and development decisions by providing a formal framework;

▮ supporting career development.

The most common approach for job evaluation/levelling in Venezuela is the point-factor system.

CASE STUDIES

The following case studies illustrate how companies operating internationally have managed their job evaluation and reward management systems.

American Express Europe, the Middle East and Africa (EMEA)

Context

American Express (Amex) employs 6,500 staff in the United Kingdom and 16,000 in EMEA. Job evaluation is used internationally to identify job grades (rather than points scores) and to underpin its company-wide competencies. Its scheme was designed many years ago, and is supported by Hay Group's job evaluation factors. There have been some minor tweaks to arrangements in the last couple of years but the process has not changed.

Process

Jobs are banded against American Express competencies, and Hay methodology is used up as backup and validation of that process. The object of the exercise is to arrive at a grade, not a number of points. Competencies are underpinned by the Hay job evaluation factors. This applies to all roles except the most senior jobs – senior vice-presidents and above. Their jobs are evaluated directly by the Hay Group.

Each region uses a similar though not identical process. In the EMEA region, there are different arrangements for three categories of staff, as shown in Table 12.1.

In the United Kingdom, a number of compensation consultants meet as a regional committee, once a month, together with at least one director, to review the jobs that come through to them. These include every new job, every upgrade or downgrade, and every job affected by a reorganization. When a job comes through that is the same as an existing role it is not put forward to the committee, just approved along with confirmation that budget and headcount has been signed off by the business.

Table 12.1 American Express bands

Bands	Roles	JE process
Bands 20–40	Roles from entry level up to and including directors	Evaluated in the UK by American Express compensation consultants, with input from HR business partners and business leaders
Band 45	Vice-presidents	Evaluated in the United States by more senior American Express compensation consultants, with input from HR business partners and business leaders
Bands 50+	Senior vice-presidents and above	Evaluated by Hay Group

Other participants join the meeting through conference calls. The business leader – the manager responsible for that job – completes a Word template before the meeting, giving brief details of what the job involves, before spending about 20 minutes presenting the job to the committee. The business leaders are supported by their relationship manager – the HR business partner. After the conference call, the committee discuss the job and arrive at a grading for it. The committee review no more than six jobs at each sitting.

There is an appeal process. If the committee does not arrive at the grading that the manager thinks appropriate, the manager can take it away, and rethink and re-present the job the following month. If it is rejected again, then it cannot be re-presented for another six months. Where there is a reorganization the committee will often advise that the proposals be complete before evaluating the roles impacted, in order to get a complete picture of what the reorganization will look like.

Outside the United Kingdom

The same process is used for Band 20–40 jobs in the rest of the EMEA region. Consistency across different businesses and between different countries is a big challenge. So when a role is outside the United Kingdom, the committee always asks first for the support of the relationship manager looking after that particular line of business, and then reaches out to the relationship leader looking after that country for alignment.

Band 45 jobs – vice-presidents – are evaluated by global committee in the United States. The process is similar, but the compensation committee is made up of more senior managers.

Pricing

Market pricing is conducted separately from the job evaluation process due to the number of salary surveys used to support different lines of business. Amex bands can be translated into survey grades. The same applies to Hay for job evaluation purposes.

Communication

The job evaluation process is not communicated to the workforce as a whole as it is considered irrelevant to them. Everyone knows their grade, and it is only managers who need to understand the process, so communication is focused on them.

The company has recently been concentrating on providing business leaders and relationship leaders with more reference material on understanding job evaluation and the processes they need to follow. A special job evaluation website has recently been set up, targeted at the HR community and people leaders.

Consistency

The key challenge for the evaluators is comparing roles across lines of business and countries and ensuring they are banded fairly in accordance with market economics. For example, should the same type of role be banded the same when one role has a larger scope of impact than the other? The reason why the evaluation committee is so large, the company says, is because it needs expertise from a wide range of people.

Advice

'Do ensure that there is a clear link between the business and the job evaluation process', Paula Holmes, compensation analyst at American Express, says. 'Everyone must be comfortable with the job evaluation process and understand it. And with the benefit of hindsight, your communication materials must be clear, as the success of what you are trying to do depends on their effectiveness.'

Other advice from Paula includes:

▌ ensure that roles and responsibilities are clearly defined and that HR partners and line leaders follow the same process;

▌ implement a tracking system for all jobs that go through the evaluation process;

▌ ensure that managers have to get sign-off for headcount and budget costs before putting a job forward for evaluation;

▌ ensure that internal competencies are aligned for each band and across regional and global markets;

▌ be aware, however, that one size fits all may not work internationally, where different rules and regulations may have to be taken into account;

▌ seek advice from external consultants to ensure that the design of the evaluation process is compliant and manageable;

▌ communicate clearly how the process works;

▌ explain why jobs need to be evaluated;

▌ train HR partners and line leaders.

Anglo American

This case study illustrate how a major multinational has applied job evaluation globally across its senior management population, not to determine a pay structure, but to get a better understanding of the organization and to manage senior level talent across the group.

Context

Anglo American is a global leader in mining. It has a range of high quality, core mining businesses, covering platinum, diamonds, coal, base and ferrous metals, and industrial minerals. Its operations are mainly in Southern Africa, South America, Canada and Australia.

The current company was formed from the merger of Anglo American Corporation of South Africa and Minorco in 1999. It is a FTSE top 20 company, with certain of its constituent divisions being equivalent to FTSE 100 companies in their own right.

The group is managed along fairly decentralized lines. Each key operating business is empowered to manage within the context of its own industry, and the different legislative and social demands of the diverse countries in which those businesses operate, subject to a number of unifying business principles.

Job evaluation history

In the early 1970s the Paterson job evaluation decision-banding scheme was implemented by a predecessor company, Anglo American Corporation of South Africa. It worked reasonably well but needed cumbersome administrative support and had difficulties with grading technical work streams compared to non-technical roles.

This scheme continued in use until the early 1990s. By then the company structure had changed, the support infrastructure for the system had broken down and the robust setting of job evaluation had fallen away. The lack of a coherent framework for grading decisions was exacerbated by the acquisition of companies that all had their own models and approaches to grading. Whereas in South Africa the company continued to maintain a highly hierarchical 23 grade structure, elsewhere there was little structure and, according to Chris Corrin, the company's head of reward, grading decisions were latterly based on no more than 'gut-feel'.

There was also an issue around the use of job titles in the group. In Minorco VP titles had been used for senior roles, whereas Anglo American had made a lot of use of the 'Consultant' job title, which did not translate well internationally or outside the group.

Rationale for a new job evaluation scheme

In 2004 it was decided to introduce a new grading system for the group. By then there had been no reassessment of the group's grading needs for over 30 years.

The aims of the new system were to:

▌ offer global consistency and understanding of roles across business units, functions and locations;
▌ facilitate talent management and career development across the group;
▌ make it easier for people to move roles within and between divisions;
▌ enable the group to recognize dual career paths for managerial and professional/technical roles;
▌ link into technical pay databases where necessary;
▌ provide an opportunity to get rid of the variety of title structures across the group so there would be more comparability and transparency about what was meant by different senior level roles;
▌ support decisions on senior executive remuneration, such as long-term incentive allocation;
▌ evaluate jobs quickly on a common basis to help in mergers and acquisitions, which happen regularly across the group;
▌ provide a common language and a tool for understanding in particular the senior population (of around 1,600 executives) around the world.

Parts of the company had been status-oriented, but it was made quite clear that the new system was not 'tied to parking places', ie not status-driven. The introduction of the scheme coincided with broader efforts within the group to eliminate existing status divisions such as management dining rooms and different tiers of travel for senior managers.

Choosing a new job evaluation scheme

Initially the company embarked on a large pilot study with Hay Consultancy, but decided not to pursue this further. It was considered too complex in a fast-moving organization where senior managers are subject to competing demands for their time and attention. Instead the company decided to implement Watson Wyatt's Global Grading System (GGS), which met the important criteria above. It was judged to:

▌ be conceptually easy and quick to grasp and use;
▌ be readily applicable to a large, devolved group;
▌ be useable without a lot of outside support but employed user-friendly software;
▌ link to pay databases in many countries;
▌ have demonstrated that it had been successfully implemented in other companies worldwide;
▌ enable technical specialists to be recognized.

When GGS was introduced to divisional HR directors, the scheme was well received. There had been widespread acknowledgement that existing arrangements were 'broken' – but it was also felt to be such a big issue to fix that no attempt had been made to do so. The HR directors welcomed the introduction of a unifying system to such an extent that, as Corrin commented, 'the floodgates opened'. The system was immediately used to deal with 'a couple of burning decks'.

Interestingly, Anglo American has been joined as a user of GGS by two of its major international competitors, which means that the bulk of the mining sector is now going to be using the same system.

How GGS works

Watson Wyatt's GGS system is underpinned by a point-factor scheme with seven factors. These are:

1. functional knowledge;
2. business expertise;
3. leadership;
4. problem solving;
5. nature of impact;
6. area of impact;
7. interpersonal skills.

As a large, complex, multinational group with a mixed portfolio of operating companies, Anglo American covers 23 of the 25 pre-determined grades in the GGS system. These grades have been reduced to a seven-band structure covering 17 of the 24 grades available, which extends from chief executive to team manager/professional level, as shown in Table 12.2.

Further bands (8 and below) cover the remaining seven GGS grades and are reserved for local banding frameworks. The broad bands have been used because of a desire to move to a more broad-banded framework, while the 23 GGS levels will underpin them. Staff will be told only what band they are in – not which grade. Bands are described as 'Talent Group' levels, emphasizing that the primary purpose of the scheme is to support career management and mobility across the group.

Table 12.2 Anglo American grades

Anglo 1	Group CEO
Anglo 2	Enterprise Leadership
Anglo 3	Executive Leadership
Anglo 4	Senior Leadership
Anglo 5	Senior managers/professionals
Anglo 6	Managers/professionals
Anglo 7	Team managers/ professionals

Anglo American found that it was necessary to make only minor definitional changes to the GGS model. The company also found that the dual management/ professional career ladder worked very well for them, eg for evaluating specialist technical roles such as geochemists and rock mechanic experts.

How it was done

Chris Corrin, as head of reward and job evaluation project leader, placed a lot of reliance on the consultants, Watson Wyatt. The head office operates with very slim resources – only around 150 staff in total, with a small HR team.

Within each division the process is owned by the appropriate HR director. Depending on the needs and preference of the division, the grading exercise has been done in different ways. However, in all cases line management has been closely involved. Typically jobs were evaluated first by line managers, supported by divisional HR and then calibrated within the division before wider calibration *within* disciplines group-wide and then *between* disciplines group-wide. Corrin has been keen not to dictate how divisions will use GGS below band 7. It is up to each division to decide on the extent to which the system will be used further, particularly since some divisions have a union interface at more junior levels.

Business unit heads have all been involved to some extent – whether within the grading group or to overview the results. On completing the initial evaluation process, divisions will have 'read only' rights on the software for senior bands (3 and above), so any changes at this level will have to go through the head of reward.

On completion of the initial evaluation process, new roles will be evaluated using a new job description, supplemented for changed roles by an additional statement, prepared by the line manager, which describes how the role has changed and why it should be allocated to a higher band. All roles will be evaluated. There will be no 'slotting' allowed and all grading records are held within the GGS system. Only those who have been trained in the GGS methodology are given access to the system.

For the top three bands below chief executive there is centralized review of results through a steering group. This group has been set up to sign-off senior roles, calibrate across divisions and deal with any grading issues or individual appeals that cannot be resolved within a division. Corrin says that where there are inconsistencies this has usually been readily obvious. To avoid delays in the decision-making process the steering group will meet as and when required, on a 'virtual' basis if necessary.

Outcomes

The scheme was due to go live in 2007 as all senior jobs had been evaluated. Corrin even believes that people have enjoyed the process. In practice, 'GGS is a fun system to use. It can be understood readily and is very user friendly.' The process of evaluating roles is quick, makes sense and follows a logical path.

The job evaluation project has thrown light on some organizational structure issues and the use of titles. For example, one division had insisted on using the title 'manager', whereas in other divisions the role would be 'director'. This made it difficult to get people to transfer across on title grounds alone. Now there is a system to help make sense of the titles.

Corrin emphasized that the scheme has not been used in a heavy-handed way to deal with any historical issues of over-payment. The purpose of the scheme is to understand the organization. The introduction of the scheme has helped to clarify what the anomalies are, but individuals who turn out to be overpaid relative to market comparators are 'red-circled' (protected). Anglo American is a fair employer and early clarification about this took the pressure off what they were doing by reducing the 'fear factor'.

Divisions can use GGS as they wish – locally it becomes more of a tool for managing pay, whereas for senior staff this is a minor feature as pay is market-driven. In certain countries there is a need to be particularly sensitive to the local environment. For example, in South Africa 'you tinker at your peril at more junior levels', as the Department of Mines in South Africa still refers to the Paterson system at this stage and the industry is highly regulated.

Learning points

▊ Anglo American threw away the old grade language. It was helpful to stop the organization talking in old grade terms – the new scheme was intended to represent a break with the past.

▊ Anglo American has a lean head office, which meant that the project was very resource-stretched. The project has been a heavy burden of time for the head of reward – ideally it would have been better to have a dedicated multidisciplinary project team.

▊ The divisional HR directors were all given a personal bonus objective to ensure that GGS was in place. It was only when this happened that the process really took off.

Advice

▊ Involve the line – if the project is owned by HR 'you've had it', and credibility is lost.

▊ There is a need to get buy-in from business units.

▊ Do little and simple things – people liked the colourful and easily understood band diagrams.

▊ 'Don't get too theological' – the last thing Anglo American wanted was to create serious staff motivation problems from the grading project. This would have been working against the business, and the reward function is 'not here to cause anguish' or lose talent because of status fear.

▌ It was essential to have multidisciplinary teams within divisions – Corrin observed the power that this gave to 'talk about things sensibly', although these were set later than was ideal.

▌ Keep the system 'pure' and emphasize the fact that it is the role that is being graded, not the person. Unfortunately, this meant that Anglo American did not keep a record of who was the incumbent in each role. This proved to be something of a problem later as new titles were being put into the system as part of the aim to improve titles across the organization that were usually different to those held on SAP. The result was that the titles in GGS sometimes ended up being different from the titles on the internal pay and other systems, which made identification of some job incumbents rather time-consuming.

Convergys EMEA

Context

Convergys is engaged in business consulting with high-tech solutions. It has 1,200 employees in the United Kingdom and 60,000 worldwide.

Overall approach to job evaluation

Convergys uses a single analytical matching scheme for its entire global workforce. The scheme enables it to be sure that a manager on a job code in one country has the same level of responsibility as a manager on the same job code in another. Pay, however, is benchmarked geographically. The company uses up to five salary surveys for this purpose, if all three of its businesses (hi-tech consultancy, professional HR services and call centres) operate within a country, and it uses the same analytical process to match all its jobs into the salary survey databases and matches all the jobs in the databases against the Convergys jobs. The databases of Hewitt Associates, Towers Perrin, Radford and Watson Wyatt surveys are routinely consulted. The team that controls the job evaluation process also sets the pay ranges.

Analytical scheme based on Mercer IPE System

The company uses an analytical matching scheme designed by Mercer Human Resource Consulting and loosely based on its International Position Evaluation (IPE) System, a point-factor rating approach that allows jobs to be ranked across an organization on a global basis. The IPE System analyses jobs according to four 'core' factors: impact, communication, innovation and knowledge, with each of these factors subdivided into 12 dimensions, all of which are individually weighted. The Convergys factors include scope, responsibility and opportunity to influence outcomes.

Global evaluation

Convergys jobs are evaluated centrally, in the United Kingdom, by a team of at least five compensation professionals, several of whom have more than 10 years' experience of the organization. Individuals speak for their geographical region: Europe, Middle East and Africa, Latin America, Asia Pacific, North America and Canada. The process is not computerized. The team is powerful; a new job can neither be created nor recognized until the team has given it a job code. Decisions are unanimous, although discussion may be required to reach a consensus decision. Deviations from the team's decisions are not allowed. There is an official appeal process, but once this has been undergone, the team's decision is final. These arrangements help to prevent pay drift, which is a priority for the company.

Middle managers and seasoned professionals forward jobs for evaluation to the compensation manager for their region, who does a sift, asking questions such as: 'Is this a new job or the result of a reorganization, and is it a new function or one that has evolved from a previous role?' An important consideration is that the 'new' job should reflect how the organization is today, not how it operated in the past. When the regional compensation manager is satisfied, he or she presents the job to the rest of the team, so the process is one team member presenting a job to other team members.

Jobs are 'levelled' (given a job code) according to very detailed written criteria, which the company describes as a verbal points system. The detail is such that Convergys believes that its scheme is defensible under equal pay legislation. The organization has just 350 job descriptions and job codes for its 60,000 staff. Job descriptions are broad, and an 80 per cent match is considered a good match. The evaluation team's encyclopaedic knowledge of jobs in the organization enable it to limit the number of job descriptions, since 'new' jobs usually turn out to be the same as existing jobs elsewhere in the company. This knowledge is indispensable, and the organization would be in some difficulties if any of the long-serving compensation professionals were to leave, says Janna Maxey, senior manager, international compensation and benefits for Europe, the Middle East, Africa and Latin America.

If a manager says that a job has changed, the job code will not be changed unless every other manager responsible for the role throughout the organization agrees. As a result of this process the compensation team is able to keep a very tight grip of earnings throughout the global organization. Job evaluation is not, however, linked to any other aspect of compensation, such as pay progression. There is no agreed competency framework in the organization, though there are some guidelines.

Communication

When managers join the company they attend a workshop in their region which explains how compensation, including job evaluation, works. In addition, there is a compensation folder on the intranet that contains full details of the job evaluation criteria, a template, a checklist and a schedule of when the job evaluation committee meets, which is every Wednesday if there are jobs to evaluate. Managers show a lot of interest in the job evaluation process. This, says Janna Maxey, is because of the links between job evaluation and pay, and the fact that the job code determines the opportunity for merit pay.

Conflict and problems

The only problem Janna has with the current analytical matching arrangements is that they make it hard to prove that jobs in Europe are as demanding as jobs in the United States. There is an assumption that US jobs are bigger jobs because markets are larger. But there is just one Federal authority to deal with in the United States as against 22 governments and sets of regulations in Europe, which makes European jobs more complex. A points-based system would make comparisons more straightforward, Janna says, and would give the process more transparency overall. Apart from this, Convergys is reasonably satisfied with the effectiveness of its evaluation scheme, which has been in place for at least the last 10 years, and has no plans to change it.

If there is ever a conflict between internal equity and paying the market rate for a job, it is dealt with by creating a job family, with market pay for the whole family.

Feedback from managers suggests that they don't always understand how job evaluation works and are frustrated by the apparent bureaucracy of the scheme and the time it takes to process jobs, but the compensation professionals believe that any negativity from managers is the result of having the levelling process taken out of their hands.

Advice

Janna Maxey advises international companies to adopt a single evaluation system for all their staff, regardless of geographical location; a points-based system is best as it is easier to understand. 'Do establish the credibility of your scheme and ensure that the results of the evaluation are absolutely final', Janna says. 'This does not mean that there cannot be an appeal, but after this the organization must accept the decision.'

ABC Limited

This case study describes how, in the United Kingdom, ABC Limited has gone about implementing a worldwide tailored job evaluation scheme, developed by its parent company outside of the United Kingdom.

Context

The name ABC Limited has been used for an international distribution company that was in the process of completing its job evaluation exercise when this book was going to press. The company has grown from a small group of founders to a world-wide business since it was formed in the 1960s. It has grown organically and by acquisition into a company that is recognised globally.

In recent years the company was bought by a large European-based company that had a background in public service provision in a single country. This meant that the parent company was still adapting to its new global positioning whilst at the same time asking the UK company to implement a job evaluation system that it planned to use world-wide. In turn, the UK company had been growing exponentially and was adapting its services to meet a range of both UK domestic and international services. For these reasons the implementation of a new job evaluation and grading system was a difficult path to take, as the external and internal environment were constantly changing.

The need for global job evaluation

The parent company had been a user of the Hay system for years, whereas the newly acquired UK operation did not have a systematic approach to grading and a large part of its workforce were covered by collective agreements, paid either on-spot salaries (operational staff) or on a pay spine (clerical and administrative staff). Elsewhere around the world there were mixed arrangements.

The parent company decided that it needed a consistent basis for grading staff worldwide, top to bottom of the organization. The company developed a classification job evaluation scheme known as the Role Classification System (RCS) with the aid of Mercer Consultancy. Initially the scheme was piloted in North America and then extended across the Americas. As the biggest European operation, the United Kingdom was targeted as the first European user of the scheme.

The grading scheme was intended to determine grades on a common basis around the world, but pay continues to be determined locally for all but the highest positions.

The scheme covers around 5,500 ABC Limited UK employees. This includes all staff in the international operation and managers/professionals only in the domestic operation. In line with the approach taken throughout Europe, the scheme does not include staff in the domestic operation who are covered by collective bargaining arrangements.

Practical implementation in the United Kingdom

Work in the United Kingdom began in 2004, with an initial target completion date of April 2005. There was a strong impetus to meet this deadline. However, the UK market was going through a period of rapid change. The company needed to accommodate a change in customer preferences and to improve profitability through a more cost-effective service model. This meant that the company had to realign its business to match the changing demand by putting in place a new structure and distribution model. The practical impact of the necessary restructuring was that the work on the job evaluation project had to be stopped, a week before the due implementation date.

As a result of the restructuring every role had to be re-evaluated, but this could only be done when the new organization had emerged. In the meantime the company had to continue using the Hay system to fit jobs into the existing grade structure. The scheme was due to go live in mid-2007.

Features of the job evaluation scheme

RCS is a classification scheme, with roles being matched to predetermined grade definitions. There are three 'career level guides' that are used for matching purposes depending on the type of role. The first evaluation decision is therefore whether a role is an 'associate', typically covering administrative through to team leader type roles, or a professional/specialist covering, for example, specialist IT and finance roles, or a 'leadership' role, ie one that focuses on team management. The purpose of the three career level guides is to represent different career paths. The decision about which career level guide to use is based on the primary focus of the role. So, although a role in the specialist/technical path may have a responsibility for other employees, the role is evaluated according to its primary focus, ie application of specialist, professional or technical expertise.

Each career level guide is defined under a number of headings. These vary slightly for each guide. The professional and specialist matrix includes:

▌ skills and qualifications (level of expertise and qualifications);
▌ impact;
▌ problem complexity;
▌ customer and stakeholder (influence of internal and external relationships);
▌ autonomy;
▌ people management;
▌ knowledge (complexity of situations to which knowledge is applied).

The leadership matrix does not include knowledge, but includes a 'process' heading, encompassing the nature of problem solving in the role.

The role of the parent company

The scheme and guidance on pay ranges was developed by the parent company, with little consultation elsewhere. This led to the need for some discussion of compensation and benefits issues. However, as the parent company increasingly shifted its focus from being a major domestic company to a major global group, more staff were being transferred across borders within Europe, which was leading to a greater sharing of ideas.

As part of the initial scheme development, it was decided that the grade structure would run from A to P. The United Kingdom is responsible for grading jobs in grades H and below. The parent company is responsible for grades H and above (UK board members and direct reports, and senior project roles) to ensure international consistency. Of the 550 or so distinct roles in the United Kingdom, around 50 are covered by the parent company.

The UK HR team were given training and a supporting toolkit by a central European HR team, and were then free to get on with implementation. This was subject to the need to discuss any cases for roles at the borderline between UK and parent responsibility.

The evaluation process

The development and implementation of the new job evaluation scheme has been fairly low key. Probably due to the single country history of the parent company, a centralized approach was taken with support from consultants – there was no international involvement in the process.

In the United Kingdom the evaluation process has been conducted through ABC Limited management. Line managers have been responsible for preparing role profiles using a standard template and guidance.

All roles have been evaluated by a six-person grading panel comprising representatives from the business (a representative from marketing and sales, IT, finance, the HR business partner for the relevant part of the business, and two operations representatives – as it represents the largest part of the business). Panels have been facilitated by the UK Reward and Recognition team. Over the course of the project around 20 people were involved as panel members.

The panel has been attended by each head of department, who was invited to explain the roles in his or her department. Each panel lasted around four hours and in this time around 20 to 30 roles could be evaluated. The process slowed down at the tail end of the project because department heads were being called in to the panel to explain roles and structure, but the evaluation panel would be dealing with one-off roles rather than a whole function.

The output from the evaluation panel meeting was an organization chart that showed the relative grading of all staff in the department, which the head of department could review and comment on. Only the panel see the career level guides, so any observations from heads of department were made entirely on the basis of the chart. It was considered that senior line managers were more interested in seeing which roles were on a par and whether the pecking order appeared right, although the lack of supplementary information has meant that this review process has sometimes been a challenge for managers. To ensure consistency, all evaluation results then went to Board members for functional approval, followed by a cross-functional board review.

Post-implementation, ABC Limited planned to continue with the same broad approach as during initial implementation. There were plans for a panel to be used, but on a reconstituted basis including more senior staff.

Implementation plan

The communication plan for implementation focused on three main groups:

1. the board, senior managers and HR business partners;
2. line managers;
3. other employees.

A set of responses to frequently answered questions was prepared along with the main briefing.

Early on in the process a union representative was invited to sit in on a job evaluation panel as an observer, even though unionized staff are not covered by the scheme. The feedback from this was positive. However, there has been no formal consultation with staff covered by the scheme.

On implementation it was intended to inform staff that the main purpose of the grading exercise was to provide greater clarity about the organization structure, so that it would be possible to benchmark internally for fairness and equity. The allocation of roles to grades was going to be put on the intranet so that staff could see what roles fell into each grade. They were not going to be told which career level guide their own role belonged to (associate, leadership or specialist/professional) or given sight of the guides.

On initial implementation it was also intended that information for staff would not emphasize a pay link, as the total reward salary ranges were still in the course of development. However, there would need to be some individual follow-up because it was anticipated that when the pay ranges were finalized, around 1 per cent of staff would be above the maximum of their grade.

Implementation did not include scope for employees to appeal, on the basis that gradings had been agreed by the heads of department and in the context of the new organization structure.

The pay link

ABC Limited in the United Kingdom was planning to move to total reward ranges that encompass base pay plus pension, cars, life insurance and private medical insurance, but exclude holidays. The plan was for these ranges to apply to all new staff, but not to existing staff, who would have their existing entitlements preserved. Although the parent company set the pay range spread between 75 and 125 per cent of each grade mid-point, it was agreed that this should be reduced to 80 to 120 per cent in the United Kingdom, as the United Kingdom applied a job family approach, so there was no need for such large spreads in salary within grades.

The UK HR function is aware that some UK-based staff in specialist areas are paid though a non-UK payroll. It was recognized that for these roles the United Kingdom would need to liaise with their colleagues elsewhere in Europe to ensure that pay levels do not get out of line with each other.

Despite the implementation delay, the UK evaluation results have been given to other European countries as example benchmarks to use in their own evaluations. All countries of operation have been given the same centralized training. Also, the United Kingdom has shared its experience with other countries.

Advice

▌ Do not underestimate the administrative task involved. This requires attention to detail. The project involved a massive coordination exercise across the company. This included understanding what distinct roles there were, preparing role profiles, creating organization charts that could be used by job evaluation panels – and the need to be able to continually track job information when job titles did not tally across these documents and spreadsheets.

▌ Job evaluation requires a lot of input from those that are providing role information, panel members and the HR/reward and recognition function. Therefore before committing to the project, take account of what other priorities there are for the human resources team and the organization as a whole.

▌ Be mindful of the impact of potential organizational change. If there is impending change, think carefully about whether it is the right time to embark on the project.

▌ Secure top management approval and commitment. This needs the leadership of the organization to really understand the implications of going ahead with the scheme. In the case of ABC Limited, stronger involvement might have meant that the board would have been able to predict the potential impact of impending organizational change on the project, which may have affected the timing of the project.

▌ Ensure that the governance processes are in place so that there is a disciplined approach to dealing with changing and new roles, and to prevent potential duplication of job titles, and variations in role profiles and organization charts.

▌ Try and start with clear job descriptions and organization structure at the outset.

▌ Invest in the appropriate tools and ensure that there are the appropriate skill sets to support the project. ABC Limited used Excel throughout. The organization management module of SAP, which would support the continual need to redesign organization charts, was due to be introduced only on completion of the project.

▌ Try to conduct job evaluation in a stable environment. Not only was the company restructured during the course of the ABC Limited project, but the chief executive and human resources director were both changed.

Greenpeace International

This case study shows how an international campaigning organization has been able to provide a common framework to evaluating roles, whilst offering a flexible approach to meet the differing needs of a highly devolved organization.

Context

Greenpeace is a global environmental organization, consisting of Greenpeace International, in Amsterdam, and 27 national and regional offices around the world, providing a presence in 41 countries. These national/regional offices are largely autonomous in carrying out jointly agreed global campaign strategies within the local context they operate in, and in seeking the necessary financial support from donors to fund this work.

The development and coordination of these global strategies is the task of Greenpeace International. It also monitors the development and performance of national and regional Greenpeace offices and provides a range of services to these offices such as the operation of Greenpeace ships and IT support.

Offices around the world have their own HR support. In large offices, such as that in the United Kingdom, there is a small dedicated HR team; in other offices the role is combined with other infrastructure support functions, such as finance or office management.

Developing a common approach to job evaluation

Across the world a range of approaches had been used to set pay. Some offices such as that in Germany had developed their own job evaluation system; in others the approach was more ad hoc. Two separate initiatives, one in the United Kingdom and one in Amsterdam, were to lead to the development of a more coordinated framework for job evaluation and grading around the world.

In 2004 the UK office decided to develop a more systematic and defensible basis for grading jobs through a tailor-made point-factor scheme. Around the same time the new head of human resources for Greenpeace International, Tascha Tinneveld, was keen to develop a new grade structure for the international office in Amsterdam and a framework that could be used elsewhere, as a number of offices were expressing interest in developing new grading structures. A more consistent approach would also support the international transfer of people around Greenpeace, which tended to be dealt with on a case-by-case basis. However, as Greenpeace is a federal organization, Tinneveld was not in a position to develop a scheme that had to be used worldwide, only to influence and provide support to the Greenpeace network of offices. This could be done through regular liaison with other offices and regular skills sharing events that brought together colleagues around the world involved in people management issues.

The first initiative took place in the United Kingdom. In late 2004 a project team, including functional and union representatives, developed a point-factor scheme. The aim was to create a scheme that was simple to administer. The outcome of the development and testing was a scheme with nine factors, all with five levels, except for an environmental demands factor, which was split into two sub-factors, each with three levels. Each level within each factor scored the same number of points, so point scores could be readily calculated and recorded on an Excel spreadsheet.

The Greenpeace International initiative started after the UK project team had already completed their scheme development. Again, the process involved a cross-functional project team including a member of the works council. Although the international project team were aware of the UK work, they initially decided to start from scratch, without reference to the UK factors. However, they were supported in the process by the same external consultant, who could share some of the learning from the UK experience. The outcome was remarkably similar. Most of the factors ended up the same or very close to the UK scheme, although the international scheme ended up with only seven factors by combining a couple of factors into one and excluding an environmental demands factor. This was because environmental demands were not as important to international office roles as some of the more action-focused UK roles, and because the UK office had found that this factor was subject to personal interpretation and potential bias, and there had been some debate about whether it should be taken out of the scheme.

Greenpeace International took its job evaluation development work one step further. Around 30 benchmark roles were evaluated using the point-factor scheme. This was then translated into a six-band matrix that could be used to evaluate additional roles with a matching process. The banding matrix further simplified the factors by combining analysis and decision-making factors within a single heading and doing the same for people responsibilities and resources (see the example of one level in Table 12.3).

The similarity between the UK and the international schemes indicated that a common framework could be used worldwide. This was also tested when

Table 12.3 Greenpeace – definition of band C

	Band C – typically:
Knowledge and skills	Has broad/deep working knowledge and proficiency in own area of expertise: may be a recognized source of expertise in this area
Communication	Applies a range of communication and interpersonal skills to interact with others on a range of issues of varying complexity – whether staff, stakeholders or external opinion formers/external bodies
Analysis and decision making	Makes decisions that impact on the delivery and quality of work in the unit within a broad framework of operational, professional or creative guidelines. Uses initiative to come up with recommendations or new working methods/approaches in own area of work by interpreting information, concepts or data from diverse sources
Planning	Likely to be involved in planning, prioritizing and organizing the work/resources of others, either within own unit or for major project strands
Responsibility for others and resources	Typically has formal responsibility for others (except where role is high-level specialist), and will have either a formal or delegated resource responsibility

staff with people management responsibilities from around the world met for a skills-sharing forum. As part of this session the group conducted an exercise to see if they could agree a set of factors that they felt would be appropriate for Greenpeace internationally. This exercise again revealed a high degree of similarity with the factors that had already been developed in the United Kingdom and Amsterdam.

The outcome of this development work and discussions with colleagues internationally meant that there was a growing awareness that the organization had a set of job evaluation techniques and tools that could be offered to other offices around the world as and when they needed it. Depending on their need and preference, offices could be offered the point-factor scheme or the role matching tool as well as accompanying guidance and job questionnaires. This flexibility was ideal for an organization where the needs of the offices differed, depending on their size, local management style and preference.

As a federal organization, Greenpeace International was not in a position to insist that other offices adopt a common approach, but Tinneveld could encourage offices to share a common starting point whenever offices were ready to review their pay and grading structure. There was also a body of knowledge within the organization about how to evaluate roles, both within the UK and International, so practical support could be offered to their colleagues elsewhere.

By mid-2007 support had been given to Brazil, China and the Nordic countries, with Brazil and the Nordic countries preferring a role matching approach, and China favouring a point-factor approach. Another four offices have shown interest in the new scheme and are likely to adopt the new approach. Tinneveld says that this flexible approach has been of real benefit to Greenpeace because it makes international exchanges much easier if offices around the world adopt the same system. Furthermore, as the offices can choose the option of the role matrix or point-factor scheme, the culture of the country, size of the different offices and their management style can fit easily to one or other of the options.

NEC Electronics (Europe)

Context

NEC Electronics, which is involved in semiconductor sales, marketing and technical support in Europe, employs 90 people in the United Kingdom and 500 in Europe. In 2002 the company brought in a new point-factor job evaluation system, based on Towers Perrin's INSitE methodology and data, to provide the foundation for a pan-European pay system to cover the eight countries in which it operates. There is now a common pay and grading structure benchmarked against the INSitE data in each country. All jobs across the organization are evaluated centrally, in the United Kingdom. The purpose of the scheme is to match pay to the market. The previous evaluation system was based on simple job titles, which failed to differentiate sufficiently between roles.

The company already used INSitE, a European survey covering professionals, middle management, support and production staff in the information and communication technology (ICT) sector, for pay benchmarking. It was keen to work with Towers Perrin to build a new pay structure that could be closely matched with the INSitE market data. Since the structure was introduced, the company has converted the INSitE factors into competencies, which are used in the performance assessment system.

Process

Together with Towers Perrin, the company set up a cross-functional project team consisting of staff from all levels in the organization. Questionnaires were completed by job holders for the 270 roles in NEC Europe and the calculation of the scores was computerized. Some jobs were re-evaluated when the scores were not as expected. Role scores were then placed in rank order, with lines drawn across at appropriate points to establish a hierarchy of grades. The resulting structure follows the INSitE career ladders, and is based on five job families (client management, corporate and engineering, technician support, business support and production/operations). Individual jobs are graded, and individuals are also allocated to one of three levels, which determines the pay range for the job:

Level 1 – 25th to 50th percentile of INSitE market rates.
Level 2 – 50th to 75th percentile of INSitE market rates.
Level 3 – 75th to 90th percentile of INSitE market rates.

Factors used by NEC in a hybrid version of Towers Perrin's INSitE:

1. Professional expertise.
2. Role complexity.
3. Innovation and creativity.
4. Autonomy and independence.
5. Networking and communication.
6. Use of resources.
7. Decision making – a) own decisions; b) informing and advising others.
8. Commercial and business impact.

Communication

A series of roadshows were held throughout Europe to explain the grading system and the new pay structure, and all the background material was put on the intranet. This included the whole of the INSitE methodology, the codes and the role profiles. Alan Berck-May, NEC's compensation and benefits manager Europe, now questions this approach, as Towers Perrin is changing all the role descriptions. In retrospect, he says, NEC may not have needed to advertise these, since individuals just need to know their grade and their level. Salary bands are advertised neither internally nor externally. There have been no challenges from individuals in the five years that the scheme has been in operation.

Maintenance

As a relatively small organization, NEC says that it doesn't really have any new jobs, other than those that are amalgamations of existing jobs. The only maintenance required is picking up on questionable gradings, which may come to light when a job is being filled. 'Sometimes a result just doesn't look right, regardless of the points score', Alan says. When this happens, Alan might go back to the score, but he emphasizes the importance of a 'sense test' or 'gut feel', and the flexibility that the INSitE methodology offers, to accommodate jobs that have to be looked at on a one-off basis. The company has a 'free and easy approach' to promotion, he says, so a post holder who is performing highly can be promoted to boost his or her salary. As pay is so tightly matched to the market, grade drift is not a problem.

Conflict and problems

The job evaluation system that underpins the market matching on which NEC Europe's pay arrangements are based generally works well. 'If your organization isn't used to facts and figures, you may need to try another approach', Alan believes. Problems arise for NEC, however, when someone the company wishes to appoint wants a salary considerably in excess of level 3, the 90th percentile for the grade. Depending on how desirable a recruit the person is, the company may choose to pay over the odds to obtain scarce skills or experience. The Towers Perrin database provides averages and percentiles, Alan says, which are extremely useful, but there will always be exceptions. 'Whilst we are aware of some issues around internal equity, we have not had any direct challenges to date. However, general managers are becoming much more knowledgeable about how the salary system works and are looking to address issues in a structured way in order to proactively manage retention and staff morale issues.'

Weighting is another issue. At the moment, factors are not weighted, which results in a flat range of scores. Weighting, especially for the impact of a job, would result in points scores representing roles more accurately than at present, Alan believes. The cost of developing and using the software has also been a problem. As a small company, NEC Europe decided not to invest in Towers Perrin's latest software. This has resulted in extra work as the old stand-alone software is creaking.

International issues

The same JE scheme is used throughout the organization, which has presented no difficulties. NEC Europe is a relatively small company and uses a common language, which helps, although job questionnaires are available in French and German, as is all the background information on the INSitE scheme, and roadshows were held in each country.

Advice

Alan says: 'Do find a scheme that is congruent with the organization; the Towers Perrin point-factor scheme is easy to explain to engineers, so works well for an organization like NEC. And involve your own staff in a project team that does the fact finding and designs the final grading structure. Communicate the how, why and when to everyone, and move to your own company language for implementation, rather than staying with the consultants' language. This will enable you to set out changes in the consultants' methodology, which NEC can't do as it is using INSitE role descriptors rather than its own.'

REFERENCES

Bloom, M, Milkovitch, G T and Mira, A (2003) International compensation: learning from how managers respond to variation in local host contexts, *International Journal of Human Resource Management,* **14** (8), pp 1350–67
Perkins, S J (2006) *International Reward and Recognition,* CIPD, London

Part 4

The Practice of Job Evaluation

13

Job evaluation in action

The e-reward 2007 survey of job evaluation produced a comprehensive picture of job evaluation in action in the United Kingdom. There were 117 respondents to the survey, 65 per cent from the private sector, the rest from the public and voluntary sectors. A summary of the survey data is set out in Table 13.1.

Two health warnings about the e-reward 2007 survey need to be borne in mind. First, the survey is something of a self-selecting sample and there is always a concern that a 'single-issue' survey like this might exaggerate the level of take-up because those actually using job evaluation – or planning to introduce a scheme – were more interested in the subject and hence more likely to respond. To safeguard against this and to get the richest possible data, replies were sought not only from organizations that use job evaluation and but also from those that do not.

Secondly, although the e-reward 2007 survey is based on a reasonable spread of replies from almost all sections of industry and commerce, there was a particularly strong response from public services and the voluntary sector – a third of all returns – and job evaluation is more widespread here than in the private sector.

The results of the survey are presented in this chapter under the following headings:

Table 13.1   Summary of 2007 job evaluation survey data

Use formal job evaluation	60%
Type of scheme:	
Point-factor	70%
Factor comparison	5%
Analytical matching	12%
Job classification	5%
Job ranking	4%
Non-analytical matching	5%
Development of scheme	
Tailor-made	20%
Proprietary brand (consultant's scheme)	60%
Hybrid (adapted proprietary brand)	20%
Computer-aided scheme	44%
Factors used in analytical schemes	
Average number of factors	5
Range of numbers of factors	3–14
Number of different factors	63
Scheme design wholly or partly aligned to competency framework	24%
Explicitly weighted point-factor schemes	53%
Scoring system progressive (geometrical)	61%
Tell individuals their job evaluation scores	
Yes	36%
No	64%
Plan changes to scheme	31%

▌   incidence of job evaluation;

▌   type of scheme;

▌   reasons for using job evaluation;

▌   use of computer-aided job evaluation;

▌   features of job evaluation schemes;

▌ operation of job evaluation;

▌ doing without job evaluation;

▌ effectiveness of job evaluation;

▌ advice on job evaluation.

INCIDENCE OF JOB EVALUATION

The survey reveals that:

▌ Six out of 10 of all the 117 respondents (60 per cent) operated a formal job evaluation scheme for at least one group of employees;

▌ just under a third of all respondents (32 per cent) have never operated a scheme;

▌ only 8 per cent of the sample had used job evaluation in the past but had since abandoned their scheme.

The e-reward figure of 60 per cent of organizations using job evaluation compares with the 55 per cent identified by the Chartered Institute of Personnel and Development's 2007 survey and the 49 per cent established by the IRS 2003 survey. These variations can be attributed to differences between the samples.

The analysis shows that the incidence of job evaluation has increased significantly since the last e-reward survey in 2003 when it was 45 per cent, but this rise may have been exaggerated by differences in the samples of organizations the surveys covered.

The 2007 survey reveals that job evaluation was more common in bigger organizations: among the respondents who use job evaluation the median workforce size (the mid-point in the range) was 3,700, while the median in the sample of organizations without job evaluation was only 250.

The number of schemes

Organizations were increasingly introducing integrated pay structures supported by a single job evaluation scheme, although they do not always include executive directors. As the Equal Opportunities Commission (2003) points out:

The most reliable and objective approach to determining equal value is to use a single job evaluation scheme designed and implemented to take account of equal value considerations and your specific job population... Those organizations, which do not operate a single job evaluation scheme covering all employees, should seriously consider introducing such a scheme.

The survey found that 74 per cent of the organizations with job evaluation did indeed use only one scheme. This figure rose to 78 per cent among the private sector respondents, while the comparable figure in the public services and voluntary sectors was 70 per cent.

Organizations without job evaluation

The analysis of the sample of 47 respondents without job evaluation shows that the vast majority – more than eight in 10 (81 per cent) – have never operated a scheme, and only 19 per cent said that their organization had any past experience of formal job evaluation. What is most striking is that among the 47 respondents who do not currently operate a formal job evaluation scheme, 45 per cent had plans to implement such a scheme in the future. Put another way, if employers' intentions translate into practice, only 22 per cent of all the organizations polled (26 respondents) will not be operating a formal job evaluation scheme in coming years.

Differences between sectors

The survey shows that job evaluation was much more widespread in the public services and voluntary sectors (79 per cent) than in the private sector (51 per cent).

Job evaluation was relatively common in the private sector amongst finance organizations (10 of the 14 respondents; 71 per cent), as well as manufacturing sectors such as engineering (seven of 13 respondents; 54 per cent).

In the private sector, the incidence of job evaluation has risen from 39 per cent four years ago to 49 per cent now, while in the public and voluntary sectors it's up from 68 to 80 per cent.

Date of introduction

A significant proportion of schemes (25 per cent) have been in use for three years or less. Many of the respondents have fairly long-standing schemes – more than two-fifths (44 per cent) have been in operation for 10 years or more. Overall, the median length of time that schemes have been in operation was 6.0 years and the average was 9.4 years. Once started, job evaluation seems to stay.

Job evaluation abandoned

Among the respondents without job evaluation, just under a fifth (19 per cent) have operated one of the main types of formal job evaluation in the past but have since abandoned it. Among the reasons mentioned were a move to broad banding, a major business reorganization, and a belief that the scheme was too bureaucratic and cumbersome.

TYPE OF SCHEME

Point-factor schemes were by far the most popular (70 per cent of the 82 schemes). The e-reward 2003 survey also found that 70 per cent of schemes used this approach. Such schemes were more likely to cover managers than their manual counterparts. Among the sample of 57 point-factor schemes in the analysis, manual workers were covered by 67 per cent of the schemes, compared with 95 per cent of professional, technical and administrative staff and 100 per cent of managers.

Of the five other types of scheme examined in the survey, analytical matching schemes were used in more than one in 10 schemes. This is a relatively new development. Analytical matching is prompted by the pressure to speed up and streamline the implementation of job evaluation. Its popularity has increased as a result of its use in a number of well-known projects including the NHS Agenda for Change programme and some universities.

The three types of non-analytical scheme – job classification, job ranking and non-analytical matching – were each operated in around one in 20 schemes.

Tailor-made scheme or consultant's package?

Tailor-made schemes were in the minority among the respondents with job evaluation schemes – only 20 per cent had them. The packages offered by consultants (proprietary brands) dominated the job evaluation market – 60 per cent of the survey sample had purchased a proprietary brand and another 20 per cent had adopted a hybrid scheme, ie a proprietary brand modified to meet the needs of the organization.

The Hay Group's Guide Chart Profile method was by far the most popular (58 per cent of the proprietary or hybrid schemes). The next most common approach was Link HR Systems, used in 12 per cent of the schemes. Towers Perrin and Pilat HR Solutions were each used in 10 per cent of the schemes.

REASONS FOR USING JOB EVALUATION

As might be expected, the reasons given by organizations for using job evaluation, shown in Table 13.2, focus mainly on developing an equitable pay structure.

The following were some of the explanations given by respondents for using job evaluation:

▌ Ensures sensible organization design, ie not too many layers, and sensible spans of control – Hay is very good at this.

▌ A language for discussing the size of roles; assist in slotting roles into new grade framework; framework for career development; facilitate global mobility.

Table 13.2   Reasons for using job evaluation

Reason	% of respondents
Provides basis for design and maintenance of rational and defensible pay structure	94
Ensures equitable pay structure	93
Helps in management of job relativities	87
Ensures the principle of equal pay for work of equal value	84
Assimilates newly created or changing jobs into existing structures	79
Compares internal pay levels with market rates	74
Facilitates lateral moves and internal mobility	40
Harmonizes pay structures as a result of merger or acquisition	34
Provides a framework for identifying and measuring competencies	20
Helps develop performance management and appraisal systems	19

∎ Defensible in terms of challenges for our employee representation body that provides representatives to sit on the job evaluation panels.

∎ We use it as part of our internal promotion process and as an opportunity to review jobs as they become vacant.

∎ May also use for measuring competencies in future.

∎ Provision of benefits.

∎ Job evaluation sits behind the grading structure, which is linked to benefits. Main use is to get market data to inform pay decisions – others, especially equal value, were considered to be 'nice to haves' but were not the main driver for its use.

∎ To prepare for eventual merger.

∎ Three key reasons for bringing a role to evaluation: new job, job upgrade, organization restructure.

USE OF COMPUTER-AIDED JOB EVALUATION

Computers were used in different ways by 44 per cent of the surveyed organizations that have formal job evaluation. While it is far from the norm, there were signs that their use is growing – the comparable figure in the e-reward 2003 survey was only 28 per cent.

However, more than half the sample used computers simply to maintain a database and record the rationale for evaluations. Those that were fully computer-aided used computers as follows:

∎ interactive collection of job information – job holders and their manager, advised by a facilitator, jointly answer series of interrelated questions on the screen and resulting data are converted into job evaluation scores (10 per cent);

∎ conversion of paper questionnaires (role profiles) into job evaluation scores (13 per cent);

∎ online entry of responses to questionnaire converted into job evaluation scores (32 per cent).

Computer-aided job evaluation is often used in national schemes such as those developed for local government, higher education establishments and further education colleges, and 52 per cent of the respondents who use it were public sector organizations. Respondents who used any of the three fully computer-aided approaches appeared confident that they were beneficial – in record keeping, speeding up the process, achieving greater consistency in evaluations, and eliminating much of the paperwork. Respondents were less convinced that fully-computer-aided approaches add greater credibility to the process.

However, computer-aided job evaluation is not all plain sailing. Some concern was expressed about the time taken to complete the process (mentioned by 27 per cent of the sample), the cost of implementation (20 per cent), and developing the skills required to operate the system (20 per cent). There was little concern about lack of transparency.

FEATURES OF JOB EVALUATION SCHEMES

The survey investigated the use of factors, weighting and the scoring system in job evaluation schemes.

Job evaluation factors

An analysis of the factor lists provided by respondents for the 69 schemes shows that:

- the total number of different factors was 63;
- the average number of factors was 5.6, while the range of factors was from 3 to 14;
- just under half of the schemes (48 per cent) contained three factors (mainly the popular Hay Guide Chart Profile method);
- as many as 80 per cent of schemes had seven factors of less;
- nearly one in 10 schemes (9 per cent) had 14 factors.

The 10 most frequently used factors in tailor-made analytical schemes in rank order were:

1. Knowledge and skills.
2. Responsibility.

3. Problem solving.

4. Decision making.

5. People management.

6. Relationships/contacts.

7. Working conditions.

8. Mental effort.

9. Impact.

10. Creativity.

Competency-related factors

Competency-related job evaluation aims to value the work people do in terms of the competencies required to perform effectively in different roles and at different levels in the organization. It is usually based on a competency framework, which provides the starting point for selecting factors and defining levels. Thus the values built into the competency framework were integrated with those contained in the factor plan. However, competency-related factors were not used to any great extent. Less than a quarter of respondents with analytical schemes reported that their factor plan had been wholly or partly designed to reflect the competencies included in their organization's competency framework. The vast majority (76 per cent) of participants said that their factor plan was 'not at all' designed to reflect their competency framework.

Weighting

The survey established that 81 per cent of the schemes used by respondents were either explicitly or implicitly weighted. Just over half (53 per cent) were explicitly weighted by increasing the maximum points available for what were regarded as more important factors, while 28 per cent were implicitly weighted by allocating more levels and therefore points to some factors than others. Implicit weighting is most likely to take place when there is a large number of factors – 10 or more – and the impact of explicitly weighting any factors is less (unless the weighting is so disproportionate that the non-weighted factors become immaterial).

Out of the 33 factors mentioned as being weighted, almost half (48 per cent), were knowledge and skills.

Scoring model

Each level in the factor plan has to be allocated a points value so that there is a scoring progression from the lowest to the highest level. A decision needs to be made on how to set the scoring progression within each factor.

There were two methods. First, the arithmetic or linear approach assumes that there are consistent step differences between factor levels – eg a four-level factor might be scored 10, 20, 30 and 40. Alternatively, geometric scoring assumes that there are progressively larger score differences at each successive level in the hierarchy to reflect progressive increases in responsibility. Thus the levels may be scored 10, 20, 35 and 55, rather than 10, 20, 30 and 40. This increases the scoring differentiation between higher-level jobs.

Less than three in 10 of the respondents with analytical schemes (27 per cent) used an arithmetic or linear approach. The remaining 73 per cent used the geometric method. The preference for geometrical progression probably arises because it provides for clear step differences and therefore indicates justified grade breaks more easily than arithmetic progression. It also increases the scoring differences between higher grade jobs, which pleases those affected, although it does not usually affect the rank order.

OPERATION OF JOB EVALUATION

One of the principal aims of the 2007 survey was to provide more information on how organizations operated their job evaluation schemes rather than to concentrate on the incidence of job evaluation, as in 2003. The results are summarized below.

Conflict between internal equity and external competitiveness

The survey questionnaire asked how organizations deal with a situation in which there is a conflict between internal equity and external competitiveness – ie when paying the market rate could mean overriding the principle of internal equity as established by job evaluation. Reconciling these conflicting requirements is usually a balancing act. Organizations cannot safely ignore equity because if they do, they will create unequal pay situations and dissatisfaction amongst employees. However, they ignore the need to be competitive at their peril.

The most common policy, cited by 46 per cent of the sample, was to use market supplements or premiums – additional payments to the rate for the job as determined by job evaluation (internal equity), which reflect market rates. Just under a quarter (23 per cent) had created a 'market group' or job family structure in which each 'family' had its own grade and pay structure that takes account of different levels of market rates between families. The size of jobs and rates of pay can vary between the same levels in different job families. As many as 16 per cent of the respondents said that they were 'market-driven' – ie they ignored internal equity and paid market rates. Surprisingly, 10 per cent said that they ignored market rates.

Information on scores

Whether or not to disclose job evaluation scores to individuals is a vexed question. Practice varies greatly. In principle, if the system is to be truly open and transparent, then all details of the evaluation scores for a job should be made known to anyone who has the right to ask for them. If such details are not disclosed, it may lead to mistrust in the objectivity and fairness of the system. It is all too easy, however, for people who have not been trained in job evaluation to misunderstand or misinterpret such detailed information, and this level of openness may create more difficulties than it solves. The survey revealed that:

▌ informing individuals of their score is a minority pursuit – only 36 per cent of respondents did so;

▌ among the respondents who disclose information, 54 per cent did so on request, while 42 per cent automatically informed all employees;

▌ more than three-quarters of respondents (77 per cent) reckoned that there have not been any problems with informing or not informing employees of their scores;

▌ among the sample making scores known to employees, problems cited by respondents include staff 'chasing' points, numerous appeals for re-grading and a host of 'amateur evaluations';

▌ some of those not disclosing mentioned concerns about lack of transparency.

Some of the comments made by organizations that do disclose scores were set out below:

▌ Although we give them the score for each factor level, we do not disclose how this impacts on the overall 'score' of the job, or indeed what the rank order of their job is or what the 'actual' weightings were. Staff do know that particular factors were either high, medium or low in terms of weighting.

▌ Results were issued to all staff and a rank order of posts was made available for all staff to see. This resulted in a lot of 'amateur evaluations' and a lot of unease between particular work groups. The difficulty we faced was that we had received several Freedom of Information requests at this time, so the decision to release the information was forced by the level of anxiety, etc amongst staff.

▌ There were issues in the past with staff 'chasing points' or comparing jobs. Procedure is to inform management of the score, who inform the post holder, if requested or at their discretion.

▌ Employees were informed of the grade of their role, rather than the specific point score. Where an employee, line manager or trade union representative is unhappy with the grade allocated to a role, they can request that it is reviewed under a grade review procedure.

▌ On implementation, everyone was informed of their score; this led to a lot of appeals for re-grading, particularly from those close to the points boundary.

Comments from respondents whose organizations do not disclose scores were:

▌ Employees periodically question the perceived lack of transparency of the scheme – usually those individuals who challenge the career band they are in. Employees were advised of their career band – and if relevant may be advised whether their job sits high or low in the range, but not of the actual evaluation score.

▌ Original evaluators will have scores – they will convey outcome to requesting manager. In some cases, in the event of an appeal, factor scores have been discussed with employees.

▌ Employees have raised complaints about their grade and requested information on how the grade was determined.

▌ Knowing scores can drive inappropriate behaviours in an attempt to increase scores.

▌ Individuals believed it impossible to lodge an appeal without sight of the scores and comments from the evaluator. This has resulted in a grievance. The procedure has recently been reviewed and a summary of information from the job evaluation committee is now given to those wishing to appeal on application.

▌ Managers can have the scores but not the employees – this causes a problem of transparency and also leads to managers manipulating information to get the grade they want.

▌ Previously individuals were aware of their Watson Wyatt grade that sat within their band. This caused too much focus upon the grade and we found individuals changing roles and applying for jobs internally just because the jobs were one grade higher despite them being better suited to and needed in their original role.

▌ It's less about the scores – much more about not understanding the whole system.

Use of analytical matching

Analytical matching has emerged in recent years as an important technique designed to speed up the implementation of job evaluation while still preserving an analytical approach. An analysis of how matching is carried out in the 10 analytical matching schemes in our sample shows that:

▌ profiles for individual roles were matched with grade or level profiles expressed in terms of the same job evaluation factors – cited by one respondent;

▌ profiles for individual roles or jobs were matched with profiles of benchmark jobs that have already been graded expressed in terms of the same job evaluation factors – cited by three respondents;

▌ both of the above – cited by six respondents.

Grade and pay structure design – decisions on number of grades

A new grade and pay structure has been designed by 40 per cent of the respondents within the last four years. The following replies were received to the question: 'How did you decide on the number of grades, bands or levels?':

- Our broad bands define benefit breaks, and we looked at the market to determine at which Hay score the various benefits were offered. We also took a view on where it would be logical to create the band breaks, bearing in mind the jobs in the organization. We ended up with just six bands.

- Looked at various options and moved to the most appropriate one, taking account of cost, assimilation and fit with the outside market.

- Management structure only – grades were determined by using grade widths of two 'know-how steps'. Four grades were sufficient to cover the range of job sizes.

- Broad-banded pay structure for head office roles only – six bands. Broad bands chosen because we had come from nothing and wanted something flexible and not too bureaucratic.

- Based on an internal analysis of the number of levels of hierarchy (or reporting levels), and an external analysis of the market data and how many levels were provided for a particular job family.

- Designed a series of job families and identified and drafted appropriate levels of activity within each family. Each job family level was then evaluated. This provided a 'fit' into a series of benefit bands. The salary ranges were determined by appropriate market data for each job family level.

- Divided the whole job hierarchy into sections where obvious gaps appeared.

- Five bands from original eight grades.

Grade and pay structure design – use of job evaluation

Respondents made the following comments on how they used job evaluation to guide the design of their grade and pay structure:

▌ We looked at where roles naturally formed clusters and for natural boundaries. As a result some bands contain a lot more jobs than others.

▌ We began by looking at the nature of roles at each point score and where the natural boundaries may be. Then, we analysed the results of the evaluations and considered whether the number of roles at each level was appropriate, and whether the boundary lines may require any minor adjustment to avoid too many roles being close to the boundaries. We see it as an iterative process.

▌ We used the rank order of jobs following the evaluation process, allowed obvious grade boundaries to be developed.

▌ The evaluation of the job family levels determined how each level would fit into a pre-existing benefit band structure, which was determined by job unit ranges.

▌ We used a job evaluation hierarchy to determine grade boundaries based on two Hay 'know-how' steps and levels of 'problem solving'. Benchmark jobs evaluated. Other roles slotted in around these.

Use of job evaluation in managing a broad-banded structure

As Table 13.3 shows, respondents still tended to use job evaluation to manage a broad-banded structure in spite of the original claim for such structures that they would obviate the need for job evaluation.

Table 13.3 Use of job evaluation in managing a broad-banded structure

Method	% adopting
Allocate jobs to bands by reference to definitions of band boundaries expressed in terms of job evaluation points	52
Determine the position of jobs in bands according to their points score	27
Use analytical matching to allocate jobs to bands	18
Influence the position of jobs in bands by reference to their points score having taken into account market rates	3

It is interesting that none of the respondents admitted to positioning roles in bands purely on the basis of their market rates.

DOING WITHOUT JOB EVALUATION

Overall, 40 per cent of survey respondents did not have a job evaluation scheme, 32 per cent have never operated a scheme and 8 per cent had used job evaluation in the past but had since abandoned it.

The survey provides empirical evidence on how organizations that do not make use of formal job evaluation schemes decide pay relativities. It revealed that the majority of the sample (72 per cent) used managerial judgement to decide pay for managers and professional, technical and administrative staff. Guidance on managerial judgement provided by market pricing was the main influence on the pay-setting process for both managers (used by 89 per cent of respondents) and professional, technical and administrative staff (79 per cent). Only 30 per cent of the sample used this approach for their manual workers. According to respondents, managerial judgement on pay levels was also based on a generally agreed understanding of relative levels of jobs and therefore grades. In some cases negotiations or custom and practice determined pay relativities, and managements saw no point in superimposing job evaluation.

Other approaches mentioned by respondents include:

▌ We abandoned the job evaluation system and left a matrix and grading system that is used and understood, but many have reservations about its efficacy.

▌ Job evaluation used on an ad hoc basis for isolated roles – in cases where new roles arise and market data is necessary to benchmark salary and also in the case of internal dispute resolution.

▌ We have a 'career ladder' structure with defined competencies, skills, business impact, etc. Roles were placed within them and then graded from market survey data.

Approach adopted by international organizations

Among the international organizations contributing to the survey, just under two-thirds (65 per cent) adopted the same job evaluation approach in all international locations. The main reason given for this was to achieve 'global consistency'.

EFFECTIVENESS OF JOB EVALUATION

One of the key issues examined in the e-reward survey was the effectiveness of job evaluation. This was done by seeking the opinions of respondents and a caveat is necessary. Self-rating can be an unreliable measure and it means that caution should be exercised in interpreting the results. The views were mainly those of reward and HR specialists, who may be predisposed in favour of their system because they were involved in its design. That said, an impressive level of confidence was expressed – 88 per cent reported that they were highly or reasonably satisfied because, for example, their scheme was credible, reputable, easy to understand and provided a robust basis for a defensible pay and grading structure. Here are some of the positive comments:

▌ We have an approach which includes a good balance between robustness and pragmatism, ensuring that the grading is robust and defensible, but which doesn't take up too much management time to administer.

▌ The scheme provides justification and has eliminated conflict for decisions on pay.

▌ Well established and credible – accepted by trade unions.

▌ We have a very open process, which has a high degree of credibility. The system works for the business.

Only 10 per cent said that they were not very or totally dissatisfied with their scheme, mentioning that their scheme had decayed, become out-of-date or was open to abuse. One respondent did not think a point-factor scheme 'lends itself to true broad-banding'.

Comments on the effectiveness of job evaluation

The most widely supported problem with job evaluation was a lack of understanding on the part of managers and employees – 73 per cent of the respondents said that it did not provide a well-understood basis for making pay and grading decisions. Another fairly common complaint (33 per cent) was that job evaluation did not prevent grade drift.

Fewer respondents supported other common criticisms of job evaluation. It was thought to be time-consuming by 29 per cent, bureaucratic by 21 per cent and easily manipulated by 19 per cent. Only 7 per cent said that their scheme had decayed and was no longer credible.

The major problem – lack of understanding – suggests that there needs to be more emphasis on communicating information about job evaluation and how it works. The inability to control grade drift emphasizes the need to review and audit the implementation of job evaluation. The advice given by respondents as summarized below confirms that these are important requirements.

ADVICE ON JOB EVALUATION

The survey questionnaire asked participants what advice on job evaluation they would give to organizations. Their answers provided a unique insight into the lessons that HR and reward specialists feel their organizations have learnt in the course of introducing and running job evaluation schemes.

A considerable number of respondents produced an avalanche of practical ideas on the key ingredients shaping success. This refreshingly clear guidance was the most fascinating and valuable outcome of the survey. There is perhaps nothing revolutionary in the list of techniques that they associate with operating effective job evaluation schemes. Indeed, the basic principles that should be considered when developing any scheme, as listed by respondents, might seem like obvious common sense. But sadly, all too often, managers do not follow them.

What strikes the reader of these responses is the vast reservoir of knowledge about the realities of organizational life, backed up by extensive practical experience, which has been brought to bear on the issues surrounding how best to operate job evaluation schemes by our survey participants.

Design

An analysis of the dos and don'ts of scheme design shows that in order of frequency the most common suggestions were:

- involve staff and trade unions;
- involve line managers;

- ▌ ensure good fit with business needs;
- ▌ communicate.

Some of the most interesting comments are given in Chapter 4.

Introducing job evaluation

The most common suggestions for introducing job evaluation were:

- ▌ communicate (overwhelmingly);
- ▌ explain;
- ▌ be transparent;
- ▌ train;
- ▌ don't treat it as an HR 'black art';
- ▌ don't underestimate the time required.

Some of the most interesting comments are given in Chapter 5.

Maintaining job evaluation

The most common suggestions for maintaining job evaluation were:

- ▌ keep scheme under review;
- ▌ regularly audit grade levels;
- ▌ keep good records, including rationales for evaluations;
- ▌ don't create a cottage industry/bureaucracy.

Some of the most interesting comments are given in Chapter 5.

CONCLUSIONS

Job evaluation is alive and well in the United Kingdom. There's a lot of it about and organizations with it seem to be pretty satisfied, although there is always room for improvement. This survey confirmed one of the key messages of the 2003 survey – that process is far more important than design. The constant theme of respondents to almost every question was the need to get communications right, to involve people, especially line managers, to explain and train, and to review and audit.

REFERENCE

Equal Opportunities Commission (2003) *Good Practice Guide – Job evaluation schemes free of sex bias,* EOC, Manchester

14

Case studies in job evaluation

The five case studies in this chapter were collected by e-reward in 2007. The main features of interest in each case are:

- *Chichester College* – this is an example of a further education college applying a national scheme based on the Pilat Gauge software. It illustrates how a job evaluation programme can be organized. All the jobs in the college were covered but the individual job evaluation scores were not released to them.

- *The Crown Prosecution Service* – this case illustrates how a large government agency applies the Civil Service job evaluation schemes, JEGS and JESP. It is interesting to note how the workload involved in evaluation was reduced by what was termed a 'dip sample'.

- *Rencol Tolerance Rings* – this is a small company which, with the help of an ACAS adviser, developed its own point-factor scheme.

- *Stockport Council* – an example of a local authority introducing a national point-factor scheme to support the achievement of single status for employees.

- *Syngenta* – this case describes how a company developed its own analytical matching scheme largely run by line management.

Chichester College

Background

Chichester College is a college of further education with about 16,000 students and 1,400 staff. It was decided in 2004 to introduce the job evaluation scheme developed by the Association of Colleges (the AoC) for further education colleges because it had been specially designed with colleges in mind.

The job evaluation scheme

The job evaluation scheme uses the Gauge software provided by Pilat UK. It is based on a 'paper' point-factor job evaluation scheme designed and tested by an AoC joint working party consisting of representatives of the AoC drawn from a number of colleges and representatives of the trade unions in the sector, including NATFE, Unison, ATL and GMB. Support to the working party was provided generally by Michael Armstrong and Ann Cummins. The conversion of the paper scheme to the Pilat software was carried out by Willie Wood of Pilat, and Sue Hastings, an expert in equal pay issues, advised on 'equality proofing' the scheme.

The scheme consists of eleven implicitly weighted factors:

1. expertise;
2. thinking skills;
3. planning and development;
4. autonomy;
5. communication and interpersonal skills;
6. responsibility for learners;
7. responsibility for staff;
8. responsibility for relationships with others;
9. responsibility for resources;
10. physical demands;
11. working environment.

The Gauge system deals with each of these factors in turn, presenting a question about the job on the computer screen together with a set of possible answers. The holder of the job plus the line manager then jointly select the most appropriate answer and a 'facilitator' provides guidance and help. The system will then interpret that answer and present a follow-up question to be answered. Different answers lead to different follow-up questions, allowing jobs of all types to be fully explored. At the end of this process the system produces a narrative description of the job demands (the job overview), built from the answers that have been given. The job holder and line manager will be asked to read this and check that it presents a fair, overall summary of the job demands – if it does not, there is a facility to return to any question and select a different answer. Once finalized, this job overview will form the agreed record of job content, from which the job score is determined. In effect the Gauge system combines the process of job analysis and job evaluation.

The job evaluation programme at Chichester

A total of about 400 evaluations were carried out using Gauge. This covered all the jobs in the college – individual and generic roles such as lecturers. The evaluations were conducted by the line manager and an individual with a facilitator. There were five of the latter involved in the programme – three members of the HR department, a member of the senior management team and the business support manager. The time taken for each evaluation averaged between one and one and a half hours. Staff were not told the evaluation score for their job.

To provide for consistency, the facilitators met every two weeks to exchange information about their evaluations and identify any issues that needed to be resolved. There was also a process of moderation. All the evaluations were reviewed by the Project Group, which consisted of trade union and staff representatives and members of the HR department, including the full-time project manager. The group could amend evaluations if they were clearly out of line.

The grade structure was developed by examining the evaluation scores, identifying clusters of jobs with similar scores, drawing grade boundaries expressed in points and aligning the 15 grades to the pay spine.

There were 50 appeals out of the 400 evaluations and half of these were concerned with assimilation to the new pay structure. Upgradings took place following only 10 of the appeals. Although moderating might change the original evaluation, this did not cause much difficulty as staff had been informed that this was a possibility.

The total evaluation programme took about two years to complete. The initial evaluations, moderating and hearing appeals took about 18 months, and assimilating staff to the new structure took about six months.

The trade unions (NATFE UCU and Unison) were cooperative throughout. They were represented on the Project Group, which met every two weeks.

Communication

A communication strategy was implemented, which involved using a wide variety of channels, including meetings, the intranet, newsletters, open sessions when staff could raise their concerns and get answers to their questions, and messages from the principal. An 'open door' policy was adopted throughout the project.

Advice

The following advice was given by Julia Sleeman, head of HR. Do:

▌ Plan meticulously – allow twice as much time as you think it is going to take.

▌ Pilot test and practice using the Gauge process.

▌ Adopt a top-down approach (the programme at Chichester started with the Principal and cascaded downwards).

▌ Communicate and keep on communicating.

▌ Be open.

▌ If using Gauge, ensure that facilitators and moderators are familiar with the help texts in the Gauge system, which provide additional information about the questions.

▌ Brief your managers well.

Don't:

▌ Leave it to HR – at Chichester it was treated as a cross-college project.

▌ Assume it can be done as an 'add-on' to an existing job – it's essential to have a full-time project leader; as was the case at Chichester.

▌ Rush things.

▌ Expect it to resolve your HR problems; it generates more problems to be solved.

The Crown Prosecution Service

The Crown Prosecution Service (CPS) has 8,500 employees located in 42 regional centres in England and Wales. As a government department, the CPS is obliged to use job evaluation, a policy initiated by the Treasury in 1992 to support job analysis and grading in the Civil Service. There are two different point-factor schemes. JEGS – Job Evaluation and Grading Support – is used for jobs up to and including grade 6 posts. JESP – Job Evaluation for Senior Posts – is used for senior civil servants, ie all those on grade 5 posts (assistant director level) and above. JEGS was updated by the Cabinet Office in 2000, in association with

Table 14.1 Civil Service JEGS and JESP weighted factors

	JEGS	JESP
Who does it cover?	All staff up to and including grade 6	Senior Civil Service (grade 5 – associate directors and above)
Factors	• Knowledge and skills • Contacts and communications • Problem solving • Decision making • Autonomy • Management of resources • Impact	• Managing people • Accountability • Judgement • Influencing • Professional competence (where appropriate)

Towers Perrin, which owns the copyright to the software. Knowledge and skills, problem solving and management of resources are the most highly weighted factors in JEGS (see Table 14.1 for a list of all the factors).

The CPS says that the most important reasons for using job evaluation are to ensure consistency of grades across the Service and to establish the relative worth of the jobs. It also facilitates the accommodation of new or revised jobs into the grading structure and helps to avoid discrimination. JE therefore underpins all the organization's pay and performance initiatives, such as the implementation of phase one of the INVEST programme on 2 April 2007, which includes performance development and a grading structure based on 15 career families. Phase 2 will involve further in-depth analysis and evaluation of roles. The INVEST programme was designed to focus on and improve the way in which the CPS and its employees work, to develop a motivated, skilled and rewarded workforce, and a management that is strategic and supportive. It aims to ensure that all staff are fully aware of what their jobs require of them, the type of behaviours they are expected to display while carrying out those jobs, how their career will develop, and how they will be rewarded in the short and longer term.

Unusually, the CPS has removed performance pay in order to drive up performance. It found that managers were not dealing with poor performance and were giving around 60 per cent of the population the top two ratings (out of five), instead of the 30 per cent that might have been expected. As there were twice as many people getting performance bonuses, and the pot was constant, each payment was worth half what had originally been intended. The emphasis now is on training managers to manage performance and only when this has been achieved will the reintroduction of performance pay be considered.

Process

To date, not every job in the CPS has been evaluated. Benchmark jobs have been looked at, and all new roles, as well as existing ones that have changed over a period of time, must be evaluated before they are advertised. There is a job evaluation protocol, agreed between the trade unions and the CPS, which sets out under what circumstances a job will be evaluated and the requirements from employees, managers, the departmental trade unions and HR staff to ensure that the evaluation is accurate, objective and fair. All jobs are evaluated independently by HR and union representatives, and are then passed to a quality assurance panel, also consisting of representatives of HR and the unions, who will determine the final assessment. There are trained evaluators around the country, although HR controls the process and policy centrally.

Roles are benchmarked against the public sector labour market, and market analysis shows that the CPS pays upper-quartile rates. Where there is conflict between internal equity and the market the CPS will sometimes pay supplements.

For new jobs, created perhaps by a government initiative giving the CPS additional responsibilities, HR consults with the trade unions and produces a job description, person specification and an 'indicative' evaluation. Once the job holder has been in post for up to a year, the job holder fills out a job analysis form and the job is re-evaluated. A job may sometimes be advertised as a temporary grade, so that applicants are aware that it may change.

There is also a rolling programme of streamlining national roles as a result of local organizational and government initiatives. In 2000, for example, there was an IT initiative that resulted in a PC on every desk, which led to a dramatic reduction in work for the typing pools that existed in all 42 regions. Most of the typists were redeployed and, despite being a specialist grade, are now doing a wide variety of other jobs that may or may not include the actual specialism for which they were initially employed.

Dip sample

The streamlining process involves taking a dip sample, so that instead of interviewing everyone in a particular role, a sample of, say, 2.5 or 5 per cent of the population are asked to complete a job analysis form, and these are evaluated by the panel to establish the appropriate grade, which could be higher or lower than the existing grade. The sample is selected by sex, age, ethnicity and disability, to reflect the profile of the whole group. Tracy Aqui, HR consultant at the CPS, says that it is important to decide what will happen to individuals as the result of such a process. If the evaluation results in a higher grade, will everyone be upgraded and how will this be funded, and if a lower grade seems appropriate, will everyone be red-circled?

Communication

Tracy comments that it is important to ensure that each step of the JE process and design are understood by all and that there is no room for different interpretations of what the design is trying to achieve. Involving the trade unions (where recognized) and training a pool of union representatives in the evaluation process will make it easier to get buy-in to changes in grades. The protocol agreed with the unions sets out details of the JE process and its scope. In addition, there is an easy-to-read process manual for staff and managers, which sets out the circumstances under which they can ask for a job to be evaluated.

It is also important that those responsible for recruitment understand what job evaluation is and why it is needed, and are aware that no job should be advertised until it has been evaluated, Tracy says.

Maintenance

The job evaluation panel meets as and when needed. In general, however, job evaluation is a weekly activity, with new or changed jobs coming through regularly. Tracy says that because the panel does so many evaluations and is familiar with the process it can do them quickly; it takes around an hour to carry out an indicative evaluation, and about half a day to do a full evaluation. The process is fully computerized, which contributes to a speedy turnaround.

Advice

Tracy Aqui says that 'if job evaluation is to be accepted, it is essential to explain to staff how job evaluation will be applied in the organization and how staff will be updated on progress. They need to know too that diversity criteria are used when selecting roles for evaluation. It is also important that everyone understands the consequences of evaluating roles in terms of possibly upgrading or downgrading roles'.

Rencol Tolerance Rings

Rencol Tolerance Rings is a manufacturing company with 85 employees based in the United Kingdom. It is the only UK manufacturer of tolerance rings – industrial fasteners – and is unable to recruit in the external labour market for staff with product knowledge, so employee retention is a priority. Manual workers make up about 60 per cent of the workforce. Rencol is a non-union company, but consults extensively and has had a works council since 2005. It introduced a point-factor job evaluation scheme for all staff in 2004, largely at the behest of employees, many of whom believed their roles were undervalued.

The scheme was designed by a joint working party led by ACAS. Once the scheme had been designed and every job evaluated, a new seven-grade pay structure was constructed, with grade boundaries established where there were obvious gaps between clusters of jobs. Rencol is happy with what it has achieved, although in retrospect it says it would have taken a more strategic approach to the whole process from embarking on JE to adopting new pay and progression arrangements.

Using ACAS

The original purpose of the scheme was to establish relativities between jobs that would be understood and perceived as fair by employees. Since it was employee feedback, expressed in opinion surveys, which prompted the adoption of job evaluation, the company believed that it was important that employees were involved. It asked ACAS to assist, and the ACAS facilitator helped to set up a joint working party to design a tailor-made point-factor scheme and take part in its implementation. The working party consisted of six people and the HR manager as an *ex-officio* member.

The company asked for volunteers and then picked people to represent different occupational areas and levels of responsibility within the business. It took around six weeks to train everyone involved and to evaluate some benchmark jobs, and another 12 weeks for all 50 jobs to be evaluated. Two panel members interviewed each job holder and completed a job analysis questionnaire. The job holder and his or her manager then reviewed the job analysis to ensure that nothing had been left out, and the factor points were added together to give a total for each job. Chris Roberts, Rencol's HR manager, describes the ACAS facilitator, who had put in some 70 schemes previously, as 'absolutely excellent'.

Although this had not been part of the original plan, it became obvious once all the jobs had been evaluated that the company needed to introduce a new grading structure. Before this, everyone had been on spot rates that had developed without any rationale over the organization's 25-year history. A seven-grade structure was put in place and staff were informed about their new pay band, though not their individual JE scores. Grades are defined in terms of a range of points scores and jobs are placed in a grade if their score is within the range. But there is no link between an individual's pay and where they sit in the band.

Another issue then arose, which was how staff were to progress within the structure. The works council, which represents the whole workforce, asked for performance-related pay. In 2005 there was a cost of living increase across the board with some staff receiving a performance-related supplement, and in 2006 the annual increase was entirely related to performance. The performance criteria are not related to the JE factors.

Rencol's factors

▮ knowledge/experience (the most highly weighted factor);
▮ communication skills;
▮ handling information;
▮ physical skills;
▮ autonomy;
▮ responsibility for staff;
▮ responsibility for financial resources;
▮ responsibility for product and physical resources;
▮ working conditions.

Communication

The company holds monthly meetings to which all staff are invited, and these, together with a monthly newsletter, were used to keep everyone informed about the job evaluation process. Once the work was finished there was a full presentation at a monthly meeting and every employee received a letter telling them about their new grade. Employees reacted favourably and most felt that the JE exercise had come up with the right results.

Performance-related pay is a bit more problematic. Employees had asked for this and they support the principle, but they are not always happy with what it means for them as individuals.

Maintenance

The JE scheme is maintained on a rolling basis by the HR manager, who evaluates one job a week. He meets every job holder, or representative where several people do the same job, to review the job analysis. Where there have been any significant changes, the job is referred to the six-member panel, chaired by Chris Roberts, some of whom were involved in the original working party. New jobs are also referred to the panel. The full JE process is used in every case.

Equity and other problems

When a job is about to be filled or a new job created, it is benchmarked against the external market. Only after this is it evaluated, because the evaluation process is based on the experience of the person doing the job. That person may not be fully aware of all the demands of the job, so the situation can arise that the internal JE score and grade are below the market rate. Even though this is dealt with through market rate supplements, the company is still concerned by what it sees as a problem of internal equity. In addition, existing staff were assimilated to the nearest point on the new pay structure, which also means that person A may be earning less than person B who has more responsibility but is lower down the grade. Chris Roberts comments that while there is a mechanism – market supplements – for paying people more in line with the market, there is no mechanism for paying less than the market in line with internal relativities.

Apart from the issue with internal relativities, Rencol is aware that there is a temptation for managers to add responsibilities to a job to get the post holder some extra money.

Advice

'Think beyond the job evaluation exercise to how you will use it to support your pay structure and pay progression', says Chris Roberts. 'We did job evaluation, then decided to sort out the pay structure and only then thought about progression, all on an ad hoc basis. It would have been better to have thought everything through before we started... And be aware that it takes a lot of time and effort to keep a scheme relevant – it's not just a six-month effort, it goes on for ever.'

Do:

▌ Ensure that you use a balanced, cross-functional team.

▌ Communicate well with all employees, both collectively and individually.

▌ Review each analysis, at least on an annual basis.

Don't:

▌ Give undue weight to one particular factor as this may distort the outcome.

▌ Publish individual scores.

▌ Assume that because nobody has said anything a job hasn't changed.

Stockport Council

Stockport Council has 10,000 employees. It started to use job evaluation in 1990; Hay for managers and the Greater London Whitley Council scheme for white collar employees. In 1997 a national agreement was reached to implement Single Status in England and Wales, that is, the harmonization of the terms and conditions of former manual workers and APT&C employees. This required a single job evaluation system for white collar and manual workers. Along with most other councils in the United Kingdom, Stockport moved cautiously towards Single Status because of the problem of having to equalize the earnings of male manual workers who have traditionally received bonuses and female workers who have not.

The Greater London Whitley Council JE scheme could only be used for white collar employees, so, for the last year, the council has been working with the trade unions to implement the Greater London Provincial Council (GLPC) JE scheme, which can be used for all employees, although Stockport is retaining Hay for managers. Jobs on the borders of the two JE schemes are being looked at carefully to ensure that someone at the top of the GLPC scheme would not earn more if they were evaluated through Hay, and vice versa.

Greater London Provincial Council JE scheme factors

▪ **Supervision/Management of People – 7 levels.** Assesses the scope of managerial duties and the nature of the work that is supervised. Accounts for flexible working patterns, deputizing, the number of staff supervised and their geographical dispersal.

▪ **Creativity and Innovation – 7 levels.** Measures the extent to which the work requires innovative and imaginative responses to issues and in the resolution of problems, and the impact of guidelines.

▪ **Contacts and Relationships – 8 levels.** Examines the content and environment of contacts required as part of the job. Measures the range and outcome of contacts.

▪ **Decisions.** Operates as two sub-factors: *discretion* – **6 levels** – identifies freedom to act and the controls in place; *consequences* – **5 levels** – measures the outcome of decisions by effect, range and timescale.

▪ **Resources – 5 levels.** Assesses the personal and identifiable responsibility for resources.

▪ **Work Demands – 5 levels.** Considers the relationship between work programmes, goals, deadlines and the subsequent management of priorities.

▪ **Physical Demands – 4 levels.** Identifies a range of postures and demands of a physical nature.

▪ **Working Conditions – 4 levels.** Examines the typical elements encountered with working inside and outside.

▪ **Work Context – 4 levels.** Examines the potential health and safety risks to employees carrying out their duties.

▪ **Knowledge and Skill – 8 levels.** Assesses the depth and breadth of knowledge and skills required. This factor is the most highly weighted.

Process

Since 1990, in excess of 2,000 jobs had been evaluated through the Greater London Whitley Council scheme. When starting to adopt the new scheme, Stockport sought to build on the existing job descriptions and evaluations and evaluated a further 80 benchmark jobs across all the non-managerial occupational groups. Panels consisted of equal numbers of union and management representatives, all of whom had been trained in union methodology. The manager of the role being evaluated attended the meeting as an expert witness, but left the meeting once he or she had answered questions about the job.

There has been a long history of job evaluation in the Council, and there is general acceptance that the process is fair. Despite this, it has in some cases been difficult to get agreement on job content between the employee and his or her manager. Managers have been urged to 'evaluate for the future', that is, to think about future challenges and incorporate them into job descriptions.

Now that the evaluations have been completed, the Council is using software to analyse the evaluations and draw a pay line through the ranked jobs. This will enable the creation of a best-fit pay structure. Grade boundaries will be established according to JE points, and jobs are allocated to grades according to the boundaries rather than individual points. All employees will be informed of their points scores and retain appeal rights.

Where there are conflicts between the market and individual pay, the council will continue to pay market supplements. These are limited to 10 per cent of basic salary and must be supported by a business case and authorized by a senior manager. Paul Whitney, pay and benefits manager at Stockport, says that the Council is considering further streamlining its procedures by basing future evaluations on job families.

Communication

Managers have been kept informed about the progress of the new scheme through the *HR Bulletin*, which is circulated every six to eight weeks. A specific communication exercise has focused on the 250 or so employees who currently receive a bonus, and some of whom will be going into pay protection arrangements; they have all received a face-to-face briefing and individual letters explaining what is happening.

Issues

The long history of using job evaluation has been helpful in some ways, but this history has resulted in considerable union expertise, and the unions preferred another scheme – the local government National Joint Council JE scheme. A Unison briefing comments that 'the GLPC scheme can be expected to deliver similar outcomes to the NJC scheme but may undervalue front-line jobs which have a responsibility for people and put emotional demands on the job holder.' Stockport did, however, adopt the GLPC scheme, along with many other councils throughout England, Scotland and Wales.

Advice

Stockport Council is reasonably satisfied with the GLPC scheme, and Paul Whitney suggests the following 'dos' and 'don'ts'. Do:

▌ Consider how your proposed scheme will fit into your particular organization.

▌ Consult and communicate widely and prepare the organization for major changes in pay relativities.

▌ Ensure you have sufficient time and resources in place to do the job properly.

Don't:

▌ Underestimate the amount of time and effort involved in job evaluation activity.

▌ Let it be perceived as purely an HR initiative.

▌ Evaluate for the past. Ensure your scheme takes on board service modernization.

Syngenta

Syngenta is involved in agribusiness – the research, development, manufacture and sale of agrochemicals, seeds, plants and lawn care products. It has around 2,000 employees in the United Kingdom.

Syngenta was formed in 2000 from a merger of the agribusiness interests of AstraZeneca and Novartis. The company wanted to move away from its existing points-based job evaluation arrangements and try to bring together the inconsistent pay structures across the business areas in the United Kingdom. It also wanted an approach to job evaluation and pay that would operate across the United Kingdom and fit the culture of the newly merged company.

In 2001 it introduced a new job grading and linked pay structure consisting of six broad bands, covering everyone in the United Kingdom except for the most senior leaders, and some workers in the manufacturing environment. This replaced a 15-grade structure.

The company previously used Hay, but did not wish to continue with the laborious and analytical processes involved in writing job descriptions to a particular format, preparing cases and getting senior managers together to review them. The complexity of the Hay system meant that managers needed technical job evaluation skills to manage the system rather than applying their knowledge and understanding of the roles and discussing their content and impact. The mathematical nature of the system also led to little ownership of the outcomes of the job evaluation system. More often than not, they were seen to be the results of a mysterious process carried out behind closed doors. In addition, even a points-based system requires judgement and interpretation, so it was decided that a less analytical and mathematical system would reduce the unproductive time spent on process and need not undermine the robustness of the final outcomes. Under the previous system it was easy for people to spend fruitless time working out how they could get additional points in order to reach a higher grade, says Nick Cansfield, head of UK HR operations.

'Syngenta wanted the new arrangements to be owned by line managers. There was a desire to use the knowledge of the managers about the roles in their functional areas to best effect in a simple, line-owned grading structure.' The system is therefore designed to encourage line managers to contribute to grading decisions and to set both pay benchmarks and individual salaries. To underpin this, the new arrangements were 'co-created' with senior managers and owned by them, says Nick.

Job matching

There are six work levels, populated with a number of generic role descriptors. The levels are defined by a number of factors, the most significant of which is level of responsibility and autonomy. The role descriptions vary in each of four business areas: research and development, manufacturing, marketing and sales, and business support. Most business activities (such as HR) have job families – a ladder of generic roles. This provides clarity for leaders and employees on potential career paths available, and supports the allocation of new roles into existing ladders. In the science area, for example, there are 10 different generic roles spread over several work levels, each of which is benchmarked against the market. To manage career progression, and recognize growth in role size and contribution, there are often two benchmarks within a work level. 'The differences in the work levels are quite significant', according to Nick, 'so the business of allocating jobs to levels is fairly straightforward'.

There is no direct linkage between work levels and salaries, although the on-target annual bonus increases by work level, and level six roles typically receive a car allowance to reflect the external market.

Process

There are three local job-sizing panels – one for research and development, one for UK manufacturing, and one for commercial and support staff. In addition, there is a UK job-sizing panel, which takes an overview for consistency between the different parts of the business. The UK manufacturing panel, for example, consists of the head of UK manufacturing, the site managers for the two manufacturing sites, the head of HR and the head of UK engineering. The UK panel consists of the site heads and other senior managers, including some from outside the United Kingdom. HR managers are members of panels alongside other managers, but their role is no different to that of the managers – 'to question, challenge and fully understand any rationale for a change of work level or benchmark'. Nick Cansfield says: 'It is important to have people on the panel who have the credibility and confidence to challenge their colleagues, even in different functional areas where they may have less expert knowledge.'

The panels tend to meet once a year and approve promotions, grade changes and changes to benchmarks. They also set the benchmarks for all the jobs for their area, following recommendations from managers and HR managers who have reviewed the salary survey data. The company takes part in a number of surveys and benchmarks the ladders of generic roles. External data influence what Syngenta pays but does not directly determine it – management judgement and data in combination will determine the final benchmark changes. Syngenta wishes to pay competitively in the markets in which it competes for talent. In practice, this means that benchmarks are often set at the median of market data.

Nick Cansfield says 'a lot of people can find the term median confusing, and in reality, whilst this is where Syngenta will start from, there are other factors that are taken into consideration before the benchmark is set. Actual pay is generally between 80 per cent and 120 per cent of the benchmark, and is very largely based on performance'.

Involving first-line managers

HR have worked with senior managers to design and implement the new structures but there is no doubt that more can (and should) be done year on year to continue to build and develop all leaders' knowledge of and comfort with the job evaluation and benchmarking systems, the company says. The HR team is now trying to provide more support to first-line managers when they are having compensation-related discussions with their employees. Information on the background to the salary budget, the link to total compensation, and how salary benchmarks are set needs to be shared more openly, and employees and leaders need to feel confident to engage in conversations about this often difficult and uncomfortable area. Syngenta is therefore trying to provide opportunities for first-line managers to discuss compensation-related matters with senior leaders so that they have the opportunity to ask whatever questions they need to deepen their understanding.

Advice

Syngenta is satisfied with its job evaluation arrangements, which it describes as 'a good balance between robustness and pragmatism, ensuring that grading is robust and consistent but that the time spent on it is focused on discussing and comparing role content and impact rather than mathematical points allocation'. It advises others introducing job evaluation systems to look for opportunities to co-create their approach with managers in the business, to involve line managers in role-sizing discussions, and to ensure that managers feel ownership of the process. It advises against having a system policed by HR, or which HR are implementing because 'they know best'. It is very easy to turn job evaluation into a mathematical process that underutilizes the understanding and knowledge of managers in the business, and makes role sizing a purely theoretical and analytical process. Resisting this temptation and balancing analysis with knowledge and judgement has proved a far better approach for Syngenta.

15

Trends and issues in role valuation

The research conducted by e-reward into job evaluation (the 2007 survey and case studies), our discussions with consultants and our recent experience have indicated a number of trends in the practice of role valuation and identified some issues.

TRENDS

The most important trends are:

▌ the extent to which formal job evaluation schemes are used;

▌ changes in the process of role valuation;

▌ the pursuit of ways in which the familiar tension between achieving both internal equity and external competitiveness can be reconciled;

▌ the use of role analysis and valuation as the basis for career mapping rather than simply as a means of designing and managing graded pay structures;

▮ a change in the language of role evaluation – there is more reference by consultants and some practitioners to the term 'levelling' to describe the processes of both career mapping and job grading for pay purposes. This applies particularly to the growing number of international organizations;

▮ a greater emphasis on linking job evaluation and human resource information systems;

▮ some initial moves to link job evaluation and human capital measurement.

Use of formal job evaluation

The e-reward surveys showed that the proportion of respondents with job evaluation schemes rose from 45 per cent in 2003 to 60 per cent in 2007. Because of the different sample of respondents, the scale of this increase needs to be regarded with some suspicion, but consultants have confirmed to us that organizations are increasingly demonstrating a need for some form of role valuation. Jim Crawley of Towers Perrin admits to having been surprised at the continuing high level of job evaluation activity. David Conroy of Mercer commented that the 'evaluation wheel has turned'.

Changes in the process of role valuation

Organizations appear to want a system that has been proven to work before, which enables them to manage grading and pay issues without being unduly complex or time-consuming, helps them to develop their career and talent management processes, and reduces their exposure to the risk of successful equal pay claims.

The overall trend is for more pragmatic adaptation rather than revolution; for simplification rather than complexity. Continued consolidation of existing methods of evaluation is taking place and there is less bespoke point-factor job evaluation – bespoke analytical matching or job classification schemes are becoming more popular. This development has been caused by the desire to simplify the process and to reduce the time-consuming nature of point-factor job evaluation schemes applied to all jobs.

Consultants and others are increasingly referring to 'levelling' rather than job evaluation. Levelling involves the definition of the levels in an organization using a standard set of descriptors, often including competencies. The introduction of management information systems is also forcing the introduction of levelling and in these cases organizations may not have the appetite to undertake full job evaluation.

Job evaluation can be used to get a better understanding of the organization, especially if the emphasis is on levelling. One consultant quoted the example of a big pharmaceutical company. It was believed that people left the organization and rejoined later to get a higher salary than their peers who had not left. The introduction of levelling enabled the organization to prove that this was not the case.

Perhaps this move away from total reliance on point-factor or factor comparison schemes to the use of matching approaches is the most important development in recent years. Organizations in the United Kingdom such as the National Health Service and a number of universities may start with a point-factor scheme but rely mainly on matching after the initial benchmark evaluations have taken place. Others such as Syngenta (see Chapter 14) and the charity referred to in Chapter 2 may do without an underpinning point-factor job evaluation scheme altogether. They rely on analytical matching or levelling, and this is perhaps the main direction that job evaluation will take in the future. David Conroy of Mercer believes that the increased accessibility of new, simple approaches will demystify the power and mystique of the consultant/external expert.

Whether a point-factor or a matching approach is used, the trend is for more web-enabled job evaluation to be introduced, as described in Chapter 2.

Equity and competitiveness

In the 1990s the mantra in Western economies was market and performance related-pay. These remain important and continuing themes, but some commentators perceive that organizations are determined to get a better balance between internal and external equity and between reliance on tried and tested techniques and innovation, or as one consultant put it to us, companies are 'wanting to have their cake and eat it'.

In some cases a better link between internal value and the external market is the impetus, so a number of the large consultancies, either have or are moving towards an integrated offering. However, this link is only of value if the consultants' database is relevant for the organization. Many consultancy databases have strengths in particular sectors or size of organization.

The use of 'extreme market pricing' removes any reference to internal calibration. A number of consultants said that US colleagues are reporting an increased interest in using valuation techniques to audit market pricing. One consultant described this as a 'born again' interest in work levelling. The exclusive use of extreme market pricing has led some organizations to recognize that they are missing out on a broader understanding of organization design and structure – particularly when it comes to explaining career progression.

Role valuation and career mapping

There are differences of view about where the future priorities for role evaluation lie, particularly in global organizations. In the experience of one consultant, the focus at senior level is increasingly on understanding and, where possible, calibrating total remuneration levels around the world, whilst career and succession planning are more relevant further down the organization. However, most practitioners have stated that at senior level the emphasis is on succession/career management and planning, whereas further down valuation tends to translate into local pay and grading systems. According to some consultants, the outcome of levelling today is frequently non-pay outcomes – or clients wanting more in return from the job evaluation process.

In some instances there may be no formal link to the pay system at all. For example, Gayle Spear, worldwide leader in the Career Map approach for Towers Perrin, reports that the main interest in the mapping methodology is to support the description of career paths, and to provide a basis for talent management and a structure for career development.

It was suggested by David Conroy that the approach to job evaluation will be determined by its purpose. If measuring jobs, it is more likely to be point-factor rating. If it is about development, carer planning or understanding organizational levels, then it is more appropriate to use matching and job families – although it may be necessary to have the safety net of a point-factor scheme.

The language of job evaluation

What has changed is the language of job evaluation. There are too many historical connotations in relation to the processes used. David Conroy commented that organizations are even seeking to avoid words like 'worth' or 'value', but instead prefer the arguably more neutral language of 'levelling'.

Thus, although many organizations are using recognizable job evaluation techniques, some would deny that they are evaluating jobs or roles. Reflecting this rejection of job evaluation terminology, the consultancies have been adapting their language by referring to 'levelling', 'career mapping' and 'pathways' and various other euphemisms, while using the same underlying processes and techniques.

Human resource information systems (HRIS)

Since the authors collaborated on their previous book on job evaluation in 2003, it is clear that an increasing, if still fairly small proportion of organizations are reviewing their need for some form of role valuation as a result of technology initiatives. In particular the larger consultancies have all reported that they have been asked to support the introduction of new management information systems such as SAP or PeopleSoft.

These major information management systems require the inclusion of a field for level within the system. These are then used to generate standard reports. Clearly, if the levels that are fed into the system are meaningful for reporting purposes it makes sense to tie them to some form of valuation that is relevant for other purposes. Some organizations count down organizational levels from the chief executive. However, this may not accurately reflect job levels and can yield some peculiar statistics. For example, if an organization has 12 pay grades, but only reflects, say, five organizational levels in their management information system, the reports generated will not be useful for the purposes of subsequently analysing pay-related data, eg for equal pay monitoring. Therefore, some organizations have introduced a form of role valuation to support their broader data analysis needs – typically a matching approach.

But what comes first: the desire to streamline HR policies or the need to streamline HR processes to fit the IT system? The answer is likely to differ depending on where the impetus for the systems development is coming from. Where the system is being introduced in response to broader information requirements, the need for better HR reporting may be a secondary consideration. Elsewhere it may be a driver, particularly where an organization is seeking to improve its human capital measurement and monitoring processes. For others the answer is probably a combination of both. One consultant told us that for people reporting a major information systems implementation, HR implications can be an afterthought.

Whether or not there is a broader information technology systems development, most consultancies now claim to provide technology support for their main job evaluation scheme. So how real are the advantages of an integrated technology-based approach? Depending on the specifics of the system, these might include:

∎ employee accessibility;

∎ guidance on the website to support devolved use of the system, by explaining tasks to be done, instructions on how to do them and hints and practical information;

∎ a linking to a broader HR database to enable managers to see, grade by grade, all components of total remuneration;

∎ integration with intelligence on pay guidelines, internal and external data and spend;

∎ modelling capability, eg grade structures and performance pay matrices.

However, the application of a technology-based method may need to be approached with some sensitivity. Perkins (2006) believes that problems could arise in some cultures, for example where face-to-face communication is important, as in Latin America. However, none of the case study companies or consultancies contacted during the course of research for this book mentioned that they had encountered this problem.

Human capital reporting

David Conroy of Mercer described how the introduction of job levelling can support the emerging focus on human capital measurement. An understanding of job levels 'helps organizations to understand their organization, the relativities, the relationship with the market, and how benefits hang on to the levels'.

The argument is that organizations are increasingly having to justify their spend on human resources. Unless an organization has some way of allocating staff to levels, it is not possible to generate appropriate statistics, eg to monitor patterns of benefits entitlement, pay levels or overall total remuneration costs for benchmarking purposes.

ISSUES

Some of the more interesting issues we identified during our research were:

I creating links between the job and the person;

I linking competency frameworks with job evaluation criteria;

I risk management in connection with equal pay cases;

I the use of job evaluation in mergers and acquisitions.

Creating links between the job and the person

Historically, job evaluation has provided a basis for understanding job requirements and assessing the 'size' of the role. Jobs are assessed against criteria that are deemed to be important to the organization for the purpose of assessing their relative worth or level in the organization. It is somewhat surprising therefore that more has not been done to make a link between job evaluation and performance management processes. Although 19 per cent of participants in the 2007 e-reward survey said that they wanted their job evaluation system to help develop their performance management and appraisal system, anecdotal evidence suggests that a smaller proportion of organizations are actually doing so. This could be the traditional reluctance in some quarters to link pay and development issues. However, it could be due as much to the separation of the learning and development function from the reward functions, particularly in large organizations. Several of the major consultancy firms we spoke to while researching this book commented on the barrier between these parts of the human resources function. If the project sponsor is the HR director, then there is more likely to be a broader based outcome, but if it is at the level of the reward specialist, it can be difficult to get broader engagement.

The link to competencies

In recent years a number of consultancies have begun to describe their proprietary scheme elements in terms of competencies. Some organizations have linked existing competency frameworks with job evaluation criteria, and the 2007 e-reward survey showed that 20 per cent of organizations wanted their job evaluation scheme to provide a framework for identifying competencies.

However, there are problems in making the connection. David Conroy of Mercer commented that where organizations have a pre-existing competency framework, retro-fitting often doesn't work – the number of levels of competencies is usually not the same as the required number of levels for classification. Also, some competencies don't translate readily into job evaluation levels. For example, it is difficult to translate a competency on 'living the organization's values' into classification or factor levels. Jim Crawley of Towers Perrin says that making the link is difficult if competencies are person-centric rather than job-centric. It's also easier to make a link between competencies and career mapping (ie matching or levelling approach) than it is to link a point-factor scheme with competencies.

Some determined attempts are being made to make the link. The Towers Perrin 'Framework' software and Watson Wyatt's 'e-level' software both provide for a link between job requirements and required behaviours. 'Framework' supports the new job evaluation/ competency link that is now available to higher education institutions that are using the 'HERA' job evaluation scheme. The 'elements' of the scheme (ie factors) are written in competency language. These enable the line manager and job holder to assess the individual's competencies in relation to the job evaluation profile for the role. The information can be used to support the performance review process and promotion decisions.

Geoff Nethersell of Hay Group explained that, historically, it was frustrating for Hay Group consultants to find that the Hay job evaluation process produced a wealth of information about jobs and roles but was not used for anything other than putting a price on the job. The Hay Group scheme suits more senior staff, but the focus at senior levels is now more on people than jobs, whereas the scheme produces a lot of residual knowledge about jobs. So there was a need to marry the two.

Fortuitously, when Saatchi owned Hay Group, it also acquired McBer, so Hay Group and McBer began working to see how the two could come together. The starting point from the Hay Group perspective was that jobs with similar scores could have quite different profiles. The 'feel' of the job was different, for example between an operational job and a staff job. McBer had a generic leadership competency approach but agreed to profile high-performing organizations by looking at a database of behavioural interviews to explore whether there were behavioural differences between types of job. Their analysis confirmed this was the case, so a platform could be provided through the Hay Group Guide Chart for aligning jobs and people.

The outcome is a matrix of level of work vs types of role, which is now used as the basis of assessment in talent management type projects. This has become the biggest strand of work for Hay Group in the United Kingdom. It is not strictly a job evaluation application, but uses the job profiles to underpin the analysis. Although the matrix does not typically use Hay Group Guide Chart language, it can link back to evaluated job size.

Risk management

The UK job evaluation market has been influenced by equal pay legislation for the last 30 years or so. Recent employment tribunal cases have shifted the focus from simply having an analytical job evaluation scheme, to how pay is managed within grades or bands. Equal pay cases have been won on the basis of unequal pay within grades (eg ACAS). This has not reduced the need for job evaluation but has caused organizations to take a broader view of how they respond to equal pay legislation, most notably with public sector organizations moving back to a stepped approach to pay increases to ensure that most people in each grade will reach the same 'target' or 'reference' salary. Job evaluation techniques can help to analyse broad clusters of jobs, for example in a broad-banded structure, so that an assessment of risk can take place.

It is not only the public sector that has continued to take account of equal pay risks. Towers Perrin reported that for one of their financial sector clients the equal pay review was funded by the audit/risk management function, rather than through the human resources function. In this case job evaluation techniques were used purely as an equal pay risk assessment tool.

Mergers and acquisitions

Several practitioners have commented on the usefulness of a simple but robust form of valuation to support either a specific merger and acquisition situation, or to provide support for a company such as Anglo American where there are frequent mergers and acquisitions. In mergers, organizations need to respond quickly when comparability has to be established and there are many other business issues to be resolved. They want a straightforward tool for quickly assimilating people into a common structure, and this is available if a matching approach is used. In this kind of situation few companies have the organizational will or appetite to conduct a detailed job evaluation exercise, particularly as the organization structure may be very fluid at the point of integration.

Having a clearer understanding of the organization can also help to manage other business risks. As businesses are thinking about defending themselves from private equity merger and acquisition activity, they need good data on the cost of human capital and understanding of metrics to be in the right shape to fight off bids.

REFERENCE

Perkins, S J (2006) *International Reward and Recognition*, CIPD, London

Appendices

Appendix A. Bibliography

ACAS (2005) *Job Evaluation: An introduction,* ACAS, London

Armstrong, M and Baron, A (1995) *The Job Evaluation Handbook,* CIPD, London

Armstrong, M *et al* (2003) *Job Evaluation: A guide to achieving equal pay,* Kogan Page, London

Arvey, R D (1986) Sex bias in job evaluation procedures, *Personnel Psychology,* **39,** pp 315–35

Chartered Institute of Personnel and Development (2001) *Equal Pay Guide,* CIPD, London

Cohen, P and Wethersell, G (2004) More to job evaluation than meets the eye, *IDS Executive Compensation Review,* No 286, December, pp 21–22

Crystal, G (1970) *Financial Motivation for Executives,* American Management Association, New York

Dewey, T (1916) Objects of valuation, *Journal of Philosophy,* **5,** pp 9–35

Egan, J (2004) Putting job evaluation to work: tips from the front line, *IRS Employment Review,* No 792, 23 January, pp 8–15

Ellis, C M, Laymon, R G and LeBlanc, P V (2004) Improving pay productivity with strategic work valuation, *WorldatWork Journal,* Second Quarter, pp 56–68

Emerson, S M (1991) Job evaluation: a barrier to excellence, *Compensation & Benefits Review,* January–February, pp 4–17

Equal Opportunities Commission (2003) *Good Practice Guide – Job evaluation free of sex bias,* EOC, Manchester

Fowler, A (1992) Choosing a job evaluation scheme, *Personnel Management Plus,* October, pp 3–34

Giancola, F (2005) Need a new system for evaluating management positions? Read on, *Workspan,* **48** (2), pp 28–32

Grayson, D (1987) *Job Evaluation in Transition,* ACAS, London

Gupta, N and Jenkins, G D (1991) Practical problems in using job evaluation to determine compensation, *Human Resource Management Review,* **1** (2), pp 133–44

Hastings, S (1989) *Identifying Discrimination in Job Evaluation Schemes,* Trade Union Research Unit, Oxford

Hastings, S (1991) *Developing a Less Discriminatory Job Evaluation Scheme,* Trade Union Research Unit, Oxford

Heneman, R L (2001) Work evaluation: current state of the art and future prospects, *WorldatWork Journal,* **10** (3), pp 65–70

Heneman, R L and LeBlanc, P V (2002) Developing a more relevant and competitive approach to valuing knowledge, *Compensation & Benefits Review,* July/August, pp 43–47

Heneman, R L and LeBlanc P V (2003) Work valuation addresses shortcomings of both job evaluation and market pricing, *Compensation & Benefits Review,* January/February, pp 7–13

Hicks, J R (1935) *The Theory of Wages,* Oxford University Press, Oxford

Hilage, J (1994) *The Role of Job Evaluation,* Institute of Manpower Studies, Brighton

Incomes Data Services (1991) *IDS Focus No 60,* IDS, London

Incomes Data Services (2006) *IDS Executive Compensation Review No 299,* January, pp 21–23

Incomes Data Services (2007) *Job Evaluation HR Study Plus 837,* IDS, London

International Labour Office (1986) *Job Evaluation,* ILO, Geneva

Jaques, E (1961) *Equitable Payment,* Heinemann, Oxford

Kingsmill, B (2001) *Review of Women's Employment and Pay,* TSO, Norwich

Lawler, E E (1986) What's wrong with point-factor job evaluation?, *Compensation & Benefits Review,* March–April, pp 20–28

Livy, B (1975) *Job Evaluation: A critical review,* Allen & Unwin, London

Madigan, R M and Hills, F S (1988) Job evaluation and pay equity, *Public Personnel Management,* **17** (3), pp 24–38

Martin, S (2006) Competencies, job evaluation and equal pay, *Competency & Emotional Intelligence,* **14** (1), pp 35–38

Marx, K (1867, translated in 1976) *Capital,* Penguin, Harmondsworth

Nielsen, N H (2002) Job content evaluation techniques based on Marxian economics, *WorldatWork Journal,* **11** (2), pp 52–62

Paterson, T T (1972) *Job Evaluation: A new method,* Business Books, London

Phelps Brown, E H (1962) *The Economics of Labor,* Yale University Press, Newhaven, CT

Plachy, R J (1987) The point-factor job evaluation system: a step by step guide, part 1, *Compensation & Benefits Review,* July–August, pp 12–27

Plachy, R J (1987) The point-factor job evaluation system: a step by step guide, part 2, *Compensation & Benefits Review*, September–October, pp 9–24

Pritchard, D and Murlis, H (1992) *Jobs, Roles & People*, Nicholas Brealey, London

Quaid, M (1993) *Job Evaluation: The myth of equitable settlement*, University of Toronto Press, Toronto

Risher, H W (1989) Job evaluation: validity and reliability, *Compensation & Benefits Review*, January/February, pp 22–36

Risher, H W (2002) Planning a 'next generation' salary system, *Compensation & Benefits Review*, November/December, pp 13–23

Supel, T M (1990) Equivalence and redundance in the point-factor job evaluation system, *Compensation & Benefits Review*, March–April, pp 48–55

Suss, P and Reilly, P (2006) *The Application of an Inexact Science: Job evaluation in the 21st century*, Institute of Employment Studies, Brighton

Watson, S (2005) Is job evaluation making a comeback – or did it never go away? *Benefits and Compensation International*, **34** (10), pp 8–12, 14

Zingheim, P K and Schuster, J R (2002) Pay changes going forward, *Compensation & Benefits Review*, **34** (4), pp 48–53

Appendix B. Example of point-factor job evaluation scheme (trade union)

FACTOR PLAN

Factor and level definitions

Factor	Levels				
	1	**2**	**3**	**4**	**5**
1. Knowledge, skills and expertise	20	40	60	80	100
2. Contribution	20	40	60	80	100
3. Interpersonal skills	20	40	60	80	100
4. Communicating	20	40	60	80	100
5. Planning and organizing	20	40	60	80	100
6. Judgement and decision making	20	40	60	80	100
7. Freedom to act	20	40	60	80	100
8. Complexity	20	40	60	80	100
9. Responsibility for resources	20	40	60	80	100
10. Demands on the role holder	20	40	60	80	100

1. *Knowledge, skills and expertise*

The level of professional, specialist, technical, administrative or operational knowledge and expertise required to carry out the role effectively

1   The use of the skills required to carry out straightforward work

2   The application of specific administrative skills gained through specialized training or relevant experience

3   The application of a range of professional, specialist, technical, administrative or operational areas of knowledge and skills acquired through professional or higher education and/or considerable relevant experience

4   The application of high levels of professional, specialist, technical or administrative expertise

5   The application of authoritative expertise in a key area of the union's activities

2. *Contribution*

The contribution made to achieving the objectives of the team, department or organization

1   Contributes as a team member to the achievement of team results within a section, department or office

2   Contributes in a supervisory or specialist role to team results in a section, department or office

3   Contributes significantly to the results achieved by the department or office

4   Makes a major impact on the achievement of objectives in a key area of the work of the union

5   Makes a considerable impact on the performance of the organization

3. Interpersonal skills

The level of skill required to work well with others, to exercise leadership, to respond to people's requests, to handle difficult cases, to argue a case, to negotiate and to exert influence

1   Requires the skills to work well with others and respond politely and competently to requests and enquiries

2   Requires the skills to exert some influence over others, getting them to accept a proposal or point of view

3   Requires the skills frequently to relate to people inside and outside the organization, providing advice and guidance, dealing with problems affecting people and exerting influence on important matters. Normal leadership skills may be required to manage or supervise a small team. The skills may be used in negotiations and/or case work on relatively straightforward issues

4   Requires the skills constantly to relate to other people at a high level inside and outside the organization, providing advice and guidance internally on major policies, and acting as the recognized representative of the union on key issues externally. Superior leadership skills may be required to lead a large team. The skills may be used when conducting important negotiations and/or dealing with difficult and sensitive cases

5   Requires the skills to represent the union at the highest level on complex and often political issues and to carry out a high profile leadership role. High levels of interpersonal skills are needed to lead major negotiations

4. Communicating

The requirement to communicate orally and in writing to individuals and groups of people inside and outside the union and to external bodies and the media

1   Communications are concerned with largely factual matters, covering well-established situations

2   Communications include detailed information, which has to be explained with care

3   Communications include the provision of complex information, which has to be presented with care and interpreted and explained to ensure understanding

4   Communications deal with complex issues and include informed opinions that may be challenged. May have to make formal presentations to groups of people inside or outside the union

5   Communications deal with very complex and sensitive issues, often at a high political level with significant implications for the influence and reputation of the union. Presentations may have to be made at major conferences

5. *Planning and organizing*

The requirement to plan, schedule and coordinate work, to allocate priorities and to meet deadlines

1   Plans own work on a daily basis although there is little variation in work schedules or need to prioritize

2   Plans own work priorities with some rescheduling needed to respond to changing demands from time to time

3   Frequently has to re-prioritize and reschedule own work because of constantly changing demands. May also be involved in planning the work schedules and priorities for a small team and coordinating their work

4   Plans, organizes and prioritizes work in a department or office. Own workload is largely unpredictable and has to be regularly re-prioritized and rescheduled

5   Plans and organizes programmes and activities that affect the whole of the union. Own work is subject to almost entirely unpredictable demands and has to be constantly re-prioritized and rescheduled

6. *Judgement and decision making*

The requirement to exercise judgement in making decisions and solving problems, including the degree to which the work involves choice of action and/or creativity

1   The work is well defined and relatively few new situations are encountered. The causes of problems are readily identifiable and can be dealt with easily

2   Evaluation of information is required to deal with occasional new problems and situations and to decide on a course of action from known alternatives. Occasionally required to participate in the modification of existing procedures and practices

3   Exercises discriminating judgement in dealing with relatively new or unusual problems where a wide range of information has to be considered and the courses of action are not obvious. May fairly often be involved in devising new solutions

4   Frequently exercises independent judgement when faced with unusual problems and situations where no policy guidelines or precedents are available. May also frequently be responsible for devising new strategies and approaches that require the use of imagination and ingenuity

5   Deals with widely differing problems calling for extreme clarity of thought in assessing conflicting information and balancing the risks associated with possible solutions. Additionally, one of the main requirements of the role may be to develop fundamentally new strategies and approaches

7. Freedom to act

The degree to which independent action has to be taken, bearing in mind the level of control or guidance provided and the extent to which the work is supervised

1 For most aspects of the work, specific and detailed instructions are given on both what has to be done and how it should be done

2 Specific guidelines and procedures exist on what needs to be done, but there is some freedom to decide methods and priorities. The work is generally carried out in accordance with specific guidelines and procedures, but there is some scope to determine methods and priorities

3 Takes independent action within defined policy frameworks

4 Takes independent action as required within broad policy frameworks

5 Actions are constrained only by union overall strategies

8. Complexity

The variety and diversity of the work carried out, the decisions to be made and the knowledge and skills used

1 Work requirements are on the whole well defined and the choice of action is fairly limited

2 There is some diversity in the work that involves a number of non-routine elements and the exercise of a variety of skills, although they are quite closely related to one another

3 The work is diverse, consisting of a number of different elements that are only broadly related to one another, and the exercise of a wide variety of skills

4 The work is highly diverse, involving many different elements that may not be closely related to one another

5 The work is multidisciplinary and involves making a broad range of highly diverse decisions

9. Responsibility for resources

The size of the resources controlled in terms of people, money, equipment, facilities, etc

1   Responsible only for the equipment required to carry out the work

2   May have two or three staff reporting to him or her; and/or monitors expenditure

3   May lead a small team, and/or manage a small budget or be responsible for a range of facilities or equipment

4   Leads a large team or department of more than 10 people, and/ or acts as budget manager for a department or office

5   Leads a major function or range of activities and manages a commensurately sized budget

10. Demands on the role holder

The demands made by the role on the role holder because of work pressures (including those arising from handling emotional situations), non-social hours or a considerable amount of travelling

1   The work can generally be maintained at a steady rate without undue pressures

2   The role involves occasional periods of pressure to meet deadlines or cope with extra work

3   The role is subjected to frequent periods of pressure to meet deadlines, deal with difficult cases or situations, or cope with large volumes of additional work

4   The role is subjected to constant pressure to meet demanding deadlines and handle very difficult situations or cases that may involve dealing with emotional and stressful issues. Anti-social hours may be a regular feature as a considerable amount of travelling may be required

5   The work is highly and continuously pressurized

Appendix C. Example of job questionnaire

Basic Details	
Job Title:	**Name(s) of job holder(s):**
Department:	

Reporting Structure	

1. Please fill in the job titles of:
   - your line manager _____
   - your department manager (if different) _____
   - people who you line manage (if applicable) _____

Job

Overall purpose of job:

2. Describe as concisely as possible the overall purpose of your job – what in general terms you are expected to achieve. (You may find this at the top of your job description).

As an alternative to completing the rest of this page you may wish to attach your job description if it accurately reflects what you do. Or you can attach the job description and provide some extra information below if you think this will help the evaluators to understand your role.

Main areas of responsibility:

3. List the main responsibilities of your job. You do not need to describe the tasks/activities in detail or go into how they are carried out. Most jobs can be described in a relatively small number of key headings.

If you think it will be helpful to get a better understanding of your job, give an indication what time that you spend on each part of your job (as a percentage of the total).

➢

➢

➢

Scope

4. Describe the extent to which your work is guided by guidelines, procedures or precedents and on what kinds of activities your job requires you to make choices.

5. Describe how regularly and on what your job requires supervision, giving examples of the kinds of things you typically receive or ask guidance on from your manager.

6. Give examples of the actions, advice and decisions you are free to make without needing guidance or approval from anyone else.

7. Does your job involve you in adapting procedures or finding new ways of working to improve how things are done, either in your own area of work or through participation in/leadership of project teams? Give examples.

8. Give examples of what you have to plan for/prioritize in your work, either for yourself or for others – and what timescale this typically covers.

Impact of decisions (this is about when work is being done to the required standard, not about the consequences of things going wrong)

9. Give examples of how the actions, recommendations and decisions that you take impact on any of the following:

- Day to day operations in your area of work or elsewhere in the organization
- Colleagues/volunteers in your own area of work, or elsewhere in the organization

- Clients, customers or other external contacts/bodies
- External perception or reputation of the organization

*In giving examples, please give an indication of the **risks and benefits** that are taken into account and the **timescale** over which your actions, recommendations and decisions take effect.*

Resources

10. Describe what resources or assets you are directly responsible for, eg planning, allocating or spending budgets, equipment (including equipment you use on a day to day basis), premises, or raising income.

11. If applicable, quantify the resource(s) involved, eg budget/quantity.

12. Do you have any other responsibility for resources that you are not directly accountable for, eg monitoring resource usage (eg, records of monies, people or equipment), ensuring their safe-keeping, or in generating or spending income? If so, please describe.

Interpersonal skills

13. Please complete this table to describe the key people or groups of people that you have to work with in your job, excluding the colleagues in your own department that you work with on a day to day basis. Include internal and external contacts.

Who (individuals or organizations)	Frequency	Purpose

16. How many people, if any, do you manage:

    a. Directly? _____

    b. Indirectly (ie report in though others)? _____

    c. Not applicable? _____

(Note: This answer should tie in to the section on page 1 about reporting structure.)

17. If applicable, describe to what extent their jobs are similar or dissimilar (to each other and to your own), and where they are based.

18. If there are colleagues/volunteers who do not report to you, but for whom you supervise/direct work, provide guidance or are involved in their development, please state who this is for, and what it involves.

Applied knowledge and skills (this is about what is needed to be able to do the job – this may not be the same as your own personal experience or background)

19. What are the basic skills, whether acquired inside or outside the organization, which are *needed* to do your job?

20. Are any specific professional, technical or vocational skills or qualifications required to do the job?

21. On what kinds of things do other people come to you for information, advice or as a source of expertise, because of the kind of knowledge and skills that your role requires you to have? Give examples – whether inside the organization or externally.

22. If your role requires you to be the sole or main source of knowledge or expertise in a particular field of work, describe what this covers.

Your comments: is there anything else about your job, not covered by the questions above, which will help others to understand and evaluate your job?

Thank you for completing this form.
Before sending the completed questionnaire to HR, job holders and line managers should both read the verification statement and confirm the accuracy of the information provided by entering the date, as requested.

Verification statement: I/we agree that this completed questionnaire accurately reflects the requirements of the job	
Name of manager	**Date questionnaire contents confirmed by line manager**
	/ /
	Date questionnaire contents confirmed by job holder(s)
	/ /

Appendix D. Example of a project plan for the development of an analytical matching scheme

---

Activity	Responsibility	Jan.	Feb.	Mar.	April	May	June	July	Aug.	Sept.	Oct.	Nov.	Dec.	Q1
Appoint consultant	**Steering group**	█												
Visioning/strategic direction														
Visioning workshops with Board	**Steering group**		█	█										
Sign-off Reward Principles/Reward Policy	**Steering group**		█											
Set up project team	**Project leader**		█	█										
Optimum meeting dates – project team	**Project team**				2x	2x	2x	2x		x1				
Detailed design work														
Job Evaluation														
Confirm no. of grades/levels required	**Project team**				█	█								
Agree criteria for level descriptors	**Project team**					█	█							
Agree basis for allocating jobs to levels	**Project team**					█	█							
1st test questionnaire and level descriptors	**Project team**						█							
2nd test questionnaire and level descriptors	**Project team**						█							
Staff/managers to complete questionnaires	**Staff/line managers**						█	█						
Initial allocation process	**Project team**							█						
Recommendations for simplifying job titles	**Project team**									█				
Pay Structure														
Analyse current structure, plot all pay points	**Analyst**					█								
Review rationale for existing structure	**Project team**					█	█							
Examine options	**Project team**						█							

Activity	Responsible
Individual Pay Progression	
Develop operating guidelines	Project team
Criteria for 'normal' progression	Project team
Guidance for deferring/accelerating progression	Project team
Guidance for what happens at top of grade	Project team
Prepare draft guidance for staff	Project team
Develop assimilation arrangements for staff falling above or below new structure	Project team
Financial Modelling	
Market data analysis	HR
Financial modelling	Analyst/project leader
Finalise/cost assimilation arrangements	Project leader
Communication/Consultation Plan	
Steering group sign offs	
Board sign offs	Project leader/steering group
All staff communication	Project leader; management team
Consultative forums: communication	Project leader; management team
Reference group review	Project leader, project team

Task	Responsible					
Develop formal consultation/implementation plan	**Project leader**	▨				
Steering group sign off consultation plan	**Project leader/steering group**		▨			
Consultative forum: final consultation	**Project leader; management team**		▨	▨		
Communication/contractual change roll-outs	**HR, management team, line managers**			▨	▨	
Implement changes	**Payroll, HR**				▨	▨
Individual reviews/appeals	**Project team**					▨

Appendix E. Example of an appeals procedure (university)

1 APPEALS PROCEDURE – TRANSITION ARRANGEMENTS

1.1   The aim of the appeals procedure is to ensure equal pay for work of equal value. The appeals process therefore looks to ensure that any anomalies within the assimilation process of job matching for all staff are addressed. This could potentially mean a higher or lower grade being applied to the post in question as a result of the appeal.

1.2   This appeals procedure is for the purpose of dealing with appeals against placement on the new pay structure, and is part of the transition process. It has no life after all transition appeals have been heard.

2 CRITERIA FOR APPEAL

2.1   The appeals procedure is available to any member of staff who, as a result of the implementation of the new grading structure, has been job matched into either a grade or job family which the employee can demonstrate is not representative of the work they carry out.

2.2 The appeal must be substantiated with evidence and reasons given. The employee must show where they feel their role differs from the grade descriptors.

2.3 Employees cannot appeal against the pay point into which they have been assimilated.

3 THE APPEALS PROCEDURE

Stage 1. Review

3.1 Appeals must be made within six weeks of notification of their new grade. The appeal should be made in writing, to the Head of Human Resources. All appeals received by that date will be acknowledged by the Human Resources Department

3.2 The Head of Human Resources will arrange to conduct a review of the matching process by meeting with the employee and their representative and discussing their reasons for appeal. The employee must demonstrate specifically by reference to the grading criteria, where they feel their post does not match the grade assigned to them.

3.3 The Head of Human Resources will consult with a trained HERA senior management team member regarding the basis of the appeal. If the reasons are valid, the Head of Human Resources will then organize a job evaluation by allocating an analyst to conduct a full HERA interview.

3.4 The results of the HERA evaluation may indicate three possible outcomes:
   ∎ The grade is incorrect and should be higher.
   ∎ The grade is incorrect and should be lower.
   ∎ The grade is correct.

3.5 If the employee is satisfied with the outcome of the full evaluation, then no further action is taken. If, once the evaluation has taken place and a grade assigned, the employee still wishes to continue with the appeal, they must follow the process from 4 onwards.

Stage 2. Appeal

4.1 The appeal should be made in writing, to the Head of Human Resources within five working days of notification of the result of the HERA evaluation. The basis of the appeal is that there is new evidence or evidence that was not taken into account by the analyst during the HERA interview or the scoring. If this is not evidenced by the employee in their appeal application, the appeal will be turned down by the Head of Human Resources, as detailed in 5.2.

4.2 If it is agreed that the appeal should proceed, the employee will be given a copy of the record of evidence and the score generated from the evaluation interview.

4.3 The Human Resources Department will then arrange for an appeal panel to be convened within one month of receipt of the appeal. If arrangements cannot be made within this timescale, the staff member will be informed of the reasons and the next available date.

4.4 The appeal panel will consist of the following: a member of the Human Resources Department, a member of the Senior Management Team (Chair) and a Trade Union representative. All appeals panel members will need to have received training on the HERA process. A note taker will be present throughout.

4.5 The employee has the right to be represented at the appeal hearing by a trade union representative or work colleague.

4.6 The chair of the appeal panel will ask the employee to detail their reasons for the appeal, and to demonstrate with the record of evidence where they feel the new evidence should be taken into account.

4.7 The panel will consider the evidence, ask questions where appropriate and ask for additional information and verification from the employees' line manager, who will be made available, if required.

4.8 The employee then has the opportunity to sum up their argument. Afterwards the panel retire to consider the new evidence and decide:

▎ Whether it is appropriate to be considered as evidence.
▎ Whether the record of evidence should be amended.
▎ Whether the score relating to that evidence should be amended.

4.9 If the panel revise the scoring, then the Human Resources representative will be responsible for amending the scores on the HERA software and producing the new score total.

4.10 There are two possible outcomes from the appeal panel:

- ▌ The grade determined by the HERA evaluation is confirmed and implemented, with effect from a specific date.
- ▌ The grade determined by the HERA evaluation is not confirmed and the grade determined by the panel is implemented with effect from a specific date.

4.11 The Human Resources panel member will communicate the outcome to the employee in writing within five working days of the reconvened hearing.

4.12 The decision of the appeal panel is final.

5 GENERAL PRINCIPLES

5.1 The employee has the right to be accompanied to any job evaluation review or appeal hearing by a fellow worker, or a full-time trade union officer or a union official who has been certified by the union as having experience and/or training in job evaluation matters.

5.2 Where the Head of Human Resources has considered:

- ▌ the review or
- ▌ the appeal

unreasonable and the employee disagrees, they must put their case in writing to the Deputy Vice Chancellor responsible for appeals within five working days of the Head of Human Resources' decision.

5.3 The Deputy Vice Chancellor will consider the case and respond to the request in writing within five working days. If a longer period of time is needed, the employee will be informed in writing. The decision of the Deputy Vice Chancellor is final.

Appendix F. Example of a job evaluation policy statement

This policy describes our job evaluation process, which ensures that roles are placed properly within the six bands. It is purely concerned with measuring the size of the role, relative to other roles in the organization. It does not determine actual pay, only the correct allocation of the role to the bands – and therefore, the correct range in the overall pay structure.

PROCESS – GENERAL PRINCIPLES

Job evaluation entails the comparison of jobs to assess their relative worth to the organization. It is a systematic process that can assess the content of jobs in a fair and consistent manner. Individual abilities, performance and ambitions do not affect how the role itself is assessed. There are other processes that deal with these issues.

The band structure reflects our values, while aiming to provide a simple, easily understandable and robust approach to job evaluation. It covers all permanent employees.

All roles can be described using a number of key characteristics that are significant to an organization. To a greater or lesser extent these factors can be found in any job within the institute. The following characteristics have been used to create descriptions of our six career bands:

1. Accountability.

2. Knowledge and skills.

3. Innovation and process improvement.

4. Leading and developing people.

5. Building relationships.

6. Physical demands (for some roles).

Roles will be evaluated under the scheme where:

▌ They are new.

▌ Where a role profile has been updated due to changing role requirements, and there is a need to confirm whether the new role responsibilities may place the role in a different band.

▌ Where a role holder has a grievance about where their role is allocated within the band structure.

PROCESS – WHO DOES WHAT?

HR will be responsible for:

▌ Coordinating the evaluation process.

▌ Undertaking evaluations.

▌ Circulating completed evaluations to the consistency review group for confirmation.

▌ Calling together meetings of the consistency review group, when required.

▌ Keeping a record of all evaluations.

The line manager is responsible for preparing a role profile for new roles, or amending an existing profile with the relevant *employee(s)*. If required, both the line manager and the employee may be interviewed as part of the evaluation process.

A consistency review group will confirm all new evaluations, and on a regular basis will review the operation of the job evaluation scheme to ensure that it is being applied consistently.

EVALUATING ROLES

There are two approaches to evaluating roles.

1. Role matching evaluation

HR will initially evaluate the role based on an up-to-date role profile. (The process for reviewing role profiles is described separately.) The evaluation will be based on the fit between the role profile and the written description of the six bands. This evaluation will take into account how roles have already been evaluated into the bands, particularly the 'benchmark' roles that were evaluated fully when the scheme was developed. If required, HR will seek additional information about the role from line management/the employee(s).

Information about the role and the proposed band will be circulated to three members of the consistency review group for confirmation. If all members agree, this evaluation is ratified. If there is disagreement, further information may be obtained from the line manager or employee, or the role may be re-evaluated using the second approach, described below.

2. Analytical evaluation

This approach may be used:

1. Where HR cannot decide on the appropriate band because it appears to fall across the boundary between two bands.

2. Where members of the consistency review group are not agreed about the proposed band for the role.

3. Where an employee has a grievance in relation to where their role sits in the band structure.

In order to undertake an analytical evaluation for existing roles, the role holder will be interviewed, based on a structured questionnaire. This information will be verified with the line manager. HR will then evaluate the role and follow the same process as in 1 above.

For new roles, HR will interview the line manager to obtain relevant role information.

If you have reason to believe that your allocated band is no longer appropriate for your role, you should raise your concerns with your line manager in the first instance. If the manager agrees with your concerns, it is likely to be because the scope of your role has changed. This will require you to work with your line manager to amend or create a new role profile for your role, before submitting this to HR with a request to re-evaluate the role.

If the manager does not agree with your concerns and the issue remains unresolved, this will be dealt with through the grievance procedure. It may involve a re-evaluation of your role.

Index